ASTR&OLOGY
RELATIONSHIPS
MARY DEVLIN

Whitford Press

77 Lower Valley Road, Atglen, PA 19310

For Shaun

Astrology and Relationships
Copyright © 1988 by Mary Devlin
Cover design copyright © 1988 Schiffer Publishing, Ltd.

International Standard Book Number: 0-914918-77-X
Library of Congress Catalog Card Number: 88-50300

Edited by Skye Alexander.
Cover design by Bob Boeberitz.
Charts by Edward Sparks.

Published by Whitford Press
a division of Schiffer Publishing
77 Lower Valley Road
Atglen, PA 19310
Please write for a free catalog.
This book may be purchased from the publisher.
Please include $2.95 postage.
Try your bookstore first.

Manufactured in the United States of America

Acknowledgments

No book like this is ever truly a solo effort; it takes the input of many people to form a coherent whole. For this reason, I extend my sincere thanks to all who helped me in producing it: to Shaun, Edward, Diane, Jean, Dana, Bob, Rose, Dorothy, Thomas, Allan, Laura, and all the others who have contributed material over the years; to all my clients who had enough faith in me to consult me; to all the other astrologers who were an invaluable help to me in my work. Special thanks go to my friends at Gordon, Edelstein & Krepack, who contributed (however unknowingly) to the efficient use of my time while I was writing this book; special thanks also go to Travis, Judy, and Lisa Pike for their contributions, especially their help with the gods and goddesses section. Special thanks also go to Skye Alexander, my editor and my friend, who has had to put up with innumerable emotional trips on my part throughout our association.

My warmest gratitude goes to my family, my children, all my wonderful friends, and to Daniel, who have made my own relationships so incredible.

And thanks to everyone out there who still believes in love. I have needed all of you!

Contents

Part One: Individual Needs and Potential 7

1 Changing Relationships in a Changing World 9
2 The Needs of the Individual 15

Part Two: Parent-Child Relationships 37

3 Parent-Child Relationships: Where It All Begins 39
4 The Twelve Signs 59
5 The Fourth and Tenth Houses 79
6 The Moon, the Sun, and Saturn 87

Part Three: Romance and Marriage 113

7 Romance and Marriage 115
8 Animus and Anima: The God and Goddess Within . 147
9 Astrology and Sex 177
10 The Neptune Connection 185
11 The Fifth and Seventh Houses 192
12 Case Studies 203

Part Four: Friendship......................... 225

13 Gotta Have Friends............................ 227
14 The Mercury Factor: Communication 243
15 Venus and Jupiter............................. 249
16 The Eleventh House 259
17 Case Studies 267

Conclusion: Astrology and Love................. 289

Bibliography 293

Part One

Individual Needs and Potential

1

Changing Relationships In a Changing World

Human beings are social animals. I don't think there is an anthropologist, sociologist, or psychologist who would disagree with this statement. Ever since the dawn of history, men and women have been most at home in groups of other human beings, sleeping, hunting, eating, playing, loving, enjoying the comfort of each other's company.

Research in recent decades has shown that this sociability is not confined to *homo sapiens* alone. Chimpanzees, baboons, gorillas, and other primates band together in large groups, and have been observed to display such characteristics as compassion, heroism, self-sacrifice, and other traits that humans mistakenly believed for centuries to be theirs alone. People who have kept many animals, whether for pleasure or profit, have noted that dogs, cats, horses, and other domestic animals often form special "friendships" with other animals, sometimes of their own species, sometimes not. We are all familiar with stories of faithful dogs or horses, devoted to their masters, who give their lives for their humans. I am primarily a cat person and can testify that the same is often true of cats.

Even non-domesticated animals sometimes form special friendships. Years ago I read a story which may have been the source for the popular round, "Three Blind Mice." In plague-ridden London of the late fourteenth century, a merchant's wife chased two rats from her home. She chased them halfway down the streets, mallet in hand, until she finally killed the leading rat. The second rat stopped still and appeared to be trembling with fear. Curious, the merchant's wife approached the animal and looked closely at him. She then could see that the living rat was blind and that a straw ran from his teeth to the teeth of the rat she had killed.

It is difficult to speculate at what point in the evolution of life on Earth an animal looked at another and sensed on some level, "This being is special to me above all others." It seems safe to assume, however, that it was only after the growth of superior intellect, as observed in human beings, that problems with close relationships began to develop. It is a strange irony that in the so-called lower animals, love appears to be unconditional. When dogs, cats, horses, and probably chimpanzees and gorillas choose another to be their constant companion, they appear to accept that creature totally, just as it is. Human beings, on the other hand, with their intellects (and egos) usually want more from those to whom they are close. We expect to gain something from our relationships, and when we don't get what we want, we feel justified in moving on to other involvements.

The scriptures of many religions proclaim that love should be unconditional, that you should "love thy neighbor as thyself." We all know how difficult this is. Too many of us do not love our neighbors—perhaps because we don't really love ourselves. We battle the concept of "I am" whenever we come up against others who have "I am" concepts of their own. We all are the center of our own Universes, and sometimes we have trouble accepting, as the Masters can, that our neighbors are the centers of their individual Universes too, not satellites circling us. Yet the same intellect that created this problem can enable us to comprehend the rights of others to create their own Universes, whether or not they coincide with ours.

It seems that more books on relationships have been published in the past ten years than in any other decade in the history of publishing. Titles such as *The Cinderella Complex, The Peter Pan Syndrome, How to Make Love All the Time, Every Woman Can Be Adored,* and *The Wendy Dilemma* grace our bookshelves. This phenomenon appears to be a reaction to the shock of changing relationships and changing values.

When I was a little girl growing up in the U. S. of the fifties, the father was the wage-earner and the provider, the mother was the nurturer who took care of the home and children. Anthropological discoveries indicate that even the earliest of human societies embraced this family structure. Theories as to the reason for such a structure abound, but one that is widespread is science writer Isaac Asimov's "sex-for-food" theory. According to this idea, since the male animal was the physically stronger of the two sexes, and since the mother actually produced the children that were to assure the continuation of the species, the male-oriented family was a natural outgrowth of human physiology. The male could take his pleasure in the female body and be assured of heirs (although it is not clear at what point in evolution the father's role in producing children was recognized), so long as he used his physical strength to bring home enough food for the female and her offspring.

This theory has a few holes in it. Recent discoveries indicate that even though the males were the hunters, the female members of society initially did most of the farming. And, of course, since men had superior strength they could rape the women whenever they so chose and thus gratify their sexual desires—whether or not they provided food for the women and children. The "sex-for-food" theory, therefore, presupposes the existence of such virtues as respect and compassion, which scientists are usually unwilling to ascribe to early *homo sapiens.* Who knows? We have no records, only theories—and none of these theories appears totally satisfactory.

Regardless of how the family structure evolved, there is no doubt that it provided a solid foundation upon which human society was to be built and re-built for hundreds of thousands of years.

Suddenly, during the 1960s, the validity of the traditional family structure began to be questioned. Why settle for one mate at a time? Why did a household have to consist of one husband, one wife, and their children? More radically-inclined young people began banding together in communes, sharing work, partners, and the children born into the group. Another change was taking place, too. Women were becoming aware of their talents and beginning to value them. Why, they wondered, did the man always have to go out and work while the woman stayed home and cared for the children—regardless of the interests or talents of the individuals involved?

In reality, the concept of woman as stay-at-home is a fairly new one. For centuries in European society, women worked as hard as their men. Lower-class women worked on farms, in factories, or served as domestics in the households of the rich. Middle-class women helped run their husbands' businesses or embarked on business ventures of their own. The industriousness of European nuns is legend. Upper-class women perhaps worked hardest of all. Even though they may have had servants to do the actual toiling, it was no small task to oversee the household and estate of a nobleman, keep the accounts, and look out for the welfare of those who worked on the estate and their families.

The idea of woman as "lady of leisure" or "woman as toy" appears to have originated in the Victorian era. Upper and middle-class women were trained from childhood to be useless. "Can you think of anything more useless than the Victorian woman?" writes Isaac Asimov. "She didn't work, she was discouraged from studying, she had servants to perform household tasks. She wasn't even supposed to enjoy sex!!"[1]

During World War II, a new American romantic stereotype emerged: "Rosie the Riveter," the patriotic woman who sacrificed her coveted status as "lady of leisure" in order to take a man's job so he could go fight for his country. The postwar years sent all the "Rosies" back home to be housewives once again, where they had no power, no creative outlets, no intellectual stimulation, and no respect. They began to get bored. Some grew depressed, became nags or alcoholics, or had affairs. Those with outside interests wished to be free to pursue them. Suddenly, relationships began to change.

As we moved into the seventies, we started wanting to know ourselves. Some sociologists have contemptuously labeled the seventies the "me decade" and called it a very selfish period in modern history. However, metaphysicians generally regard the consciousness movement of the seventies, during which time disciplines such as est, Silva Mind Control, Transactional Analysis, and Transcendental Meditation flourished, as a positive development, for only when we understand ourselves can we genuinely understand others.

This book is being written in the 1980s, when emphasis is being placed on the quality of our relationships. We find that we can no longer take our partners for granted. Nor are we willing to stay blind and deaf to our partners' faults in order to "save the marriage."

During no other period in human history have relationships been analyzed so thoroughly and deeply. Books offer advice on how to understand our loved ones and our connections with them. Various schools of family and relationship therapy abound. Seminars and encounter groups are popular. Yet we all seem to be missing the "why" of relationships, the reason people are drawn to us and we to them, why one special person can give us so much joy or so much pain.

One reason for the current emphasis on happiness through relationships is the rapid approach of the Age of Aquarius. The Piscean Age is believed to have ended in the early sixties when the vernal equinox moved out of the constellation Pisces. The vernal equinox actually will enter the constellation Aquarius in the late twenty-first or early twenty-second century, bringing with it the Age of Man, which, in astrology, is associated with friendships and human interactions. The god of the Age of Aquarius is the god within each individual—not the warm and nurturing Earth Mother worshipped during the Age of Taurus, or the warrior gods of the Age of Aries, the savior-martyrs of the Age of Pisces—but that portion of the Divine which exists within each human being.

This transition may bring an interesting change, but it also presents a frightening new sense of responsibility. With the approach of the Age of Aquarius, humankind no longer can blame its misfortunes on its governments; we elected them. No longer can we blame career problems on our employers; we chose them. And no longer can we blame all our misfortunes in our relationships on our partners, because something in us caused them to treat us the way they do.

Perhaps during the Piscean Age the answer to relationship problems was to shave your head, put on monks' robes, and go hide in a monastery somewhere, thus avoiding close relationships altogether. But the Aquarian deity is God moving among people. The way to god-consciousness will not be joining a monastery and meditating for hours, but through increasing contact with other human beings. One of the enlightened heralds of the Aquarian Age, Paramahansa Yogananda, maintained that commitment to another human being was the first step toward total commitment to God. One's attitudes toward other people are indicative of one's relationship with God. And, perhaps most practical of all, psychologists and metaphysicians now maintain that our relationships provide us with mirrors, reflecting who and what we actually are.

If we accept this idea, it appears that through understanding our relationships and attempting to make them successful, we will enable ourselves to fulfill our potential and be all that we can be. There are many different schools of thought, consciousness-raising methods, and types of therapy to help us achieve this end. One of these is, of course, astrology.

Many astrology books that deal with human relationships concentrate on chart comparison. Chart comparisons measure compatibility. This, of course, is vital to understanding attachments to others, but the needs of the individual and his or her capacity to function within a relationship are at least as important. I also believe that the karmic connections between two people are a significant factor in their relationship.

I have spent more than a decade studying karmic ties in relationships. I have found this field fascinating, since understanding long-ago attachments helps me gain deeper insight into relationships today. We meet very few individuals whom we have not known in former incarnations. In the course of our lives, we have become attached to many people and traumatized by others—and, for the most part, these experiences are still with us. We sometimes repeat useless past-life patterns in our present-day relationships, and the persons with whom we repeat these patterns may or may not be the same entities with whom we began the pattern.

For the sake of this book, I have classified all relationships into what I consider three basic categories: parent/child, friendship, and marriage. I believe that all other relationships are simply variations on these three. Teacher/student, employer/employee, doctor/ patient, priest/parishioner, etc., all fit into the parent/child category. Siblings, business associates, casual acquaintances, and so on are all similar to friendships. All serious, committed love relationships, whether legally binding or not, are the equivalent of marriage; the heart doesn't make legal distinctions. Some business partnerships actually are more like marriages. I have a friend who is in the process of breaking up a business partnership of many years' duration. This breakup has proven more painful to both parties than many divorces I have witnessed.

Experts agree that the most influential relationship is the one between parent and child. I believe that we do not carry around with us the weight of all the traumas of our prior lifetimes; such a burden would be too great to bear. Instead, something in the current life, probably in early childhood, recalls a long-buried memory of some past-life trauma, and it becomes firmly entrenched in the current psyche as a pattern. The first relationship any of us experiences in the present life is with mother, usually followed by the relationship with father. Both can and do lock into the psyche past-life relationship hangups which can prove crippling in later life.

I once read about two identical twins who were reflecting on their childhood with their drunken father. One said he was determined never to fall into the same trap his father did and thus avoided alcohol. He also stated that he was determined to succeed in whatever he tried and to earn the respect of others. The second twin followed his father's example, becoming a lazy, shiftless drunk, and alienated everyone who might have loved and respected him, including his twin brother.

Why would two people who shared an identical heredity, identical environmental factors, and nearly-identical astrological charts react to the same situation in such different ways? The answer could be that the father's drunkenness triggered different past-life patterns in each of them.

Relationship patterns, initially locked in by parent/child interactions, continue into friendships and marriage. These patterns can be destructive, over-idealistic, sadistic, masochistic, servile, or total fantasy. But whatever they are, they affect the person's knowledge and evaluation of him- or herself, and for this reason we study them further, from reincarnational, psychological, and astrological viewpoints. Through understanding our relationships, we can better understand ourselves.

Notes

1. Isaac Asimov, *Fantasy and Science Fiction,* August, 1971.

2

The Needs
of the Individual

In judging relationships, modern astrology often places too much emphasis on chart comparison and not enough on the individuals whose charts
are being compared. This is not to say that chart comparison is unimportant. Synastry—one method of comparing two charts—judges compatibility, and compatibility is a big factor in whether or not a relationship
will work. But it is only half the story. To use a cliché, an Australian bushman and an erudite Oxford professor could have the best chart comparison in the world, yet it is extremely doubtful that they would become fast
friends because of the vast cultural differences between them.

To be sure, it is unlikely that an erudite Oxford professor will come
to an astrologer asking about the potential of a relationship between herself and an Australian bushman. However, sometimes I find that I am
asked to compare two charts that indicate a high level of compatibility,
but reflect two individuals with very different needs and viewpoints.

During my years of practice as an astrologer, the majority of my
clients have consulted me about their romantic relationships. And they
almost always have asked for a chart comparison. Although when analyzing a relationship I usually do a comparison, I won't stop there. I also look
at the two individual charts and try to determine the needs of each person
to see if they are "in sync" with the partner's. In this era of rapidly changing values, it is not uncommon for the individuals to have very different
viewpoints, and since we now believe that the needs and desires of every
human being are important, we are less inclined to sacrifice our needs
for the sake of someone else's. So despite our desire for long-term, committed romantic relationships, problems continue to occur.

For those who are not already familiar with synastry, it is a technique that involves taking the planets from person A's birth chart and overlaying them (by sign and degree) on person B's chart. The astrologer then analyzes how person B will be affected by person A's planetary influences. This method can be used to examine the interaction of two people in any type of relationship: love, parent/child, business, etc.

All individuals in any sort of relationship need one thing: unconditional love and acceptance. This need exists in everyone. According to Swami Muktananda, in *The Perfect Relationship,* the guru-disciple relationship is the only relationship between two human beings in which unconditional love exists; the guru totally accepts the disciple as he or she is, without passing judgment upon the disciple's personal habits, background, profession, or even deeds of the past.[1] Jesus, too, accepted His disciples completed as they were. His love for and acceptance of them was not contingent upon their changing.

Although everyone needs to be loved and accepted unconditionally, for us flawed human beings, this is not only difficult, but impossible. We are not Yogananda, Muktananda or Jesus. We cannot love everyone unconditionally; some people's needs are impossibly different from ours, and those we find hard to accept.

It is only through studying our own birth charts and the charts of our prospective partners that we understand our capacity to love particular human beings unconditionally, as they are, without expecting our partners to change themselves to suit us.

This does not mean that *behavior* cannot be changed. Our behavior and what we are at the core of our very beings are two entirely different matters. If our behavior annoys our partners, we can, if we so desire, change it in order to make our partners more comfortable in our presence. For example, a man with a Mercury-Mars-Uranus combination in his chart may be a frustrated race car driver who enjoys driving at excessive speeds. Should he become involved with a woman who objects to reckless driving, he certainly has the capability to change his driving style. In fact, his partner has the right to expect him to alter his driving habits. However, he cannot change the basic desire for adventure and excitement symbolized by Mercury-Mars-Uranus, though he can learn to channel it into more creative directions. His partner also needs to consider her objection to his behavior behind the wheel: is it the driving she dislikes, or is she afraid that his craving for excitement and adventure eventually will cause him to leave her?

The following case history illustrates this point. A young woman came to me with her chart and the chart of the man she had planned to marry. Her lover had thrown her over—for a man. My client was bewildered, since their relationship had seemed wonderful. Why had this happened? What, if anything, could she expect in the future from this man?

The chart comparison showed a high level of compatibility, with strong Venus-Mars and Venus-Pluto aspects. Yet my client's chart revealed a woman with domestic leanings and a healthy respect for traditional values. The chart of her friend showed a strong sex drive (he was a double Scorpio, with Pluto rising in Leo) and a desire for an unusual love life (Venus-Uranus square). Although Venus square Uranus is often associated with homosexuality, I find that such an extreme does not always manifest. The actual effect of Venus-Uranus is an unusual love life. This man's chart suggested that he would be game to try any kind of sexual practice, including gay sex.

After considering the man's whole chart my judgment was that he was not inherently gay. Rather, he was a highly-sexed individual interested in experiencing all kinds of sexual expressions. The Venus-Uranus square in his chart was being activated at that time by a Pluto transit and I felt that when this transit passed, he would return to a more traditional love life.

My client's chart, however, showed a heavy Cancer-Capricorn influence, and she needed a more conservative lifestyle. I wondered if a woman with such traditional desires could be happy with a man whom she knew had had a male lover and who would always crave an unusual love life. As it turned out, my client met someone else who was inclined toward a more traditionally-structured marriage.

The romantic attraction represented by Venus-Mars and Venus-Pluto matchups feels wonderful, but its importance in a lasting relationship pales besides that represented by shared values and ambitions. And while such factors can be measured to some degree in a chart comparison, compatibility is best judged by studying the natal charts of the two individuals.

Judging the needs of the individual can be somewhat tricky, because what a person thinks he wants and what he really needs in a relationship (and thus subconsciously seeks) often can be quite different. This dichotomy is most apparent when there is a Venus-Neptune affliction in the birth chart, a planetary combination that produces romantic delusions. Neptune at her best can express the highest form of spiritual love—*agape*—but for most people, Neptune confers a strong sense of romance along with some illusions and unrealistic expectations.

I use the pronoun "he" in the above paragraph because in my experience it is most often men who are plagued by such romantic delusions. Women, even those with Venus-Neptune afflictions, are generally more practical than men when considering their relationships. They are just as susceptible to charm and good looks, but usually take the time to get to know their partners before deciding whether or not to marry them. Men, on the other hand, especially those with Venus-Neptune afflictions, rarely consider a woman's needs and desires. I can't count the times I've heard male clients declare, "I almost always know right away whether I would want to marry a woman or not," yet these same men have had very few successful relationships.

Part of the reason for this, of course, lies in social conditioning. For thousands of years in patriarchal societies, it has been necessary for a woman to marry a man who could provide a stable home for her and her future children, and she was taught that good looks and charm didn't necessarily make a man a stable provider. Men, however, traditionally were brought up to believe that a good wife subordinates herself to her husband, and if her needs and desires conflict with his she must sacrifice them. Though attitudes are changing, centuries of social conditioning don't disappear overnight. Consequently, even today when a man meets an attractive woman who excites him physically and emotionally he often believes this is all that's necessary to make that woman his lifetime partner. Needless to say, this idea no longer works. Modern women consider their needs and desires just as important as their men's—and when they clash the relationship often crashes.

Before I continue, I wish to emphasize that I am not denigrating the traditional roles of man-as-provider and woman-as-nurturer. Even in these changing times, this sort of relationship can work beautifully if it is what both partners genuinely want. I merely point out that many people today wish to expand their horizons, on either an intellectual or financial level, and for these people such arrangements often prove unsatisfying, even if such a family structure is what they have been brought up to expect.

The Animus and the Anima

Swiss psychologist-astrologer Carl Jung first expounded upon the themes of the man within each woman and the woman within each man, and named them the *animus* and the *anima*. According to this theory, every human being seeks an outer partner who is a reflection of the inner partner—that part of a man which is female or which, in a woman, is male. These inner counterparts may be influenced by many different factors, which include subconscious memories of prior incarnations when you were of the opposite sex, childhood recollections of your parents, polar opposites of your own masculine or feminine traits, and romantic archetypes.

In this age of movies and television, our inner partners are probably more susceptible to the influence of the archetypes disseminated by the mass media than in past eras. A man's inner partner may take on the characteristics of Loni Anderson, a woman's animus may bear a strong resemblance to Tom Selleck. Although this influence is not always negative, for most people it appears to be confusing at the very least. According to the animus-anima theory, a person cannot fully experience a relationship with the outer partner until he or she comes to terms with the inner partner—and coming to terms with this deep unconscious side of oneself can be difficult if the true nature is clouded by images of romantic archetypes.

Astrologically, the anima in a man's chart is represented by the Moon and Venus, and their signs, house positions, and aspects. In a woman's chart, the Sun and Mars and their various positions in the birth chart represent the animus. By analyzing these horoscopal positions we can formulate a picture of the individual's animus or anima.

The Shadow Self

Perhaps you are aware that within you lies a darker, more "evil" side, which is unconscious and buried within the layers of the psyche. This negative side of yourself repels and yet fascinates you—and so you are attracted to, and at the same time repulsed by people whose traits are similar to your shadow self. Many people form intense attachments with partners who reflect their darker sides. Often we are traumatized by such relationships, not because our partners are cruel or evil, but because they mirror traits that we cannot abide in ourselves. So how can we love and accept unconditionally someone who possesses those same traits?

In a romantic relationship, this reflection of the shadow self can produce a kind of glamour and fascination—what back in the twenties used to be called "It." In the early stages of such an attraction, there is intense passion, sometimes to the point of obsession. Such relationships rarely last, however, and almost never result in a lifetime commitment. When the glamour fades and the partner is seen in a true light, we often are turned off by this shadow reflection of ourselves. We then tend to magnify it, projecting all our own negative traits, perhaps unfairly, onto the partner. Needless to say, much pain and anguish often result from such attachments. If you get to know your shadow self you have a better chance of avoiding such painful entanglements. At least, you will recognize them for what they are and not to try to build too many hopes around them.

In the natal chart, Pluto, its house position and aspects, is perhaps the most accurate portrait of the shadow self. The negative side of the sign in which the Sun, Moon, or Ascendant is positioned and the negative features of any aspects in which they are involved can also show characteristics of the shadow.

The Parents

All your relationships throughout your life are colored in some way by the relationship you had with your parents. Some psychoanalysts maintain that no matter whether you are male or female, all your relationships with men are influenced by the relationship you had with your father, and the way you interact with women is contingent on how you related to your mother. In my experience, this holds true most of the time; however, in some cases, I find that the roles are reversed. Sometimes, when the father is a retiring, quiet type, and the mother the more domineering parent, the child's future relations with women are based on the father.

The reason for this appears to be rooted in the fact that infants and young children are totally dependent on the parents for their very survival, and therefore the parents become as gods, whether or not they are worthy of the child's love and respect. No matter how kind or how thoughtless the parents may be, they represent survival and security. Unconsciously, then, we seek to perpetuate that "security" by re-creating the relationship we had with our parents—however hurtful or destructive it may have been.

Hence we see women who were beaten by their fathers and who attract abusive partners. Because the first man they ever loved beat them, they only feel at home with abusive men. The other extreme is the woman who worshipped her father because he eagerly did or gave her anything she wanted. Her adult relationships may fail because no one can ever measure up to her father. Whether our parents are good or bad ones, our adult love relationships can be affected adversely *if we allow it.* The best way to avoid this trap is to recognize your parents for what they were—fallible human beings whom you loved.

Astrologically, the Moon represents the mother and Saturn represents the father. Aspects to those planets, as well as to the fourth and tenth houses, reveal the nature of the relationship you had with your parents and how those relationships affect your future connections with the opposite sex.

Progressions and Transits

Sometimes an effect that is not indicated in the natal chart will occur at some time during the individual's lifetime, triggered by a progression or transit. During this period, such individuals may find their attitudes and standards changing. Karmically, they may have something to work out through the influence of the transit, but this does not mean they will live under the effect of that transit for the rest of their lives. Sometimes the effect ends when the transit passes; other times, attitudes are altered completely and irrevocably with the transit. Though the primary effect of the transit may pass, the altered views may color the person's relationships for the entire lifetime.

For instance, a man I know whose Moon is in Cancer in the eleventh house opposing Venus in Capricorn in the fifth had always embraced a traditional viewpoint toward marriage. He believed in total loyalty, one partner at a time, and one marriage for life. He was rigid in his attitudes and judgmental toward others who chose to "play the field," considering them "loose." He was especially intolerant of women who dated more than one person at a time.

However, when he was thirty-two, transiting Pluto squared his natal Moon-Venus opposition, and his marriage broke up. (Pluto signifies transformations and often the end of something.) Shortly afterwards transiting Jupiter conjoined his Moon and opposed his Venus. Suddenly he found himself attracted to many different women, and his rigid views relaxed. He went through a six-month period of promiscuity, during which time he met and dated many different types of women. He found that he could enjoy being involved with more than one woman at a time. He also discovered that women who dated without planning for marriage could be worthy of his respect. When the Jupiter transit passed, he married again and settled into a traditional marriage structure—but his judgmental attitudes were gone forever.

In another case, a woman who had always been something of a tomboy had enjoyed a healthy heterosexual love life until transiting Uranus squared her natal Venus. She became involved in a passionate love affair with another woman, a relationship that complicated her life in many ways. Her family was bewildered and many of her friends dropped her. Yet she made no effort whatsoever to hide her involvement. She felt that the relationship awakened her awareness of her masculine side and, at the same time, put her in touch with her femininity. When the Uranus transit passed, the lesbian relationship ended, and once more she began going out with men. She has no regrets about her affair and feels she is a much better person for the experience.

As these case histories illustrate, it is always important to consider the progressions and transits in a person's chart when examining his or her needs in a relationship.

Chart Comparisons and Past Lives

Clients often ask me if there is a way to use a chart comparison to discover if they have known somebody in a previous lifetime. At this stage of astrological research, so far as I know, there is none. However, the very fact that you are involved with someone in this lifetime suggests that you have known each other before. If you wish to judge whether or not you share karma with a particular individual, however, the following formula is one I have found to be effective.

If you and your friend both have what I call *karmic configurations* stretching across the same polar axis, chances are you have karmic needs that are similar, possibly identical. The chart comparison aspects between planets in the two karmic patterns should tell you more about how you are meant to work out this karma together.

Briefly, a karmic configuration or karmic pattern involves one or more of the personal planets or major cusps *and* one or more of the outer (or karmic) planets or the Moon's nodes. Such a combination is posited across one of the six polar axes: Aries-Libra, Taurus-Scorpio, Gemini-Sagittarius, etc. Although not every natal chart contains a discernible karmic configuration, charts that do reveal a great deal about that person's past-life experiences and attitudes, and how they affect the current lifetime.

The Karmic Side of Relationships

Whenever our group of researchers is interviewed regarding reincarnation, we inevitably are asked, "How many people do we meet in this life whom we have not met in former incarnations?" The answer is, "Very few." Often I am asked how you can tell when a person is someone you've known before. In most cases the very fact that an acquaintance is made is enough to suggest that you have met that person in a prior life. Perhaps the clerk at the supermarket who checks your groceries and the service station attendant who puts gas in your car are entities whom you have never known before. These are superficial acquaintances that probably will never progress further. However, if any kind of close connection exists between you and another individual, there is probably karma existing from previous incarnations.

Don't overlook karmic attachments to admired public figures, either. The number of teenagers who swooned over the Beatles and the men who nourished fantasies of Marilyn Monroe are legion; yet attraction to a public figure often reaches far beyond the usual star syndrome. I had an actor friend named Bob who all his life had been strongly drawn to Marlon Brando. When Bob himself became an actor, he made Brando his role model. One evening Bob was invited to a dinner party given by a director. One of the other guests was Marlon Brando. Bob spent a very pleasant evening with the star, who gave him many pointers on acting and the ins and outs of making it in the business. Later, when Bob was regressed, he discovered that in a recent past lifetime one of his associates—one he had looked up to—might have been the entity who is now Marlon Brando.

My father nourished an almost pathological hatred of the late John F. Kennedy, an emotion so strong it still persists more than twenty years after the former President's death—and which has little to do with JFK's politics. One of my own regressions revealed that my father was chief of an Irish clan that constantly warred with the tribe of Cinnedi. ("Cinnedi" is the Roman spelling of the Celtic name Kennedy.) JFK may or may not have been his own ancestor in that long-ago era, but it really doesn't matter. The Biblical quotation, "The sins of the fathers are visited on the sons" unfortunately runs true. The ancient cult of ancestors still lies deeply ingrained in the human psyche.

There is nothing mystical or magical about meeting someone you knew in a previous lifetime. We all do this practically every day. The nature of each involvement and how it affected you in a past lifetime, as well as how it affects you now, are the important issues. Interpersonal relationships with other human beings and how we handle them are the more important part of our spiritual development on this planet. According to metaphysical theory, we all began as one with God, and for reasons beyond our comprehension, God expanded the Divine Essence to become a multitude of different entities. These entities assume many different personalities over the eons in order to eventually work their way back to oneness with God.

I was once regressed to the point of the beginning, to the moment the Essence which gave birth to my soul split off from God. The feeling I experienced was one of intense emotional pain, of loneliness and isolation; I wanted to return, but realized I had to go on. Other people have been regressed and revealed the same type of experience.

It appears, then, that deep down in the furthest recesses of each individual's memory bank lie traces of this intense anguish and a longing to experience unity once more. Few of us possess enough awareness, however, to realize that what we seek is union with the Divine—so we look for it among our fellow human beings. And we are constantly disappointed because the very fact of our separate physical existence precludes true union. This disappointment pervades our waking consciousness, and since few are aware of the true source of our disappointment, we often blame the person with whom we are seeking unity. This blame may manifest in many ways, but regardless of the form it takes, it mars our psyches. If the relationship is an intense one, the blame cuts very deep and affects our relationships not only in this lifetime, but in future lifetimes as well.

I often hear the comment, "I must have done something terrible to him [or her] in a previous lifetime," when someone has been treated badly by another. This speculation may or may not be true. The trauma you experience with a parent, friend, or lover in the current lifetime may relate to a prior-life experience with that entity. Or, it simply may reflect an attitude you assumed in prior incarnations about relationships in general, an attitude that has been reinforced in the current existence, often in early childhood, probably by one of your parents.

Astrologically, past-life karma that is meant to be emphasized in the current incarnation generally can be discerned by studying karmic configurations. (For a detailed study of such patterns, see my earlier work *Astrology and Past Lives,* published by Para Research, Inc., 1987.)

Virtually all our attitudes toward relationships have been conceptualized in prior incarnations and locked into our current personalities by our parents. However, if the Moon and/or Venus in a man's chart, or the Sun and/or Mars in a woman's chart, appear in a karmic configuration, the individual's attitudes toward relationships, and his or her needs therein, are an important part of the purpose of the current incarnation.

The Polarities

The six polar axes are extremely important in karmic astrology. However, the polarities are also important when considering a person's relationship needs. All of us feel most comfortable with someone who shares our basic traits, tendencies, and outlooks. At the same time, however, we also seek a partner who will balance us. For instance, a man with Sun, Moon, Ascendant, or a heavy concentration of planets in Aries will feel most at ease with someone who shares his fundamental need for freedom, independence, and leadership. Simultaneously, though, he looks for a partner who possesses what he lacks—the Libran traits of sociability, compromise, and harmony—to balance his shortcomings and bring an added dimension to the couple's public image. He is looking for a person who can be both his twin and his opposite.

This quest is not as impossible as it sounds. We all have come in contact with people who combine traits that appear to be diametrically opposed to each other. Not all such people combine these characteristics in a creative manner, but the potential is always there.

The person whose birth chart contains a heavy Taurus-Scorpio influence seeks a balance of Taurean openness, affability, and practicality and Scorpionic shrewdness, secrecy, and passion. The Gemini-Sagittarius individual looks for a blend of Geminian logic with the vision and expansiveness of Sagittarius. The Cancer-Capricorn individual wants a partner who can blend a desire for a public life with a healthy respect for privacy. Leo-Aquarius people attempt to balance personal love with altruism, personal creativity and group involvement. Virgo-Pisces people seek partners who express both analysis and synthesis, serving in the mundane and spiritual realms. (For a more detailed analysis of the six polar axes, see *Astrology and Past Lives.*)

The Planets

Obviously the planets are quite important in analyzing the needs of the individual in personal relationships. Any planet in the fifth, seventh, or eleventh house—the relationship houses—will influence your personal involvements. The fourth and tenth houses rule the parents, and, as discussed earlier, your parents color all relationships you will have in your life. So any planet positioned in these two houses as well as any aspects to it will affect your relationship with the parent ruled by that house.

Astrologers still disagree about which house is associated with which parent. I find that a good rule of thumb is that the fourth house describes your nurturing parent, be it mother or father, and the tenth house rules the more dominant parent. Surprisingly, in about half the cases I've seen, the father, rather than the mother, was the nurturing parent.

The Sun

In a woman's chart, the Sun indicates her animus, or the male within her, whom she constantly seeks in a romantic partner of the opposite sex. The strength of the Sun by sign, house, and aspect reflects the strength of the woman's self-esteem and her ability to see her inner partner and her outer partner in a clear, unclouded manner. If the Sun is well-placed by sign and house and well-aspected, the woman's self-image is strong. She is likely to seek relationships that are realistic for herself, which fulfill her needs and desires, and probably will avoid the trauma of disappointing attachments.

If, however, her Sun is weak by sign or house and stressfully-aspected, the woman's self-esteem is low. She lacks confidence in herself and her abilities. Often she is too dependent, first on her parents and then on the men in her life. She may look for a substitute parent in her mate and be unhappy with any man who is unwilling or unable to play that role.

In the chart of any individual, the Sun represents the basic will and ego-drives, viewpoints, outlooks, and characteristics that he or she seeks to match and to balance. As mentioned before it is not impossible or even uncommon to find a partner who satisfies both needs. The challenge is understanding that these basic needs exist. When this is acknowledged, the individual can understand self and others much more clearly.

The Moon

The Moon represents your emotional stability and your ability to empathize with the feelings of others. If the Moon is weak or badly aspected, the individual might be most comfortable with a partner who is not especially sensitive and who is capable of dealing pragmatically with another's emotional instability. If the Moon is strong, however, the individual can accommodate almost anyone, but is less patient with people who lack sensitivity and feeling.

In a man's chart, the Moon represents the anima, or the woman within. A strong Moon indicates that the man is in balance with the feminine side of himself, that he likes women and enjoys their company. Therefore, he seeks a romantic relationship with a woman whom he can admire on all levels. A weak Moon, however, shows that the man probably is threatened by his own feminine side, and thus he sees women as threats. This person is probably happiest in a relationship where his partner is submissive or offers him no competition. If the Moon's strengths and weaknesses are mixed, the man's attitudes are likely to change and grow as he matures, therefore his relationships probably will be happiest in his later years.

Mercury

Mercury represents the ability to communicate—an important factor in any relationship. If Mercury is strong and well-aspected, the person has good communication skills and can be content even in a relationship with someone who lacks this talent. A person with a strong Mercury can break through the partner's barriers and, to use a cliché, "communicate well enough for both of them." If Mercury is weak, however, the individual has trouble communicating with others and would have problems in a relationship with another non-communicator. This individual needs a partner who either has no interest at all in talking or who can handle both sides of the conversation alone.

Venus

Venus represents the ability to love. If Venus is strong and well-aspected, the individual is capable both of feeling and expressing love in a open, joyous, and tactful manner. If Venus is weak, however, the person is incapable of either feeling, expressing, or understanding true, unconditional love, especially if the planet is afflicted by Saturn. To be romantically involved with such a person requires independence, self-esteem, and a thick skin.

If Venus is afflicted by Neptune, the person's approach to love is clouded with fantasy and unrealistic expectations. Such people are susceptible to many disappointments in love. This individual needs a partner who is not dependent on outward expression of feeling, and who doesn't look to the partner for validation of his or her desirability. In a man's chart, Venus is a significator of the anima.

Mars

Often Mars is associated with sex, but modern research indicates that Pluto may be connected more closely with sex, per se. Mars relates to sex as a reflection of the basic energy that a person channels into a relationship. If Mars is strong in the chart and well-aspected, the person probably has a great deal of energy to channel into everything, including romantic attachments. Surprising enough, even though a prominent Mars can bring high spirits and a competitive nature, which could result in quarrelsomeness, a person whose Mars is strong can only be truly happy with a strong partner. Such people have little patience with passive, "shrinking violet" types. Conversely, an individual with a weak Mars probably would feel threatened and uncomfortable with a partner whose Mars is strong. In a woman's chart, Mars is one of the significators of the animus.

Jupiter

Jupiter represents tolerance and an easy-going nature, along with friendliness and optimism. A person whose chart contains a well-aspected Jupiter is probably lots of fun and can get along with anyone. A person with an ill-aspected Jupiter, however, lacks self-esteem and good feelings, and requires a partner who is willing to reinforce his or her self-esteem. It is difficult to imagine Jupiter having a negative effect upon any relationship, but a weak Jupiter can be strongly affected by other negative factors in the chart. By the same token, a well-aspected Jupiter can intensify the good effects. Jupiter should be considered in light of other factors in the chart. Remember, the keywords for this planet are exaggeration and abundance.

Saturn

Traditionally, Saturn has been called the "Greater Malefic," and is said to deny and obstruct any matters in the chart which fall under his influence. Modern astrological research, however, seems to be a bit more broad-minded. In some cases Saturn may deny, but in most cases he merely indicates anxieties, rigidity, and that which is most important to the individual.

When positioned in the fifth, seventh, and eleventh houses, or in aspect to the relationship planets, Saturn suggests that relationships are important to the individual, and he or she has the ability to make commit-ments and to stick with them. If Saturn is strongly placed and well-aspected, the individual is willing to work at making relationships successful and does not take commitments lightly. If Saturn is weak, the person's resolve is proportionately weak. He or she may avoid close attachments entirely or lack a strong sense of commitment to them. Or, the person may desire intimacy, but tend to attract destructive involvements and stay in them even at the cost of personal well-being. People with Venus-Saturn afflictions seem to be especially vulnerable to the latter effect. A strong Saturn in the chart, whether it involves the relationship houses and planets or not, seems to be essential to a person's desire and ability to form commitments and keep them.

Uranus

Uranus appears to indicate a desire for freedom within a relationship. If Uranus is involved with the relationship houses or planets in any way, the individual needs plenty of independence and does not respond well to a partner who is jealous or overly possessive, or who demands an excessive amount of attention. There is a powerful attraction for unusual or unconventional relationships.

If Uranus is strong and well-aspected, this individual's partner can count on loyalty and true friendship, even though the attachment seems looser than most. If the planet is weak and poorly aspected, however, the individual may seek a so-called "open" relationship and may do what he or she pleases without much consideration for the partner. If this person's partner does not share his or her viewpoint, a great deal of pain might result. However, the capacity for friendship, if not romance, remains and will increase as the individual grows older.

Neptune

Neptune represents ideals, illusion, and fantasy, and if she aspects the relationship planets or houses, the individual is a romantic. If Neptune is strong and well-aspected, the person has the capacity to experience the highest and purest form of spiritual love (agape). There is potential for both partners to benefit psychologically, spiritually, and emotionally in the relationship. Such a love can enable the individuals involved to make the best use of their potential as human beings on all levels.

If Neptune is weak or poorly aspected, especially if the planet activates the relationship houses or planets, the desire and capacity for agape still exists. However, people with this placement often experience relationships that are fraught with fantasy. They rarely see potential partners as they really are. They choose to believe that everyone is capable of unconditional love, though few are. These individuals fasten their affections onto people who are not worthy of them, yet they reject potential partners who might come closer to fulfilling their ideals. This tendency towards fantasy can lead to confusion, disillusionment, and anguish. Such people need to take a good long look at their fantasies and try especially hard to see potential partners as they actually are.

Pluto

Like Saturn, Pluto often scares people. Pluto is associated with secrecy and manipulation, as well as treachery and death, and it is easy to jump to conclusions when analyzing a chart that shows Pluto involved with the relationship houses or planets. While the unpleasant characteristics of Pluto may exist in a relationship, it does not have to be that way. Pluto represents the transformational factor in relationships, and when it appears in the relationship houses or aspects the relationship planets, the implication is that the individual will experience transformation and regeneration through relationships.

People with this type of Pluto placement will be drawn to powerful, magnetic people, often those who are extremely willful and who may dominate their lives. Their attachments often enable them to see parts of themselves that they would never have realized otherwise. In such relationships, sex takes on an exaggerated importance. If treachery, manipulation, or death are part of the individual's relationships, such events will have a regenerative effect on him or her. The highest possible manifestation of Pluto is transformation.

Case Histories

Great Harry

England's well-loved King Henry VIII was notorious for bad luck in relationships. Henry, a second son, came to the throne of England in 1509, at the age of eighteen. His elder brother, Prince Arthur, heir to the throne, had died a few years previously. Henry's first decision as king was to marry his brother's widow, Catherine of Aragon, a Spanish princess five years his senior. Catherine was gracious and intelligent, and at first Henry was quite taken with her. For years their marriage was a strong one. As the years passed, however, Catherine grew stout and matronly and her intelligence, which once had fascinated Henry, suddenly seemed pedantic. Henry was still a magnificent man, and ladies of the court constantly sought his eye, and he finally settled on a dark-eyed, auburn-haired enchantress: Anne Boleyn.

Vivacious and sensual, Anne refused to become Henry's mistress; she would only be his queen. In a sensational power play, Anne won Henry to her side. He split from the Church of Rome and divorced Catherine, citing John the Baptist: "It is not right for you to have your brother's wife." Henry and Anne were married. But Anne was flirtatious and soon there were whispers that she was not faithful to the king. Henry, an insanely jealous man, chose to believe the rumors, though historians now believe that Anne was only a coquette, not an adulteress. She was arrested and beheaded for treason.

Henry's third wife was a rather plain, bookish young gentlewoman named Jane Seymour. Unlike the charismatic Anne, Jane attracted little attention from other men, and she spent most of her time doing good works and caring for Henry's children. Jane is said to have been the only wife whom Henry genuinely loved, but whether that love would have stood the test of time we'll never know. They had only been married for a short time when Jane died while giving birth to Henry's only son.

The fourth marriage was arranged without the couple ever meeting. Anne of Cleves, a German princess, had her portrait painted by the artist, Hans Holbein, and sent it to Henry. The story goes that Henry was pleased with the portrait and agreed to marry her. When she arrived in England, however, he dubbed her a "great Flanders mare" and maintained he was repulsed by her ugliness. Historians have long puzzled over Henry's declaration; even allowing for the fact that the Holbein portrait flattered her, contemporary likenesses of Anne of Cleves all indicate that she was not unattractive. Yet the marriage probably was never consummated and Henry had it quickly annulled.

Henry's fifth wife, Catherine Howard, was Anne Boleyn's cousin, said to have been the most beautiful of Henry's wives. Yet her behavior was even more scandalous than Anne's, and she was known to have had an affair with a young knight named Thomas Culpeper. She met the same fate as her cousin Anne, and her last words were, "I die a queen, but I would rather die the wife of Culpeper!"

Katryn Parr was Henry's sixth wife, a rather nondescript woman who cared for Henry for the rest of his life and proved a devoted stepmother to his children. Though Henry never loved her as he had loved Jane Seymour, he did feel a strong affection for Katryn, and demanded on his deathbed that she be cared for so long as she lived.

The six marriages of Henry VIII greatly affected the course of world history. But why did such a handsome, exciting man as Henry was in his prime fail to attract a good marriage? Let us consider Henry's chart.

When we consider Henry's wives, we notice that he seemed to have little or no luck with attractive women. Any king can have his pick of lovely women of suitable background, and this should be especially true for a handsome king like Henry. But Henry's wives' portraits all reveal one astounding fact: by no stretch of the imagination could any one of them, with the exception of Catherine Howard, be considered beautiful. (Anne Boleyn was sensual and vivacious, but except for her incredible black eyes her features were rather ordinary.) The wife whom Henry is said to have loved most—Jane Seymour—can only be called plain. To most of us, this seems rather odd, especially since Henry's mother, Elizabeth of York, was considered to be one of the great beauties of Europe.

Which brings us to an interesting question. If we accept that the mother forms the basis for all our relationships with women throughout our lives, we must ask: could the beautiful, kindhearted Elizabeth have so traumatized her son that he was insecure with women and never able to have a successful marriage?

Remember, though, that Henry was Elizabeth's second son. In the entire history of the British royal family, the eldest son, the heir to the throne, has always been valued most. Prince Arthur lacked Henry's good looks, his brilliance, his magnetism. Yet throughout Henry's youth, his mother lavished most of her care and affection upon his elder brother—and his child's psyche apparently made a decision (possibly one that had past-life associations as well), "All beautiful women are treacherous." Perhaps in a former incarnation, the entity who became Henry may even have been an unfaithful woman.

If we study the Moon and Venus in Henry's chart we find that Henry valued other qualities over beauty. His Moon in Aries, involved in a wide grand fire trine, indicates that he liked a woman with spunk. Because Neptune is involved in that trine, we can see that he idealized this type of woman and, at least in the initial stages of the relationship, did not

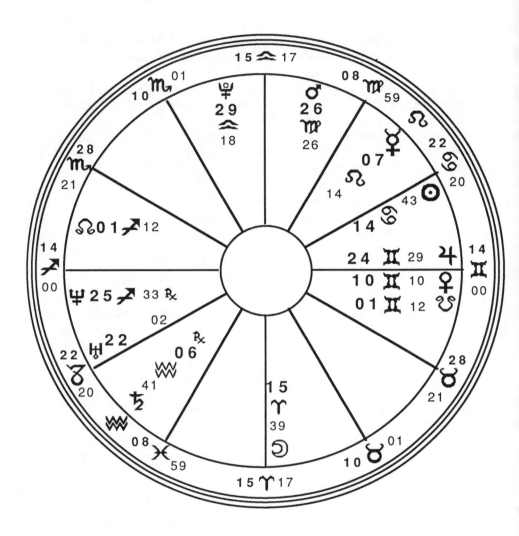

Figure 2.1
King Henry VIII
June 28, 1491 5:55 pm
Greenwich, England
Placidus house cusps

see such women as they actually were. The Arien Moon squares his Sun,
indicating a clash between the anima and the individual will. A square
between the Moon and Uranus denotes upsets and separations from this
type of woman, hence the failure of his marriages to the passionate Anne
Boleyn and the lovely Catherine Howard.

Venus in Gemini implies that Henry especially valued intelligence in women, hence the happiness in his early years with Catherine of Aragon and his attractions to the plain-but-educated Jane Seymour and Katryn Parr. The trine between Venus and Saturn suggests that a relationship with an intelligent woman would probably last much longer than one with a fiery, passionate type. However, Venus only makes one other aspect, a wide sextile to Mercury, hinting that even this type of relationship for Henry would go nowhere; hence his eventual boredom in his marriage to Catherine of Aragon.

The Sun in his seventh house indicates that much of Henry's energy would be centered around marriage, and Jupiter's presence in that house suggests several marriages. The square to Mars and the opposition to Neptune imply that there would be lies, treachery, and deceit in his marriage. Henry both plotted against his wives and was deceived by them—and, in the case of Anne of Cleves, about them.

The Gemini-Sagittarius pattern across the first-seventh axis indicates a karmic obligation involving relationships which concerns balancing intellect (Gemini) and intuition (Sagittarius). Neptune is involved in this configuration, and is positioned in the first house, so it would appear that Henry was meant to trust his intuition over his intellect. On the surface, it seems that he was governed more by fantasy than by ESP—at least where his marriages were concerned. Also, Henry chose to believe gossip and rumors about his wives rather than using his logic or his intuition.

Finally, we must consider Henry's own shadow self. Pluto is posited in Scorpio in the tenth house. We must deduce from this that Henry craved power and relished the role of despot—but he was a populist king; the English people loved him. So he dared not show this tyrannical side of himself to the public, and actually refused to acknowledge it himself.

With his Cancer Sun, Henry projected a family-oriented image. He may have had many women in his life, but he usually married them. He was known to have had only two mistresses—fewer than any other English king except William the Conqueror.

There was a sensuous side to Henry as well. He loved good food and good wine; in his later years he grew quite corpulent, and in his last year of life had to be hoisted around by a crane-like device. Henry's shadow side was a power-mad, sensual, unconscious self—traits which were clearly reflected in the passionate, power-hungry Anne Boleyn.

What kind of woman would have made Henry happy? From analyzing the positions of the Moon and Venus we can see that he would have been happiest with a woman who combined intelligence, independence, a spirited nature, and a touch of romance. How strange it is to realize that the one woman among all his six wives who came closest to reflecting his anima was the one he spurned: Anne of Cleves, who left the land of her fathers to marry a man she had never met, who inspired a famous artist to paint a beautiful portrait of her, who held her head high during Henry's public rejection of her, and who courageously carved out a satisfying life for herself after the divorce.

It appears that toward the end of Henry's life, he realized this. On his deathbed he called her "the pick of the bunch." In his will, he left her a surprisingly generous legacy. We cannot help wondering if in subsequent lives these two entities met again and completed—or made progress towards completing—whatever karma there was between them.

Like the Waves upon the Sand

Our next case concerns an intelligent young man, born to an upper-middle-class suburban family, well-educated, and trained from childhood to be an entertainer. At the age of eighteen he became involved with Swami Muktananda, and has been an ardent disciple and Seeker on the Path ever since. His upbringing and his spiritual inclinations dictate a high standard of behavior, but a part of him—his shadow self—is drawn to the seamy side of life (possibly a result of at least two previous incarnations when he lived outside the law).

When he moved to Los Angeles to enter the music scene, most of the people he associated with were street people, drug dealers, and other unsavory types. On one level, these associations were destructive, but on another level, his companions provided a cathartic release for him. Unlike upper-class scions and spiritual teachers, they imposed few restrictions on his behavior and allowed him the freedom to express all sides of his multi-faceted nature.

Success in the entertainment industry, a goal to which he aspired, demanded a strange combination of shrewdness and behavior of the highest caliber. He was constantly at war with himself, trying to be polished but also relaxed among Hollywood's low-life, and the two different parts of himself were frequently at odds with each other. The two conflicting sides of his personality also made it impossible for him to have a successful relationship with a woman.

When we study his chart, we find that the Moon and Venus suggest an anima with a sensitive, quiet, artistic, and spiritual nature, possessing some intelligence (Moon conjunct Mercury in Pisces), who is also active, independent, an individualist, and a leader (Venus in Aries). The placement of Pluto in Leo in the fifth house, however, indicates a shadow self that is sensual and self-indulgent. The negative side of Aries involves childishness, selfishness, and a quick temper. As discussed previously, we can and do experience powerful attractions to people who reflect our shadow selves. So while this man often found himself drawn to would-be

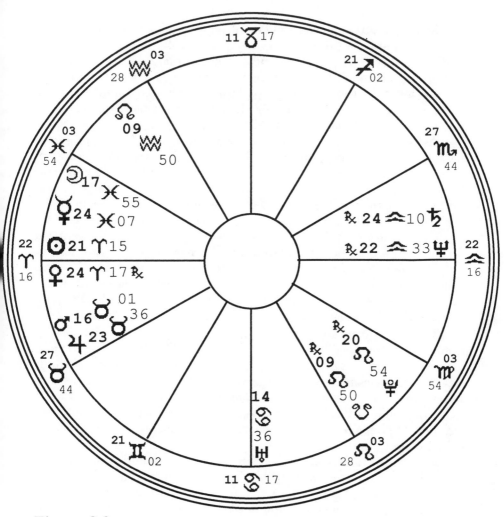

Figure 2.2
The Aspirant
April 11, 1953 5:57 am
Toronto, Canada
Placidus house cusps

actresses and singers who spent most of their time hanging out in bars and doing drugs, a part of him could not accept their way of life. That part wanted these women to embrace the spiritual path, and he fervently believed that they would change their evil ways.

Of course, the success of a relationship cannot be contingent upon one or both partners changing. Not surprisingly, none of this man's early attachments lasted and most ended with bad feelings.

Some years later, he became involved with a woman who appeared to reflect his anima in almost every way. She was, like him, from the upper middle class, socially conscious, and on the spiritual Path. Yet he became disillusioned with her when he realized that she was unable to accept his shadow self. This time, it was his partner who wanted him to change, to become more rigid in his behavior. The pressure of her demands upon him eventually affected his health.

Astrologically, we can see that this man would have problems throughout life in his relationships with women. Venus is opposing Saturn and Neptune. Saturn both restricts involvements and binds a person to them, even if these relationships are destructive. Neptune clouds the perceptions and keeps the individual from seeing partners as they actually are. Uranus, which squares the Venus-Saturn-Neptune pattern, inclines a person to unconventional relationships. Uranus also indicates a need for lots of freedom, and a lack of regard for the partner's needs and desires.

The Moon in Pisces shows the ability to love two women at the same time. For this man to have a truly successful relationship, he needs a woman who is secure and independent enough to let him have his freedom and not feel threatened if he expresses an attraction to someone else.

The Venus-Neptune opposition presents serious problems, resulting from his failure to see his partners as they actually are and his attempts to force them into his prescribed mold. The Neptune placement also indicates a strong desire for unconditional love and true friendship, as well as romance, and for someone he can look up to and admire. It will take a determined effort on his part to see beyond the Neptunian fantasies, but once he trains himself to do so, the positive Neptune effects will be more apparent in his life.

Pluto in the fifth house indicates a pattern of transformation through love affairs, and indeed, as traumatizing as this man's affairs have been, he has become a better person as a result of them. His early involvements with Sunset Strip women left him more determined to make the most of himself; his last affair purged him of much of his Arien arrogance and cruelty, while grounding him more firmly in reality. The Venus-Neptune-Saturn pattern indicates that perhaps this man will not find romantic happiness until late in life—but it will be sweeter for having been delayed. Clearly part of this entity's karma, indicated by the Aries-Libra karmic configuration, is to work to transform his attitudes toward relationships.

Notes

1. Swami Muktananda, *The Perfect Relationship,* (San Francisco: SYDA Foundation, 1982).

Part Two

Parent-Child Relationships

3

Parent-Child
Relationships:
Where It All Begins

The most significant and karmic of all relationships is the one between parent and child. We like to think of romantic relationships as being the most important; however, according to most researchers, this is not the case. Usually, the strongest karma we share with others in any lifetime is with our parents. It is our parents who provide our first impressions of the outside world and of other people. It is through them, too, that we become aware of our separateness. Our parents either give or deny us love in our formative years, thereby determining our level of self-esteem, which lays the groundwork for later success and happiness. It is our parents who build the foundations for our world views, our lives, and our selves. The relationships we have with our parents form the backbone of all our future relationships with other human beings.

No matter what karmic condition an individual chooses to complete in any particular lifetime, the parents to some degree participate in that karma. It is the parents who provide the child's physical body and its genetic makeup, as well as the individual's psychological beginnings, sociological and economic environment, educational and spiritual background. Even if the child is an orphan, the karma of the parentless condition represents a pattern begun in previous lifetimes that the entity has chosen to complete in the current incarnation. The parent, by dying or abandoning the child, helps to create the necessary karmic situation.

Cases of adoptive parents and children are complex. Usually, the adoptive parents provide the social, educational, economic, and spiritual background, as well as all the psychological effects which result from the interplay between the parents and the child. Yet the child retains a strong karmic bond with the natural parents, even if he or she never knows them. For it is the natural parents who have given the child its physical body and genetic background—and created the condition whereby the child becomes orphaned and must make a new life with adoptive parents. Regardless of the circumstances, they are totally appropriate to the karmic need, and the child has strong karmic bonds with both sets of parents. Adoptive parents also have much to gain karmically by rearing a child born to someone else.

Archetypal Images

The parent-child relationship becomes even more complex when we add archetypal images to the mix. Deeply ingrained within the psyches of all of us are the image of the warm, nurturing mother, and the strong, authoritarian, but still loving and protective provider-father. Of course, these archetypes don't always apply to the flesh-and-blood individuals who eventually become parents. Too often mothers are selfish, irresponsible, not really interested in their children, and fathers can be shiftless and undependable, unable to hold a job—then the child becomes confused. Its parents don't fit the images of father and mother. Resentment often builds in the child as he or she wonders why mother and/or father don't act like a *real* mother or father.

In cases where a parent is absent—either by death or divorce—the archetypes often fill the gap left by the human parent. Therefore, the child's dead or absent parent may become in that child's mind some kind of paragon of virtue, representing all the noblest qualities of the archetypal parent—which may hurt the child's relationship with the remaining parent and profoundly (and too often negatively) affect future relationships with other members of the absent parent's sex. In cases of adopted children, when the child's relationship with the adoptive parents is less than idyllic, the child often will fantasize about the natural parents, mentally building them up into the perfect parents according to archetypal images. The result is that the hangups based on the child's relationship with the adoptive parents, *and* his or her unrealistic fantasies of the natural parents confound the child's future relationships.

Parents, too, may find themselves battling the image of the archetypal child: well-behaved, obedient, loving, loyal, grateful, dutiful, accepting the parents' guidance without question. How many parents look forward to the birth of a baby with this fantasy image in mind, only to discover in later years that the child has ideas of its own? The parents can become disappointed not only in the child, but in themselves as well. How did they fail?

In cases where parents have lost a child, the bereaved parents often find their memories of the dead child clouded by ideals based on the archetype—and their surviving children may suffer by comparison. I have also seen cases where clever children played the role of the ideal child in order to manipulate their parents.

Responses and Responsibilities

Undoubtedly, our parents have a profound effect both on our psychological makeup and our relationships with others. It is interesting, however, to see how different individuals react in surprisingly unique ways to the same set of circumstances. Parents have a great deal of responsibility to their children, and the children also have responsibilities, not only to their parents but to themselves as well. They are responsible for making the most of their own potential, in spite of all obstacles, and to be the best they can be.

Sigmund Freud emphasized the parents' role in forming the child's psychological and emotional foundations. However, later psychologists used Freud's discoveries to make the parents scapegoats for every individual's hangups. Of course, a person's outlook and attitudes, as well as his or her relationships, are directly related to those of the parents.

But no matter how unbalanced a parent may be, no matter how much a parent's hangups interfere with a child's development, something in the child always meets the parent halfway. There is an individual measure of dependency or independence, a touch of self-esteem or insecurity, of mental health or neurosis which makes each child react positively or negatively to a parent's influence. One child might react to a drunken parent's beatings with a determination to stay away from alcohol and never to hurt any living thing. Another child could respond to a parent's kindness and understanding with rebellion and scorn, and decide never to become a "mealy-mouthed-goody-two-shoes."

Let's consider the case of Jane, a young woman who has Leo rising and thus a desperate need for attention. Throughout her childhood, Jane's father showed little interest in her. She first tried to get him to notice her for her dancing talent, then for her good grades in school, but her abilities failed to impress him. Jane made another plea for attention, this time by behaving outrageously, associating with unsavory companions, and running away. The attention she got from her father was anger, punishment, and beatings. Jane developed a severe lack of confidence that she carried into adulthood and her marriage. Whenever her husband became involved with other interests and failed to pay as much attention to her as she desired, Jane responded by becoming ill.

Jane's father had nothing against Jane. He was simply an intelligent, talented, self-centered, and somewhat withdrawn person who ignored all of his children. Jane's older sister was independent and, from an early age, managed to look after herself. Her younger brother was introverted and spent most of his time reading and painting. Neither sibling seemed to need attention as much as Jane did, so their father's aloofness didn't affect them in the same way.

Contrary to what early psychiatrists believed, a child's mind is not a blank slate, to be composed and created by the parents. Each child is an individual from birth, and he or she will react to both flesh-and-blood parents and parental archetypes in a unique way.

Seeing the Parent and Child in the Birth Chart

When analyzing parent-child relationships and their possible future reverberations, astrologers can trace these individual reactions by first studying the child's natal chart. We can see the basic nature of the human being indicated in the chart. Such things as the potential for self-esteem, dependency and independence, selfishness and compassion are revealed through certain chart factors, therefore, we can estimate how the child will react to parental shortcomings and whether he or she will make the best of childhood circumstances and use them constructively.

We can also look at the parent's chart to discover whether that parent is patient enough, responsible enough, aware enough, or compassionate enough to actually make the most of his or her responsibilities toward the child. And above all, do both parent and child possess enough awareness to give each other the unconditional love and acceptance that each of them needs? Can they transcend the influence of the archetypes and love each other, not for what traditional fantasies say they should be, but for what they really are?

The astrologer-psychologist has a unique job in analyzing family relationships and their future effect on both parent and child. If the astrologer sees two people whose relationship has a lot of potential and only a few trouble spots, that job is easy. It is more difficult, though, when the two charts indicate people with entirely different attitudes and world views, and the comparison of the two shows little compatibility. How can you tell a young man, for example, that the mother he worships is someone with whom he has little in common, and that his problems with her will probably foul up his future relationships with women unless he acknowledges these problems and works through them? How do you tell a father that the son he has centered all his hopes on will probably always be a ne'er-do-well, and that the father's karma may be to learn to love and accept his son regardless?

When analyzing a parent-child relationship, the astrologer looks at the parental houses in the child's chart: the fourth and tenth. The planetary rulers of the signs on these houses, as well as the Moon and Saturn, are also important factors to consider. How are these planets and houses aspected? Are the planets strong or weak by sign and house? Does the child's chart show the parents to be strong figures, or weak? How do the parental houses tie in with the child's Sun, Ascendant, and ruling planets? Are the aspects between these planets supportive or detrimental?

How do these parental houses and planets connect with the Sun and Mars in a woman's chart, or the Moon and Venus in a man's? How are the individual's future relationships to be affected by the relationships he or she had with the parents? Does Neptune afflict the parental planets, indicating a strong influence from the archetypes?

In the parent's chart, what planets rule or are in the fifth house (or, in the case of step-parents, the eleventh)? Are these planets strong or weak by sign and aspects? How do these planets tie in with the parent's Sun, Moon, and Ascendant? When we compare the two charts, do we find two individuals who are basically compatible, or whose attitudes are so diametrically opposed that they will probably never be friends? Whatever the findings, it is a challenge for the astrologer to discern the best way for the parties to make the most of the relationship.

Karmic patterns in the charts of both the parents and the children should be considered, too. In the parent's chart, is the ruler of the fifth house (or, if appropriate, the eleventh) involved in a karmic configuration? If so, children are to some degree part of the overall karmic purpose of the parent's incarnation, and the relationship is likely to be intense. In the child's chart, is the ruler of the fourth or tenth house, or are these houses themselves, involved in a karmic configuration? Do both charts have karmic patterns across the same polar axis? If so, the effect is intensified. The involvement can be, but need not be, an actual physical involvement in each other's lives. It is also possible that the ghost of the parent will always remain with the child and affect the child's self-image, relationships, attitudes, and behavior in one way or another.

Case Studies

Doreen

Doreen's childhood was marred by her parents' divorce and the subsequent departure of her father. She and her elder sister lived with their mother. Doreen's mother had been a great beauty in her youth, and Doreen's sister established herself as the "pretty one" in the family before Doreen was born. As a result, Doreen (erroneously) believed herself to be homely, and at times seemed to be trying to make herself unattractive. Her relationships with men were always rather explosive, and she seemed at times to avoid romance, preferring to keep the men in her life as "friends." Her chart shows the Sun conjunct the Moon in the eleventh house, the house of friendship.

Doreen's relationship with her mother had always been difficult. The mother was a strong, overbearing personality, who, it seemed, tried to boost her own ego by putting her daughter down. Doreen's life pattern appeared to be a continual search for substitute mothers who would typify the archetypal mother. When the substitute mother proved to be a human being, Doreen would return to live again with her natural mother, where she faced the same problems but never resolved them. Doreen's need for a substitute mother made her friendships with other women difficult, and her frustration carried over into her relationships with men as well.

For a time, noted metaphysical author Marcia Moore served as Doreen's fantasy mother. Marcia welcomed Doreen into her home with open arms, but Marcia thought of Doreen more as a colleague than a daughter. Eventually, Marcia became too busy with her writing and lecturing to give Doreen the attention she so desperately needed—and one day Doreen simply disappeared. She had returned to live with her natural mother again. I called her from time to time over the next few years, but she spent so much time complaining about her mother that I eventually stopped communicating with her.

Doreen's tendency to idealize females is shown by the position of the Sagittarian Moon and the placement of Venus and Neptune conjoining the MC in her chart. The conjunction of Saturn to Venus, Neptune, and the MC, squaring Uranus, suggests blocks and upsets regarding all matters ruled by Venus and Neptune. In Doreen's case, the tenth house represented the mother as her mother was a forceful, aggressive career woman who constantly urged her daughter to get out of the house and make something of herself. Doreen's father was a quiet and unassuming accountant whose business kept him sequestered in an office. His favorite pastime

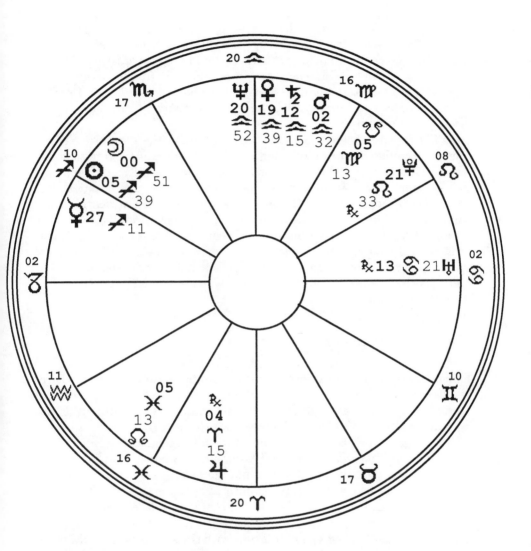

Figure 3.1
Doreen
November 29, 1951
South Gate, California
Placidus house cusps

was retreating to a cabin in the desert. He was always available, by telephone if nothing else, to listen sympathetically to Doreen's woes and extend a helping hand when she needed it. Obviously, her father was the nurturing parent, represented by Doreen's fourth house.

The situation is confused, however, by the placement of Neptune on the tenth house cusp. Neptune suggests that a parent was absent, and one would normally assume that this referred to Doreen's father since he didn't live with her. However, her mother actually fit the image of the absent parent better than the father since she expressed little interest in her daughter and often drove the young woman out into the world to seek substitute mothers.

The prominence of idealistic Sagittarius and the romantic Venus-Neptune conjunction, complicated by Mars, Saturn, and Uranus, would seem to indicate that Doreen would have tremendous difficulty overcoming her tendency to idealize all human beings and women in particular. But a ray of hope exists in the placement of practical Capricorn on the Ascendant. Capricorn's vibrations often don't come into full flower until the individual has reached maturity. When I last spoke to Doreen, she was still very young. She is now thirty-six and may be mature enough to make use of her Capricorn Ascendant. While not abandoning her ideals, perhaps she has learned to be more realistic about them and about the people with whom she lives.

The Mad Booths of Baltimore

One of the most revered actors of the nineteenth century was Junius Brutus Booth. Small in stature but magnetic and handsome, Booth was famous for his portrayals of all Shakespeare's characters, but his most highly acclaimed role was that of the infamous Richard III. Changeable and high-strung, Junius Brutus was known for his eccentricities and boyish escapades. He also was a devoted humanitarian and champion of the downtrodden, particularly children and animals.

Booth was also quite amorous, and was sued for paternity twice before he was seventeen years old. He married young, to a woman named Adelaide who bore him two children. After they had been married for some years he fell in love again, this time with the woman who would share the rest of his life: Mary Ann. Shortly after he met Mary Ann, he informed Adelaide that he had booked a series of performances in America—and left England with Mary Ann. They settled on a small farm near Bel Air, Maryland.

Although he was already showing signs of insanity, Junius Brutus was quite successful in America. The audiences loved him, in spite of— or perhaps because of—his growing tendency to cut performances and goof around on stage.

Booth never told Adelaide about Mary Ann, but managed to maintain two different households, one in London, one in Maryland. He kept Adelaide happy with letters and infrequent visits. He would book a play in London, move back in with her for the run of the play, and then return to his fast-growing family in America. Biographers still debate whether Adelaide ever knew about her husband's second family.

And an impressive family it was. Mary Ann bore Junius eight children, three of whom died in infancy. Of the five who survived, three were to become actors almost as famous as their father: Junius Brutus, Jr., Edwin, and John Wilkes.

Junius' father, Richard Booth, had wanted his son to become a barrister, but Junius was hardly suited for the bar. Junius Brutus himself believed that actors had no place in politics. Yet he agreed with many of his father's viewpoints, and was quite eloquent in expounding on current governmental affairs. He was known for enthralling listeners with his vigorous monologues on republicanism, and one of his favorite pastimes was going to a local saloon and debating political issues with Sam Houston.

Idealistic political opinions were a large part of the conversation in the Booth home when the children were growing up. Particularly vulnerable was Johnny Wilkes, a vivacious, charming child who amused and captivated everyone around him, and was his mother's favorite.

If Junius had a favorite, however, it was Edwin. A quiet and unassuming child, Edwin became his father's constant confidante and devoted companion and guardian. It was Edwin to whom Junius turned for comfort whenever he lapsed into one of his increasing fits of alcoholism or insanity; it was Edwin who showed the same studious interest in acting as his father. Eventually, Edwin travelled with his father on his many theatrical engagements. During Junius's fits of depression in which he retreated to bars, determined to take a night off, Edwin often chased after his father and pleaded with him to keep his commitments, most of the time successfully. Colleagues observed that young Edwin could actually command his father—and at times Junius would meekly obey.

Junius' attention to Edwin awoke resentment in Mary Ann who believed that he had forgotten her favorite, young Johnny. Historians have often lamented that most photographs of John Wilkes Booth show him as somewhat saturnine in appearance. He was in fact strikingly handsome, as well as courteous and joyous, with a gentle and loving disposition. He was mischievous as a boy, and lacked the scholarly quality that his father so admired in Edwin. Still, Johnny's sensitivity and affection endeared him to both family and associates. On one occasion, when dashing out of a theatre, Johnny accidentally bumped into a street child and knocked the boy down. Unaware that he was being watched, John Wilkes Booth kissed the child and filled his hands with coins.

All three of Junius' sons grew up to be actors. It was said that Junius Brutus Jr. ruled the West, Edwin the East, and John Wilkes the South. Edwin was considered the intellectual actor, like his father; he researched each role carefully before attempting to play it. Reviewers praised

Edwin's personal magnetism, as well as his vivid imagination, timing, poetic feeling, and powerful expression. Johnny's charismatic and vivacious
personality carried him as an actor. Still, few reviewers north of the Ma-
son-Dixon line considered him great. And Junius Brutus Booth, though
proud of Johnny, considered his son Edwin to be the greatest performer
of all his three sons.

The South was kind to John Wilkes Booth. He performed widely
throughout all the Southern states and received rave reviews. The people
loved him and often threw money and flowers on stage after his performances. He was a prince among admiring subjects and wanted to continue
that role.

When the Civil War broke out, Johnny wished to serve the South,
but not as an ordinary soldier. He longed to do something spectacular,
something for which his "subjects" would cheer him. And so the plot to
abduct Abraham Lincoln was born.

It was difficult for Booth to find followers. Few took his politics seriously; most people laughed at his wild ravings about secession (which were
probably reminiscent of his father's earlier debates on republicanism).
Eventually, Johnny surrounded himself with a group of Southern misfits
who planned to kidnap President Lincoln and hold him for ransom. Not
only would the ransom include money, but also a written declaration by
Congress recognizing the South's existence as an independent nation,
which would end the war.

When Lee surrendered at Appomattox, however, all Johnny's plans
collapsed. He went into a fit of despair for several weeks, lamenting the
fall of his beloved South. And then one night, in a drunken rage, he determined, not to abduct, but to kill President Abraham Lincoln.

The rest is history. President Lincoln died at Booth's hands in the
Ford Theatre, and later (it was believed) Booth died in a burning barn
in Virginia. Edwin's only reaction to the news of his brother's crime was
astonishment.

What factors turned John Wilkes Booth, a talented, well-loved actor,
into a crazed assassin?

Before we consider Johnny's birth chart, we should first look to the
natal chart of the father whose attention Johnny craved. Junius Brutus's
acting talents are represented by the Jupiter-Ascendant conjunction in
Pisces and the opposition of Neptune to the Sun-Mercury conjunction.
These conjunctions and the Moon-Pluto conjunction in the twelfth house
also indicate Junius Brutus's tendencies to escape into fits of alcoholism
or insanity. The prominence of Mercury in the chart implies that Junius
would value studiousness and research. Venus in Gemini hints at his biga-
my.

The placement of the Moon and Pluto in radical Aquarius in the
twelfth house suggests Junius's unconscious leanings toward radical poli-

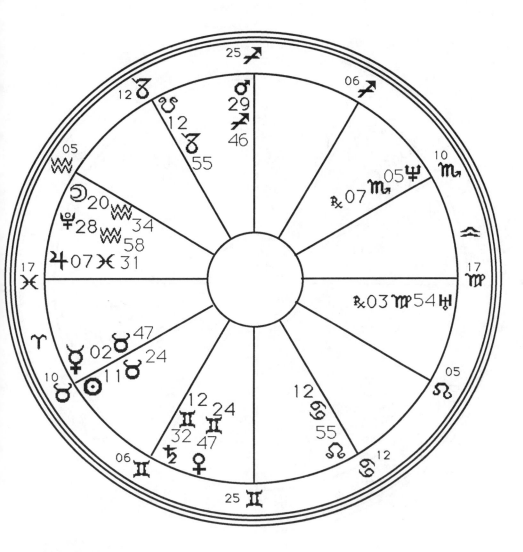

Figure 3.2
Junius Brutus Booth
May 1, 1796 3:00 am
London, England
Placidus house cusps

tics. His Aquarian humanitarianism is well-known. On one occasion, for
example, he missed a performance to help fight a fire and rescue those
in the house. Although Junius was quite vocal about his politics, he never
acted on his views. In fact, he firmly believed that an actor had no place

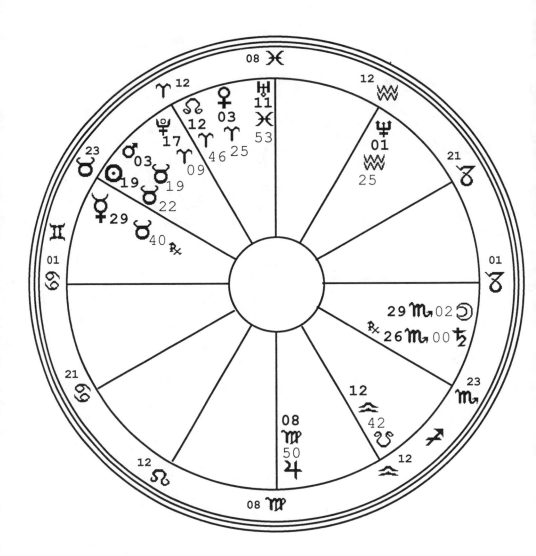

Figure 3.3
John Wilkes Booth
May 10, 1838 7:30 pm
Bel Air, Maryland
Placidus house cusps

in politics. Is it too far fetched to surmise that at times he wistfully may have said that if only he were not an actor, he would gladly participate in the governing of his chosen homeland?

Psychologists realize that often a child will play out a parent's fantasies without either party actually knowing about it. The prim, Victorian mother can raise a promiscuous daughter; the workaholic father sometimes rears a playboy son. The chart of John Wilkes Booth reveals a great deal of impressionability. Water signs predominate: Cancer is rising, the Moon conjoins Saturn in Scorpio, the MC conjoins Uranus in Pisces. And the involvement of radical Uranus in the water-sign concentration, along with the presence of Mars, Pluto, and the Sun in the eleventh house, indicate strong tendencies toward an erratic nature and radicalism.

Johnny's strong attachment to his mother—shown by his Cancer Ascendant—suggests that in this case, the mother was the nurturing parent, and therefore ruled by the fourth house. So we can look to his tenth house to see what effect his father had on him.

The presence of Uranus in the tenth house suggests not only an eccentric parent with radical leanings, but some sort of separation from the father as well. Young Johnny was separated physically from his father on two occasions, when his father toured and visited Adelaide in England. However, it appears that the physical separations were less important than the psychological separations resulting from Johnny's attachment to his mother and Junius's preference for Edwin.

Neptune, ruler of his tenth house, is in the eighth house squaring Mars and the Sun in the eleventh. This combination implies that the father and his unconscious influence (Neptune) brought about a conflict (the square) with Johnny's will and ego drive (Sun) and caused intrigue and violence (Mars) involving radicalism (eleventh house). The quincunx between Jupiter and Neptune, the co-rulers of the tenth house, plus the opposition between Jupiter in the fourth and Uranus in the tenth, suggest a strange subconscious turmoil regarding the father. This, added to the intensity and passion of the Scorpio Moon, and the stubbornness and fixity of Taurus, indicates that Johnny would have stopped at nothing to accomplish what he wanted—whether it was obtaining his father's approval or helping to liberate the South.

When comparing the two charts of Junius Brutus and John Wilkes Booth, we find Junius's Moon-Pluto conjunction in Aquarius squaring both the Sun and the Moon-Saturn conjunction in the chart of John Wilkes, suggesting that Junius's radical leanings (Aquarius) brought about conflicts involving Johnny's values (Taurus-Scorpio). The conjunction of Junius's Mercury to Johnny's Mars suggests explosive communications between the two, and the fact that both were obstinate Taureans probably didn't help relations between them. Yet the conjunction between the MC-Uranus bond and the Jupiter-Ascendant combination im-

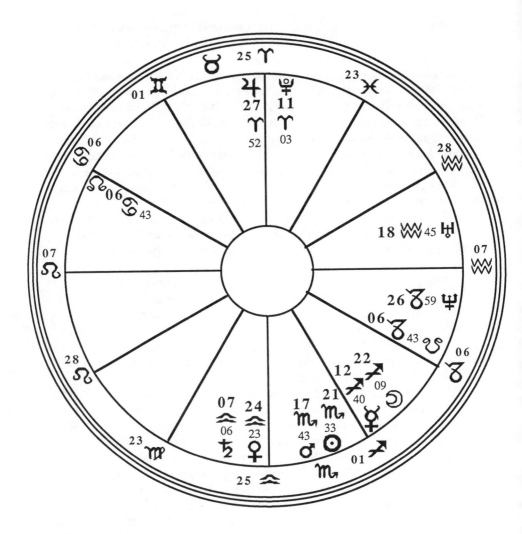

Figure 3.4
Edwin Booth
November 13, 1833 10:03 pm
Bel Air, Maryland
Placidus house cusps

plies that in spite of everything, there was a strong love-bond between father and son; hence Johnny's need to emulate his father, both as an actor and as a political activist.

The chart of Edwin, the favored son, reveals that his destiny probably was to become a famous actor. His birth occurred during a spectacular meteor shower (and the presence of Jupiter, high in the sky, conjoining the MC, probably added to the beauty of the night). He also was born with a caul, signifying a life full of good fortune. The Leo-Scorpio combination (Ascendant and Sun) is found in the charts of many actors; the charm and charisma of Leo blend well with the magnetism of Scorpio. Venus in Libra conjoining the fourth house cusp suggests eloquence and social grace, and the Mercury-Moon conjunction in Sagittarius implies the scholarly nature which Junius so respected.

Edwin's closeness to his father hints that in his case, the father was the nurturing parent (though on the surface it appeared that Edwin was the one who nurtured his father) and the conjunction of Venus to that cusp suggests a powerful love-bond between the two. The two Venuses, in Edwin's and Junius's charts, are in an exact trine, which reinforces the love-bond. The conjunction between Edwin's Moon and Junius's Mars, both in Sagittarius, implies a mental and emotional bond, and that they would invest a significant amount of energy in the relationship. The trines between the Jupiter-Ascendant conjunction in Junius's chart and the Sun-Mars combination in Edwin's reinforces the good feeling between the two, which contributed greatly to Edwin's will and ego drive (Sun) and Junius's outer persona (Ascendant).

It does not appear strange, then, that John Wilkes Booth, trying desperately to obtain his father's approval, attempted not only to try to match Edwin as an actor, but to do what Edwin never considered doing: fulfilling his father's fantasies and playing an active role in politics. It is not unreasonable to presume that even though Johnny chose the South as his battleground, if the North instead had given Johnny the acknowledgement he had never received from his father, he would have aspired to become the hero of the North, perhaps even an anti-slavery fanatic like John Brown—and the eventual triumph of the North may have averted Johnny's violent deed. Unfortunately, we will never know if this could have been the case.

Diane

Diane is an attractive, intelligent, accomplished career woman, who, because she was having problems making sense of her relationships with men, turned to psychotherapy and past-life regression in order to gain insight into them. Although Diane is an interesting person with much to offer a man, her love life has always been somewhat erratic, possibly owing to the influence of her Aquarian temperament and her changeable Geminian Ascendant. "I have had several relationships," she told me, "which (in typical Neptunian fashion) were confused, based on misconceptions and delusions, or which seemed to dissolve without my ever really understanding why."

With her Piscean Moon, Diane is also a born romantic. "If a relationship isn't really incredible," she once said to me, "why even bother?"

When I first considered Diane's chart, I looked to her relationship houses to see what she needed in a romantic relationship and what she could expect. I noted the Aries-Libra pattern involving the fifth-eleventh house axis (signifying a karmic need to learn to handle relationships, particularly friendships and love affairs). I also noted that she preferred an unusual type of man, unpredictable and adventurous (Sun in Aquarius), but at the same time one who valued society and its conventions (Mars in Libra). Observing the Mars-Neptune conjunction, with Mars squaring Uranus and Neptune squaring Mercury, I advised Diane to be on the lookout for lies and deception on the part of her lovers. "You're right about the lies and deception," was her reply, "but I'm afraid that it's been mostly on my side."

This may be the result of her Uranus-Mars-Neptune pattern which indicates a basic distrust of men. This observation is born out by the opposition of Saturn in the fourth house to Diane's Piscean Moon, which implies that her relationship with her father put an undue strain on her emotions. Also, the Leo-Aquarius pattern in Diane's chart, involving the Sun, Pluto, Jupiter, and Venus indicates karmic lessons to learn involving love given (Leo) and love received (Aquarius).

It would appear that although Diane is a bright and creative person and devoted to her career, part of the purpose of her current incarnation is to learn to handle close relationships and work on developing more trust in those whom she loves.

Diane's propensity for unusual men was centered first of all in her father, Jack. She believes she is the unloved daughter of a homosexual father. Upon examining her father's chart, I first noted his Aquarian Moon, conjoining Diane's Sun within two degrees, and her Venus within eleven degrees. Conversely, his Venus also conjoined her Uranus, which in a chart comparison denotes a powerful attraction. Unloved? I doubted it. Astrologically, all the indications were that Diane's father loved her very much—and vice versa.

Homosexual? I doubted that as well. There are two particular planetary afflictions which almost always have to be present for a person's sex drive to manifest as true homosexuality: Venus-Uranus and/or Venus-Neptune afflictions. Neither is present in Jack's chart, and therefore I doubted that Jack was in fact a true homosexual.

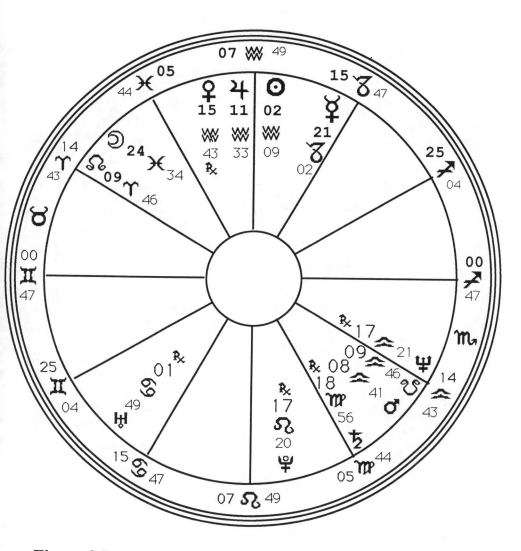

Figure 3.5
Diane
January 22, 1950 1:55 pm
Pittsburgh, Pennsylvania
Placidus house cusps

I wish to pause here to draw a distinction between what I call *apparent* and *true* homosexuality. True homosexuality may be defined as a condition whereby a person is passionately attracted only to sexual partners of his or her own sex. This is regarded by metaphysical researchers as a

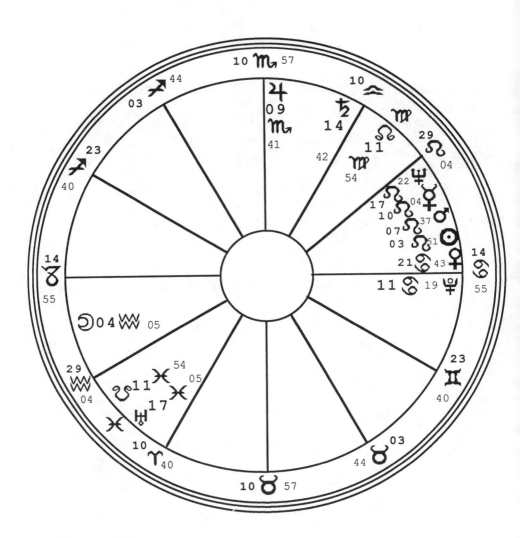

Figure 3.6
Jack
July 27, 1923 6:00 pm
Boston, Massachusetts
Placidus house cusps

karmic condition related to a history of confusion on the part of the soul/
entity regarding sexual identity, and may be locked into the current personality by hormone imbalances, precocious sexual development, an over-
attachment to the mother, or any one of a dozen possible factors proposed
by psychologists.

Apparent homosexuality, however, perhaps is defined best as a pattern of homosexual behavior on the part of a person whose primary sexual inclination is actually heterosexual. This phenomenon may be caused by social pressures, as in ancient Greece where homosexual practices were quite fashionable among both men and women, or in today's society by such things as the tendency of some radical feminists to idealize lesbianism. Apparent homosexuality also can be caused by disillusionment with the opposite sex, or by an extremely sensual and highly sexed nature which leads the individual to try any kind of sex. In my practice as an astrologer and psychotherapist, I have had many clients who fit into at least one of these three categories—and some of them fit into all three. Judging from Jack's chart, my guess is that he would fall into the last category.

My conclusion is drawn from the Venus-Pluto conjunction. Venus-Pluto aspects, particularly the conjunction, square, and opposition, produce an individual who has a strong sex drive. Many of these people believe that "if it feels good, do it," and if they are approached by a gay person of the same sex, they are more inclined to try gay sex than a heterosexual person without the strong sex drive produced by Venus-Pluto aspects. Jack not only has this Venus-Pluto conjunction in his chart, but also an Aquarian Moon in the first house, indicating rebelliousness and a deep emotional need to revolt against the conventions to which he nonetheless was deeply attached (the strong Cancer-Capricorn pattern).

Often, apparent homosexuality can be triggered by a transit. Two of my closest friends (both astrologers themselves) have a daughter who, at the age of twenty, became involved in a gay relationship. When they learned about her involvement, they were disturbed until another astrologer, who was more capable of being objective about the situation, pointed out that there were no indications of true homosexuality in their daughter's natal chart. However, at the onset of the relationship, transiting Uranus had squared her natal Venus, producing the classic Venus-Uranus effect of an unusual love life and possibly homosexuality. The astrologer predicted that when the transit passed, the daughter would end the gay relationship and return to heterosexual practices. And this is exactly what happened.

As I studied Jack's chart, a picture began to form in my mind of a man who was very much attached to convention, but also quite impatient with it; who loved his wife, Margaret, but found her too competitive (shown by Sun-Moon-Mars afflictions in their chart comparison). He also probably found her unresponsive sexually, as her chart is air-sign dominated, and pure air types rarely have much interest in sex. As years passed, the dissatisfaction created by these situations grew until it became like water pressing against a weakening dam.

My guess is that during the period when Uranus was passing through Libra (late 1960s to early 1970s), squaring Jack's Cancerian Venus and his Capricorn Ascendant, the dam burst; Jack rebelled. He was probably approached by a gay man and decided to give it a try. His home broke up, and, sadly enough, he sacrificed his relationship with the daughter whom he loved very much.

The gay community has conventions too; one is an almost universal rejection of closeness with women. I live and practice in Los Angeles, where the gay community is quite open. I have had many gay men as friends and have grown quite fond of some. However, these relationships never progressed beyond the status of "good friends"; I never became intimate with any of my gay friends (though I do know a few women who have had close friendships with gay men). For the most part, the gay community is very tightly knit, keeping pretty much to itself; few women, not even family members, are allowed to invade the clique. As is typical, Jack probably didn't know how to handle the love he felt for his daughter—hence, as a good Cancer-Capricorn type, he bowed to convention and ignored her, causing her to feel unloved. Diane went through life believing herself unloved, seeking the love of her father in other men, men who were rebellious, erratic, and at the same time conventional. At one time Diane even had a lover whom she knew was bisexual.

Diane's mother probably helped to reinforce Diane's sense of rejection by her father. The lines of communication were much more open between Diane and her mother (both have air-dominant charts). Also, as mentioned above, the Sun-Moon-Mars afflictions in the chart comparison between Jack and Margaret implies that they were constantly competing with each other—and, when parents compete, one of the first things they compete for is the love of their children. Margaret probably did compete for Diane's love, and consciously or subconsciously encouraged her daughter to believe her father had rejected her.

Can this breach, and hence Diane's mistrust of men, be healed? I prefer to believe that it can. The Venus-Uranus transit in Jack's chart has long since passed; he may no longer be inclined to keep women at a distance. My recommendation to Diane was that she continue with her therapy and past-life regressions and become more sure of herself. At the same time, she should use her own analytical skills to look objectively at her father's situation and to understand his point of view. (One excellent technique she could use is to pretend to be her father—then write a letter to herself, trying to explain why he did what he did.) When Diane feels ready, she can work actively on clearing up her relationship with her father, and in doing so eradicate her confusion about men. It undoubtedly would help him as well as her.

4

The Twelve Signs

Studying the relationships of parents and children by analyzing their horoscopes can be fascinating. The prominent signs in the chart, the positions of the Sun, Moon, and Saturn, and the planets placed in the fourth and tenth houses are of primary importance in this type of study.

This chapter deals with the basic energies and characteristics of the twelve signs of the zodiac as they apply to parents and children. When I say "the Aries Parent," I am not talking simply about people born between March 22 and April 21. The Arien energy in a chart can be the Sun, the Moon, the Ascendant, or a grouping of several planets, and, with only minor variations, the basic effect is the same. All prominent signs in the birth chart should be considered. The importance of each can be gauged by the strength of the planet according to its sign, house, and aspects.

Remember, however, when considering planets in the fourth and tenth houses that these planetary positions may not reflect how the parent actually was, but rather how the child saw him or her. And if Neptune is prominent in the chart—especially if it aspects the planets in the fourth or tenth house—the individual's perception may not be very accurate.

Aries

The Aries Parent

Aries parents have a hard time adjusting to the parental role because they have never really grown up themselves. Unlike the rather attractive child-like manner of the Geminian and the Sagittarian, the childishness of the Arien is immaturity, and in a parent it can be a handicap. If the Aries factor is well-aspected, the parent is progressive and can give the child the advantages of his or her leadership. If the Aries factor is afflicted, however, the parent can be hot-headed with a tendency to throw temper tantrums. The parent's anger often is focused on the child, and blame and guilt are the weapons.

The Arien parent enjoys the position of authority that a parent has over a child. If the Arien factor is well-aspected, the parent can make use of his or her authority to give the child sound guidance. However, if the Arien factor is afflicted, the parent can misuse that power, often resorting to corporal punishment—even punishing a child without first making certain that the child is to blame. The Arien parent needs to be aware of a tendency toward "jumping to conclusions." The possibility of violence also exists, and thus, the parent should attempt to analyze each situation as objectively as possible before taking any kind of action.

The child should try not to react to an Arien parent's outbursts of temper and/or violence with tantrums, but attempt to remain cool even in the midst of the most unwarranted anger. Rather than being defensive, the child must try to explain each situation as calmly and dispassionately as possible, and "smooth the ruffled feathers" of the parent. In this way, much stress and strain can be avoided in the parent/child relationship, and the parent perhaps can learn from the child's example. It is not uncommon for extremely mature children to take the parental role with an Arien mother or father.

The Aries Child

Aries children, on the other hand, are usually bright and charming "free spirits" who capture the imaginations of everyone. Natural leaders, they often are at the top of the sibling pecking order and are looked up to by their brothers and sisters. It is often difficult for parents and grand-parents to avoid expressing partiality for the Aries child, in spite of the fact that the child's temper sometimes shows itself in episodes of brattiness. The Aries child always wants its own way and often pits its will against the parent's. If the parent is too easygoing and allows the child to take the upper hand too many times, the child can grow up to be selfish and bossy.

In my practice, I often have heard parents of adult Aries children moan about how their Arien offspring was "such a great kid" or "a model child" who turned out wrong. My experience is that the child did not change, or turn out wrong; the problem appears to be that the free-spirited and easygoing nature of the Arien is admired and encouraged in children, but as the child grows up, the parents, teachers, and other authority figures try to force the independent Arien to conform to socially acceptable modes of behavior.

This produces a "double message" which tells the child that it is okay to be yourself when you are a child, but as an adult you have to be what others want you to be. The Aries children who accept this dictum turn out to be bored and unhappy adults; those who don't accept it often try to appear as though they are conforming, but on another level continue to do what they want, often confusing and confounding others who are close to them. Depending on other factors in the chart, the child should be encouraged to be independent and true to him- or herself, but be advised from an early age that there are parameters of social acceptability within which astute people will always operate. In this way, the child will be better able to adapt that free-spirited nature to society's norms without compromising individuality.

Taurus

The Taurus Parent

Unlike Arien parents, Taurean parents are often too placid and accepting, and at times they feel that disciplining a child is not worth the effort. The Taurean parent is kind, loving, and generous, if a touch stolid and indolent. There is a strong tendency to think of the child as a possession, as an extension of the parent, instead of as an individual.

The Taurean parent can become so stuck in his or her own viewpoints that seeing things from the child's perspective is impossible. Unlike the Arien, however, the Taurean parent is very patient and understanding, and will listen intently to the child. Sometimes the Taurean parent can be too understanding and patient, and perhaps out of laziness or lack of initiative, allow a child to "get away with murder."

Rather than being progressive, like Arien parents, Taureans rarely keep up with trends and new ideas that interest young people. Therefore, their children may see them as "boring" and will not seek the parents' company.

The Taurean parent is quite generous with both money and gifts, but if the Taurean factor is afflicted, there can be a tendency to try to "buy" good feelings and to end quarrels by giving presents instead of by working through the problems. The Taurean hates emotional confrontations, preferring peace at any price, but parents need to grit their teeth and face disagreements at times. The child needs to confront the Taurean parent with kindly, quiet opposition instead of speaking violently and unpleasantly, so that differences can be worked out while keeping emotional explosiveness to a minimum.

The Taurus Child

The Taurean child rarely exercises, preferring reading, coloring, playing music, or other artistic pursuits to outdoor games with other children. Many parents fear that this preference will cripple their child socially and retard its physical development. This rarely happens, though. Although they do prefer a sedentary life, Taureans are often quite robust and healthy, as well as socially adept.

A good compromise might be for the Taurean child to become involved in dramatic, rather than athletic games with peers. I once counseled a concerned mother whose Taurean daughter put on puppet shows with neighbor children instead of playing dodgeball and baseball. She wondered if there was something wrong with her child, but I told her not to worry.

If the Taurean factor is afflicted, however, the child can become too lazy and indolent, and might not go out at all. The parent should make an effort to encourage friendships with other children of an artistic bent, so as to help their child come out of its shell. The Taurean child also loves sweet foods and may tend to be overweight, in childhood or later on; therefore, any parent of a Taurean child should keep sweets to an absolute minimum. And even though the Taurean is not competitive in nature and not especially interested in baseball, football, and other team sports, the Taurean child should be encouraged to exercise. He or she probably would enjoy walking, swimming, hatha yoga, and other non-competitive forms of exercise.

Gemini

The Gemini Parent

Geminian parents can be lots of fun. They are curious, spontaneous, quick, and enjoy observing and learning along with their children. These are the parents who take swimming lessons with their children, who participate actively in Little League, are Brownie and Cub Scout leaders. Since there is a little bit of Peter Pan in every Gemini parent, these people seem to identify well with their children—they have never quite outgrown the wonder and curiosity of a child. They encourage their children to venture forth into society and cultivate the friendships which they themselves enjoy so much. However, Gemini resists close involvements, and Geminian parents are no exception. There is always some distance and dispassionate logic in all Geminian relationships, even in a parent's love for his or her children.

If the Geminian factor is afflicted, the parents can confound and bewilder their children when they change abruptly, reacting differently at different times to the exact same situation. Their moodiness can also be a source of confusion for their children, who are too young to know how to deal with them. The Geminian parent needs to be aware of this changeability and unpredictability, and make an effort to curb these traits when dealing with children.

Children, when dealing with a changeable Geminian parent, need to cultivate flexibility in themselves so that they are prepared for any mood swings or abruptly altered plans on the part of the parent. Children of Geminian parents also need to realize that this changeability has nothing to do with them personally; it is innate within the parent and is part of that parent's *dharma* in the current lifetime. In this way, such offspring can understand their parents better and find greater satisfaction in their future relationships as well.

The Gemini Child

Geminian children can be a joy to their parents, as they are generally bright, vivacious, talkative, inquisitive, and eager to please. Extremely sociable, they often are quite popular, and their parents may bask in the reflected glory of their Gemini children. Although Geminian children tend to be bright and learn more quickly than most, their attention spans are short. Therefore, their marks in school, while rarely poor, don't always match up to those of their steadier contemporaries.

Geminian children are fond of reading and writing little stories or poems, and they should be encouraged to do so. They also love to talk and to share what they know; therefore, they can be good at teaching other children. If the Geminian factor is very strong in the chart, the child may talk incessantly and ply parents with endless questions. The parent needs to cultivate patience with this part of the child's personality; curiosity is a natural part of growth, and the Geminian child is more curious than most.

Mood swings are typical of this sign. If the Geminian factor is afflicted, the child can experience sudden fits of uncontrollable anger and outbursts of temper, sometimes over what appears to be nothing. When this happens, the parent needs to be loving, but firm. One of the most important lessons for all Gemini people to learn is discipline, and the younger they start, the better.

Cancer

The Cancer Parent

Cancerian parents are often regarded by astrologers as the ideal—and, when it comes to nurturing, perhaps they are. Both mothers and fathers of this sign are warm, sympathetic, understanding, supportive, and devoted to making the home a comfortable and secure haven. They enjoy such activities as cooking, sewing, and home decoration. Cancerian men and women alike have a gift for picking homes that grow with their families.

If the Cancer factor is afflicted, however, the parents have a way of clinging to the children, and might see their offspring as extensions of themselves rather than as unique persons in their own right. Parents with afflicted Cancer factors in their charts may give the children their all, then blackmail them or try to make them feel guilty, saying "After all I've done for you!" Cancerian parents can be very possessive of their children and may want to go on controlling the lives of offspring long after they've reached adulthood. Perhaps the hardest lesson for these parents to learn is letting go.

The children of Cancerian parents must be determined and firm in their desire to untie the apron strings. They need to learn to return their parents' warmth and love without becoming too dependent on them.

The Cancer Child

Cancerian children have an intense need to belong, to feel a part of something, and for this reason they are very family-oriented and attached to family members, especially their mothers. They are loyal and steadfast, and generally eager to please. Often they are fond of pets and like to surround themselves with stuffed animals, whether or not they are allowed to keep the real thing. The fondness Cancerian boys usually develop for their mothers can help them to be warm, affectionate men who genuinely like women and are skilled at tending to their desires. However, if the mother is not responsive to her Cancerian child's needs, the child may resort to possessiveness and clinginess.

Parents who are socially and athletically inclined sometimes find a Cancerian child frustrating, because these children generally prefer staying at home to being out in the world. If Sagittarius, Aries, or Leo is prominent in the chart, this stay-at-home tendency can be offset somewhat. To the Cancerian, home is his or her castle. These children like to bring friends home and, because of their warmth and sympathy, they attract many companions. Mothers may find themselves called upon to entertain the neighborhood children more often than they would like; in these cases rules need to be laid down and followed accordingly.

Like the Taurean, the Cancerian child enjoys good food, but mostly because food is symbolic of love. Parents of Cancerian children need to give their children expressions of love in other forms, otherwise, later in life the child may look to food as a substitute for love and develop eating disorders. Most importantly, parents of Cancerian children must try to satisfy their children's intense emotional needs and to provide a secure environment for these children to grow up in.

Leo

The Leo Parent

Leo parents are often heroes to their children, and they enjoy this role immensely, cultivating it and encouraging their children's adulation. Often they are charming, magnetic, and powerful in their presence. They possess an unquestioned belief in their own capabilities and can convince others of their indomitability. Leo parents can be kind, loving, and quite generous with their time, energy, and whatever material wealth they have.

Leos are natural actors and some Leonine parents can live with a child for twenty years without ever fully exposing their human failings. When they do, however, the children's disillusionment can be overwhelming, and the result may be an estrangement that lasts for years. Leo parents would be wise to allow their children to love them as they really are rather than seeing them as invincible monarchs or "stars."

The children, in turn, should try to realize that their Leonine parents are human beings, and not put them on pedestals that are too high. In this way the love and generosity inherent in this sign can be appreciated more fully and realistically, and the child will not become so dependent on the idealized parent.

The Leo Child

Leo children can be the light of their parents' lives. It is the Leonine children who are made over most by family, friends, and strangers, and these children thrive on admiration. Leo children quickly seize upon this advantage to get their own way, and they are the first to use tears, theatrics, and emotional blackmail. If Aries or Gemini is also prominent in their charts, these children also may use temper tantrums to get what they want. Too many parents are quick to respond to such manipulation and to reassure the child of their love by giving in. Actually, a firm hand is what's needed here. Allowing such emotional blackmail can lead to bitter resentment in both parent and child.

Leonine children, like Leo parents, are natural actors, and if Neptune is prominent in the chart, they are capable of manufacturing elaborate lies. The parents, because they don't want to think badly of their children—especially the charming Leos—usually choose to believe them. Maintaining a cool head and some healthy skepticism is good advice for the parents of Leonine children. Regardless of how much the child may cry and protest, in the long run he or she will respect a parent's strength.

For the most part, the Leonine child is a joy to have around. His or her imagination, creativity, and loving nature can be the source of great pleasure and pride for parents, and, depending on other factors in the chart, the Leo child often grows up to be a person of whom parents can be proud.

Virgo

The Virgo Parent

Virgo parents run the risk of becoming so involved with their day-to-day tasks that they fail to notice their children or to give them the attention and support they need. Extremely critical of themselves and others, Virgo parents endlessly strive for perfection, and are unforgiving of themselves when they fail to attain such perfection. They also are very critical of their children and demand perfection from them, too. Rather than giving encouragement and love, Virgoan parents tend to criticize their children almost mercilessly when they fail to be perfect.

If Aries is also prominent in the chart, or if Mars or Uranus is strong, when the children do well the Virgo parents act as if that was what was expected instead of praising their children. However, if the children fall short of the mark, the parents might indulge in rages and fits of anger. If the Virgoan factors are afflicted by Mars or Uranus, the parents may berate the child endlessly for getting a 90 instead of a 100 on an exam!

Virgo parents are inclined to be reserved and have difficulty demonstrating affection for their children. These parents need to limit their unreasonably high expectations and find other, more constructive ways of showing their love for their children. They also should take time out from their mundane tasks to listen to their children and get to know their sons and daughters as individuals. These parents can learn to use their logical and discriminating minds to help their children rather than to criticize them.

Children of Virgoan parents need to realize that their parents' expectations of perfection are only projections of the desires they once had for themselves, and their criticism has little to do with the children's own failings. These children need to learn to close their ears to their parents' criticism and make an extra effort to find worth in themselves as human beings in spite of the sometimes unreasonably high expectations of their parents.

The Virgo Child

Virgo children have an intense need to be appreciated and needed. This is why so many Virgoan children end up being "Mama's little helpers" and are so eager to assist with household tasks. Because they have a tendency to be unreasonably critical of themselves, these children need to be encouraged and praised more than those of any other sign. On occasion, when criticism is absolutely necessary, they need to be reassured that the parent loves them, but advised to change their behavior. It is unwise for parents of Virgoan children to be harsh or critical, for unlike Leo or Aries children who think they're great no matter what anyone says, Virgoan children take criticism to heart and can develop self-esteem problems easily. As a result, this child is likely to grow into a supercritical adult—who in turn will be overly critical of his or her own children.

Virgo children are more willing than others to help with household tasks; however, parents must try not to take the child's help for granted and then fail to acknowledge it—especially if other children are messy and less helpful. Virgoan children can become resentful and, when the natural rebellion of adolescence rolls around, they may suddenly decide helping out isn't worth it and stop altogether.

The parents of Virgo children need to make an extra effort to give these children all the encouragement they can. With positive reinforcement, the Virgoan tendency to seek perfection will cause the children to strive for the highest goals without becoming traumatized if their ideals are not reached.

Libra

The Libra Parent

Libran parents are concerned with appearance and social position. They are intelligent, loving, and considerate, yet their expression of love—even for their children—is always quite "correct," and often these parents keep some distance between them and their children. (This is typical of all air signs.) Their manners are impeccable and their gifts for conversation beyond reproach, and they expect the same of their children. Libran parents often train their children to do what is socially correct, and to be diplomatic and fair in all situations.

Because they are concerned with what people might think, though, Libran parents are more likely than others to hide problems—their own and their family's—for the sake of appearances. They also will try to soothe troubled feelings without taking time to get to the root of the problem. It is Libran parents who are the most likely to stay together "for the sake of the children," and to be less than honest with everyone, including their children, about problems in the marital relationship. They are quite good at projecting the appearance of happiness and contentment, but especially if the Libran factor is afflicted, they tend to build up deep inner resentments that eventually result in an explosion, probably triggered by a progression or transit.

Too often, spouses or children of Libran parents sense that appearances are important to the Libran and use this to manipulate him or her. Libran parents must realize that even though their tranquility and social image may be damaged temporarily by a problem in the family, if they attempt to resolve it, the family's contentment will be enhanced. The children, too, will be happier knowing that they are just as important as the family's image.

The Libra Child

Libran children are often the peacemakers in the family. Their diplomacy and wisdom enable them to help family members see the others' viewpoints, and they are good at mediating disputes and finding workable solutions to problems.

Because of the Libran tendency to do what is considered correct, Libran children frequently conceal their true needs and desires and to do what their parents want. Even if the parent is open-minded and flexible, and wants the child to do what he or she chooses, the child still conceals true needs and desires in order to please the parent.

At least superficially, these children strive to do what would give them recognition and status, with their peers and their parents. The parent of a Libran child needs to be perceptive to discover what the child really wants and needs—for if the child thinks the parent wants something else, he or she will place the parent's desires first. Parents of Libran children need to encourage their sons and daughters to pursue their own interests from a very early age, for Librans are so concerned with appearances they are the least likely of all the signs to admit to problems or "make waves."

When suppressed anger and resentments do surface—as they eventually must—the Libran child can be severely traumatized. If Neptune is prominent in the chart, such a person may turn to alcohol or drugs to anesthetize the pain while continuing to keep up appearances. The Libran child is lovely, intelligent, and well-mannered, but must be watched closely by parents to make sure he or she is really living, not merely trying to keep up appearances.

Scorpio

The Scorpio Parent

Scorpio parents can be secretive and are not likely to share much of their lives with their children. If the children are caught up in lives of their own, this reserve may have little effect on them. But, if the children are sensitive and their parents' opinions are important to them, this secrecy can affect the children profoundly and make them wonder if it is due to some failure on their part. Scorpio parents who have sensitive children ought to use their powerful intuitive and psychological awareness to understand their children's needs and make an effort to communicate— even though it goes against their basic nature.

If the Scorpion factor is afflicted, the parents can see their children's dependency upon them as an opportunity for power plays. If the Scorpion factor is badly afflicted, the parent may enjoy threatening the children and seeing them "quaking in their boots"—often over matters that are inconsequential. If their marriage is shaky, Scorpio parents are more likely than others to use their children as pawns against each other.

After a marriage has ended, the Scorpionic parent may harbor extreme hatred and vindictiveness toward the former mate, and the children often find themselves caught between two parents whom they love. In situations like this, the children need to summon every ounce of awareness they have and refuse to take part in such power plays. I know of a father with a Scorpio Sun and a mother with a Scorpio Moon who divorced and carried on a custody battle for years; their three children were caught in the middle and thoroughly confused. The main issue was not the children, it was that neither parent wanted to lose out to the other. All three children ended by leaving home at age sixteen and making their own ways. Unfortunately, not all children are as intelligent and independent as these three were, and such a situation as this can have tragic results.

If the Scorpion factor is well-aspected, however, the Scorpio parent can be extremely loyal and passionately devoted both to the marriage partner and to the child. The child, therefore, can count on the parent to be there when needed. The children of Scorpionic parents need to develop independence at an early age—for their lives might become entangled in their parents'. Scorpionic parents should recognize their tendency to cling to their children and make an effort to train their children to be independent.

The Scorpio Child

Scorpio children have a deep need for love and acceptance which should be gratified from an early age. The Scorpion child is devoted and loyal to loved ones, and wants to have these qualities acknowledged by the parent.

Scorpions have a reputation for being sexual and passionate, but some modern astrologers believe that this characteristic is not as strong as has been believed popularly. The keyword for Scorpio energy is transformation, and Scorpions have taken incarnation to use their inner powers for the purpose of regeneration. One of the most dynamic regenerative forces in the Universe is that of polarity, which in the material world manifests as sexual energy, and the Scorpion often makes a study of sex in this context. They also have a deep need for love, and if this need isn't fulfilled in early life, Scorpios can confuse love with sex. They may indulge in promiscuity or many overly romanticized relationships in search of ideal love through which they will be transformed.

The healthy rearing of Scorpio children requires emotional gratification. If the child is given acknowledgement and encouragement from infancy, probably the more negative manifestations of the sign can be offset and the positive effects will be brought to the forefront.

If the Scorpio factor in the chart is afflicted, such children can indulge in manipulation and power plays, even when they are very young. As they reach adulthood, these power struggles can degenerate into using sex to control and manipulate their partners. The Scorpio child is often wise and insightful beyond its years, and is capable of using this insight to manipulate and control parents, too.

Sagittarius

The Sagittarius Parent

Sagittarian parents are, like Ariens and Geminians, still very childlike themselves, and as a result, they often make good companions for their children. These are the parents who try to be "pals" to their sons and daughters. They love sports and games, and encourage their children to be interested in such pursuits as well. They enjoy the company of their children and their children's friends, and are well-liked by all of them.

Too often, however, Sagittarian parents like the pleasures of parenthood, but don't take their parental responsibilities too seriously. They may be too casual about paying bills, supervising their children's education, or other important but unexciting tasks associated with parenthood. Because of this, the children of Sagittarian parents need to be trained to take care of themselves when they are very young.

The Sagittarian parent is so caught up in Utopian ideals that he or she often fails to take time to develop close personal relationships with the children. These parents may radiate self-confidence and enthusiasm, but often are very insecure inside. They know how they would like the world to be, but they also are too intelligent not to see the differences between their perception of the ideal world and the world as it truly is. Many times they experience bitter disillusionment and intense moodiness, which can confuse their children. The children of Sagittarian parents need to realize that this moodiness has little to do with them—only with father or mother's unrealistic expectations of the world and the people around them.

This idealism may cause Sagittarian parents to view their children in light of archetypes, and thus they can be unaware of their children's true character and needs. Consequently, these parents may be very much interested in their offspring when they are little, but as the children grow older and develop unique personality quirks and less-than-ideal character traits, the parents appear to lose interest. If the Sagittarian factor is badly afflicted, these parents may not actually love their children as individuals. They love the ideal of the child, but are less than enthusiastic about dealing with a child who does not fit the archetype. Therefore, it is necessary for these children to develop not only independence, but strong beliefs in themselves while they are still very young, before the confusion of adolescence hits them. In this way, they are less likely to be traumatized by their Sagittarian parent's attitudes toward them.

The Sagittarius Child

Sagittarian children are generally charming and enthusiastic. They aspire to the same Utopia that Sagittarian adults do, but they are too young yet to have met with much disillusionment. Usually they are popular with their peers and teachers, and are therefore a source of pride to their parents. As they grow older, however, and suffer the first sting of disillusionment, they can be moody, prone to fits of crying.

Sagittarian children tend to idealize their parents and are quite proud of them. Therefore, they constantly search for approval and respect from their parents, while simultaneously longing to be free of the restraints which the parents represent. Too often, because they believe that their parents are special and matchless, they feel it is impossible to measure up to them, so they don't even try. They grow up irresponsible and seemingly uninterested in planning for their futures, preferring to seek companionship, camaraderie, and fun rather than studying for a successful career. Sagittarian girls are particularly vulnerable to this tendency since our society usually encourages boys more than girls to have a sense of responsibility and to "make it" in the career world.

Parents of Sagittarian children need to encourage them to develop whatever interests they may have, perhaps focusing on Sagittarian fields such as law, philosophy, or higher education. Strangely enough, however, it is my experience that few Sagittarians are actually interested in making these fields their life's work, unless other factors in the chart reinforce it. They are more likely to become "fireside politicians," and frequently prefer to keep these interests on an intellectual level, rather than putting them into practice. I have counseled several Sagittarian girls who said they wanted to become actresses, but who actually spent very little time pursuing their careers; instead, they supported themselves with brief, menial jobs or depended on men to take care of them. They are more interested in the idea of being a star than in the sometimes grueling work and discipline that acting entails. The biggest challenge for the parents of Sagittarian children is aiding them in developing a sense of responsibility and helping them to focus their interests in a field that they enjoy enough to make it their life's work.

Capricorn

The Capricorn Parent

Capricorn parents want to go places in life. They are tradition-oriented and prefer the time-honored family structure of the breadwinning father and homemaking mother, and from the beginning they instill in their children a strong respect for this structure.

Capricorn fathers are usually ambitious and hard-working. Often they are respected members of the community, but they can be distant and seemingly cold in their relationships with their families. Care of the children may be left entirely to the mother. It is the Capricorn-headed family which usually looks to the mother for guidance and nurturing, but reserves all disciplinary action for the father. This is the "Wait till your father gets home!" syndrome, which is always unhealthy and does not encourage loving respect for the father. Instead, it makes the children fearful of him and anxious to avoid facing him at all times. Capricorn fathers are ambitious for their children and have no patience with them if they don't measure up, so when they punish, they punish hard, which adds to the children's fear of their father. It can be difficult for the Capricorn father to alter or modify his behavior, even if he is aware of the possible consequences of it and wants to do so. In this, he needs the support both of the children and of their mother.

Capricorn mothers, especially in these changing times, are powerful and controlling figures. They can be very much involved in careers of their own, or they may be ambitious for their mates. The Capricorn mother might try to maintain a nurturing interest in her children because of her respect for traditional values, but she is always somewhat distant and, unless other factors in the chart offset it, her interest in her children doesn't actually run very deep.

Capricorn parents have a wry, sardonic sense of humor and can tell a funny story or make a teasing comment while keeping a perfectly straight face. This can be advantageous when they are dealing with adults, but children can be confused and sometimes even frightened by it—they can't tell whether the parent is joking or not. The Capricorn parent should make sure the children realize he or she is only joking.

It is important for the children of Capricorn parents to understand that their parents' ambition and detachment enables them to seek and fulfill responsibility, and to pursue the ambitions that were clearly the parents' dharma in this life.

The Capricorn Child

Capricorn children are often too serious. From the time they are toddlers they develop a sense of determination, self-management, responsibility, and control. They are usually very mature, sometimes to the detriment of their social lives and their relationships with their peers. Natural leaders, they decide very early that they want to get somewhere in life and set lofty goals for themselves. It is the Capricorn child who goes to the head of the class, runs for student council president, and makes college plans while still in junior high school. There is a tendency for them to be too hard on themselves if they fail to reach a goal. Their parents need to be aware of this and reassure them that one failure doesn't necessarily set the pattern for a lifetime.

Capricorn children can stifle their emotions and may be afraid to express their feelings for fear of appearing weak. They also have a tendency to distrust everyone, including parents and siblings, and for this reason they need to be taught to discriminate between those whom they can and cannot trust. A home life that encourages spontaneous emotional expression could help them modify their natural tendency to remain cold and distant from those around them. Capricorn girls especially tend to keep their distance from their peers because they feel they are unattractive.

I have known Capricorn women who seemed to go out of their way to look unprepossessing, and others who were beautiful but didn't think they were. Parents of Capricorn children can help them develop a sense of their inner worth and teach them how to make the most of whatever assets they possess, so that when they reach adolescence they won't lack self-confidence.

In pursuing their life goals, all Capricornian children need encouragement and support from their parents. The parents can help not only with lessons, but also such things as college recommendations, membership in fraternal groups, summer jobs, and involvement in organizations that can contribute to the young Capricorns' advancement. In this way, the parents also add to their children's self-esteem and help focus their ambition in productive and positive directions.

Aquarius

The Aquarius Parent

Aquarian parents live in their minds and prefer ideas and concepts to close, interpersonal relationships—even with their children. Therefore, the children of Aquarian parents often find themselves virtually adrift in the world, left to fend for themselves while the parent is involved in other things: science, politics, social work, humanitarianism, or metaphysical studies. The atmosphere in an Aquarian household is often impersonal, and the house is generally full of books, maps, etc., so that it sometimes feels more like a library than a home.

The Aquarian parent is usually something of a misfit, and espouses opinions that the rest of society considers strange or odd. Often the child has difficulty dealing with this, and may find the eccentricities of father or mother embarrassing.

Usually quite intelligent and scholarly themselves, Aquarian parents encourage their children to be the same way, and they are not above showing a marked preference for the brighter children in the family. In dealing with life situations, Aquarian parents tend to be theoretical, but they are not always able to utilize their ideas and theories in practical, down-to-earth ways.

Children of Aquarian parents have a distinct advantage; they are exposed early to knowledge and ideas, and the parents are always willing to help the children improve their minds in such ways as assisting them with schoolwork. The practical necessities of life, however, are far less important to Aquarian parents and the children must learn these things independently, or from other authority figures such as teachers, grandparents, or family friends.

In a relationship with an Aquarian parent, the child must be able to blend the pure knowledge and theory so beloved by the parent with practical application in life. Also, he or she needs to realize that the parent's eccentricity is nothing to be ashamed of. Those who embrace new ideas often improve the condition of humankind.

The Aquarius Child

Aquarian children are frequently more precocious than others, and therefore, from an early age they often are set apart from their peers. They prefer the company of adults to that of other children their own age, and the approval of their parents and other adults is extremely important to them.

Aquarian children feel themselves to be misfits, somehow "strange" or "different," and as they mature and move further into of the world of ideas, they tend to seek out the company of groups who share their philosophical views. If these groups welcome the child, they may offer such a strong sense of belonging that the child can become obsessed with the group's activities, even to the detriment of his or her physical health. The parent must understand the child's need for these involvements, yet help the child to balance commitment to the group (or idea) with commitment to him- or herself. It is difficult to convince an Aquarian of this, but if the parent points out that the child will not aid the cause by wearing him- or herself out, the message just might get through.

Aquarian children, like Aquarian parents, have a difficult time learning to deal with the practical realities of life. They always have a theory for each situation, but their theories might be useless in application. Parents need to start ingraining practicality into their Aquarian children while they are still very young.

These children often do well in school academically and are quite active in school clubs, groups, and organizations. (I have counseled several former exchange students who had strong Aquarian influences in their charts.) They might not be active in sports, however, unless other factors in the chart confer this interest. If the Aquarian child has enough sociable chart features to offset the rather impersonal characteristics of this sign, he or she can be a leader looked up to by peers, and a source of great pride to parents.

Pisces

The Pisces Parent

Piscean parents have a tendency to be worrywarts, and as a result they can be overprotective of their children, fretting if the kids are out of sight for even a little while. Sensitive and intuitive, these parents have a way of "sensing" pain in others, therefore, it is not easy for their children to try to hide hurts and rejections.

Pisceans are susceptible to the pains of the entire world; thus, Pisces parents often try to erect a wall between themselves and the rest of the world. This wall may manifest as a psychic barrier, which even their children will be unable to penetrate at times. Or, these parents may hide behind a wall of fat (Pisceans can have a terrible time battling their weight, and often don't even bother). Piscean parents can become abusers of alcohol or drugs, too, and use these substances as the "wall."

The children of Pisces parents often find their parents' behavior bewildering. One moment, the parent is extremely concerned for the child and will not let him or her disappear from sight for a moment; the next minute the barriers are up, and the child cannot get through to the parent.

If the Piscean factor in the parent's chart is afflicted, the result might be the "martyred parent." This is especially true of Piscean mothers. The parent will serve the child kindly and patiently, taking care of his or her needs without complaint, then one day, in a fit of paranoia, wail, "After all I've done for you!" The child may find such behavior confusing, and, if he or she is sensitive, may assume an undue burden of guilt. I know one Pisces mother who constantly played this role, until her daughter, at age sixteen, decided she would never take any favors from her mother again. The mother, who actually enjoyed doing things for her daughter, was hurt and confused. Pisces parents need to watch this tendency to play the martyr; it can only hurt their relationships with their children. Children of Pisces parents need to realize that the martyr role doesn't mean necessarily that the parents don't want to do things for their children—they probably wouldn't stop doing them for the world!

The Pisces Child

Pisces children are dreamy and imaginative, often surprising adults with their precocious ability to tell stories. They also are intuitive and know when their parents, siblings, and friends are troubled. They have excellent memories and can remember things that happened to them when they weren't much more than babies. It isn't uncommon for them to remember their own past lives, too, though parents often smile and dismiss such memories as the products of the child's vivid imagination. If the child comes up with too much interesting information, however, the parents might feel threatened, and ridicule the child's insights. This sort of reaction from a parent may cause the child to put the lid on his or her memories and imagination, which can hamper creativity.

Piscean children are more likely than others to assume guilt, and to go out of their way to do things for their parents in order to expunge that guilt. They are very sensitive and always know when something is wrong in the home, despite parents' attempts to shield them from it. The parents of Piscean children need to be aware of this sensitivity and, when something is wrong, should explain it to the children in a kind and tactful manner rather than trying to hide it—for the intuitive Pisceans will sense something and may feel alienated if the parents don't help them to understand the situation.

The parents should also encourage rather than ridicule the Pisces child's flights of imagination, for this creative potential can lead to exalted artistic endeavors later in life. Unlike other artistic signs such as Taurus or Leo, the Piscean is more likely to indulge in art for art's sake rather than for glory or financial gain, and the parents must be prepared to accept an adult offspring who prefers the lifestyle of the "starving artist" rather than pursing a successful commercial career.

The parents should also encourage the child's interest in spiritual and metaphysical studies, in exploring the reality "behind the veil." These children are more apt than others to make spiritual and metaphysical pursuits their life work. The parents need to accept, however, that unless other factors in the chart offset it, the Piscean child will probably never have a firm grasp on earthly reality, and may look to the parents to be his or her advisors for life.

5

The Fourth and Tenth Houses

Perhaps one of the areas of biggest contention between astrologers is which house, the fourth or tenth, rules which parent. Tradition connects the mother with the fourth, the house associated with the Moon and Cancer, and the father with the tenth, the house associated with Saturn and Capricorn. Probably these links were based on the traditional viewpoint that mother was the nurturer and father the authority.

Many modern astrologers reverse this idea, connecting the tenth house with the mother and the fourth with the father. The idea is that the mother inculcates into the child most of the attitudes that affect its relationship with the external world. My belief is that these astrologers base this conclusion at least partially on observations of clients who either grew up during the Great Depression or who are the children of Depression Era parents. In these families, the father was overly concerned with earning enough money to ensure that his children would never have to suffer as he did. Therefore, he was often so exhausted by the end of the day that he played a passive role in their rearing; the mother had to be both nurturer and authority figure.

It is my experience that the sex of the parent has little to do with whether he or she is represented by the fourth or tenth house. The fourth house describes nurturing, and thus the "inner link" parent, while the tenth rules the authoritative, or "outer link" parent. In these changing times, either parent can assume either role. (The aspects to the Sun, Moon, and Saturn also will be important in determining which parent played which role.)

Sun in the Fourth or Tenth House

The Sun in the fourth or tenth represents a happy and productive relationship with the parent indicated. If the Sun is in the fourth and well-
aspected, the relationship with the nurturing parent was a strong one, and
therefore the individual's self-esteem and sense of personal worth are
well-established. Such people believe they deserve to be loved and probably will enjoy strong, nourishing relationships throughout their lives. If
the fourth-house Sun is weak by sign or aspects, the person will be less
self-assured, but will still be capable of both giving and receiving love.

If the Sun is in the tenth, the individual received support and encouragement from the outer link parent. Such people have a great deal of confidence in their outer selves and their ability to succeed both socially and
professionally. If the Sun is weak by sign or aspect, however, the outer
link parent probably had few "people skills" to pass on to the children,
and therefore, the individual's social and professional ambitions often interfere with relationships. It takes a great deal of patience and understanding to be involved either on a friendly or romantic basis with someone who has an afflicted tenth-house Sun.

Moon in the Fourth or Tenth House

The Moon in one of the parental houses signifies a strong emotional bond
with the parent ruled by that house. Probably the individual has a strong
emotional need to identify with the parent ruled by that house. If the
Moon is in the fourth, there is a powerful identification with the nurturing
parent, and if the Moon is well-aspected, the person's ability to love and
be loved is well-developed. If the Moon is weak or afflicted, however, the
person exudes a sense of desperation in forming relationships, and seems
to be saying, "Love me! Please!" Anyone involved with such a person
needs to beware of this partner's need for continuous reassurance.

If the Moon is in the tenth, the bond is with the outer link parent,
and the individual identifies with the social and professional standards
of that parent. If the Moon is weak, this can indicate a person who follows
the parent's occupation, whether or not his or her abilities are commensu-
rate with that profession. Such a choice undoubtedly will cause problems,
not only with that individual's career, but with relationships as well. Long
periods of depression may occur, often triggered by a progression or transit. If you are a friend or partner to this person you need to be able to
recognize these periods of depression for what they are without feeling
slighted and give the tenth-house Moon person space to go through them.

Mercury in the Fourth or Tenth House

Mercury in one of these houses indicates that the parent ruled by that house was bright, quick, and vivacious. Because of this, individuals with this planetary placement often are interested only in friends or lovers who display intelligence. An afflicted Mercury in either house implies that the person lacks confidence in his or her mental abilities; the parent may have been so clever that the individual believes he or she cannot match up.

If Mercury is in the fourth house, the nurturing parent passed intellectual values on to the child when it was very young, thus creating a strong bond between the child's thinking and feeling. This person seeks relationships with partners who have a similar connection between reason and emotion.

If Mercury is in the tenth house, the outer-link parent pursued a career that utilized the intellect, and therefore the child is likely to do the same. Friends or romantic partners are probably involved in the same or related occupations, and the relationships are likely to be marked by much communication and exchanges of ideas. People with this planetary position have a need to display their intelligence to everyone they meet, in an attempt to prove that they are indeed the intellectual equals of their brilliant parents.

Venus in the Fourth or Tenth House

Venus in one of these houses indicates that the parent ruled by that house was attractive, charming, outgoing, and loving. The individual with this planetary placement formed a strong love-bond with that parent and probably will retain a powerful attachment to that parent throughout life. Friends and romantic partners must accept that they will have to share this person with the parent.

If Venus is in the fourth, the nurturing parent passed on to the child a deep emotional desire for a beautiful home, therefore, his or her home and surroundings will always be warm, inviting, and cheerfully decorated. Family is important to this person, and family will always come first.

If Venus is in the tenth, the outer-link parent was popular and well-liked socially, and the individual will tend to follow that example. Social skills are an asset this person uses to advantage in his or her professional life. Such people may be involved in careers that require a lot of socializing and "networking," and friends and lovers need to be prepared for an active social life. These individuals are generally charming, loving, considerate, and pleasant companions—like the parents they seek to emulate.

Mars in the Fourth or Tenth House

This planetary placement implies that the parent ruled by that house had a quick temper, and that relations between the individual and the parent were somewhat explosive. Perhaps the parents fought constantly, creating a tense atmosphere in the home. As a result, this person may have developed a fierce temper, or, at the very least, a certain defensiveness that can manifest as a "chip on the shoulder."

If Mars is in the fourth, the nurturing parent was the one with the temper, and therefore, the child lacked the support and love necessary from this parent. This is not to say that the parent did not love the child, only that his or her quick temper made the child feel as though he or she was walking on eggshells when around that parent. Thus, the child might have avoided contact with that parent in order to avoid any unpleasantness in the home.

If Mars is in the tenth, the outer-link parent was the one with the bad temper, and therefore the child missed out on contact and learning from this parent. The child probably was forced to learn social and professional "people skills" independently. Discipline in the home probably took the form of spankings, and the parent may have guided through fear rather than love.

If Mars is well-aspected, the person will probably make an extra effort to give loving guidance to his or her own children. If Mars is afflicted, the individual unfortunately may repeat the pattern set by the parent, and compensating for this person's bad temper and behavior probably will fall to the marriage partner.

Jupiter in the Fourth or Tenth House

Jupiter in the parental houses indicates a jolly, good-natured parent, and a beneficial and mutually supportive relationship between parent and child. More than one person may have played the role of that particular parent; the second person could have been a stepparent, grandparent, aunt or uncle, even a teacher or family friend. In some cases, one parent was absent for some reason and the parent ruled by the house in which Jupiter is placed played both roles.

If Jupiter is in the fourth, supportiveness came easily to the nurturing parent, and therefore this ability was passed on to the child. The individual's capacity to love and be loved is vast, and a partner will find the relationship quite pleasant on an emotional level. If Jupiter is afflicted, the person may scatter the energies represented by this house among too many people; friends or romantic partners may find this tendency frustrating, but probably will have to learn to live with it—this individual isn't likely to change.

If Jupiter is in the tenth, the father or mother was well-known and respected professionally. Therefore, this person is comfortable and confident in his or her professional life, and may receive much gratification from the occupation. Fame is even possible with this Jupiter position. The benefits of such professional success certainly will affect this individual's relationships. If Jupiter is well-aspected, the person's success will enrich relationships; if Jupiter is afflicted, he or she will scatter energies and not be able to focus attention on any one friend or partner.

Saturn in the Fourth or Tenth House

Saturn positioned here implies a coldness on the part of the parent and a distance between parent and child. Both may have held strange attitudes that interfered with the relationship. If Saturn is in the fourth house, the individual never got a fair share of nurturing and support— perhaps none at all. Therefore, such people are themselves markedly deficient when it comes to nurturing and being supportive. Friends or romantic partners will find relationships with these individuals difficult and frustrating at times.

If Saturn is in the tenth, the parent was hardworking and well-disciplined, but probably put career ahead of all relationships, including the one with his or her child. Therefore, this individual is apt to do the same. People who have Saturn positioned here may experience some delay in realizing their ambitions. Partners may find early life with such people to be a hard climb upward for both parties.

If Saturn is well-aspected, the individual most likely will obtain ultimate success, but if the planet is afflicted, the delays and frustrations probably will persist throughout life. These problems may make it difficult for such people to concentrate on the development of their relationships. If they have children, they may be too absorbed in their outer-world struggles to pay much attention to their children, and the pattern of coldness and distance may be repeated. If there are children, this individual's partner might be called upon to fill both mother and father functions.

Uranus in the Fourth or Tenth House

This planetary position suggests some kind of separation from the parent ruled by that house, often one that is abrupt and unexpected; hence there is an unusual relationship with the parent ruled by that house. The parent was an eccentric and unusual person, and may have fluctuated between wanting to be independent of the child and wanting to cling to him or her. This undoubtedly will leave its mark on the individual's future relationships, with friends, lovers, and his or her own children.

If Uranus is in the fourth house, the nurturing parent alternated between playing the "perfect mother" (or father, as the case may be) and declaring his or her independence. Perhaps the parent even went so far as to be absent from the home for long periods of time.

If Uranus is in the tenth house, the outer-link parent pursued an unusual, independent, or avant garde occupation, perhaps involving modern technology, scientific thought, or astrology. The parent's interest in this occupation was passed on to the child. Perhaps the parent changed careers frequently, and the child picked up an interest in many different fields. This planetary position also can indicate an abrupt break in the career at some time in the individual's life—and the partner should be prepared for an uprooting or other instability as a result of this sudden change.

Neptune in the Fourth or Tenth House

Traditionally this placement is associated with the "disappearing parent." The parent may have been taken away by death or divorce, and there is generally an aura of mystery about the absent parent. In some cases, this planetary position has been associated with illegitimacy. (King William I of England, whose nickname was William the Bastard, had Neptune conjunct Mars in the fourth house. His father was killed on a Crusade.) Neptune's placement in the parental houses can also be associated with the "fantasy parent." In either case, as pointed out earlier, when the real parent is missing, the archetype rushes in. This could cripple the individual's future relationships with members of the same sex as the missing parent, for few human beings can live up to the archetypal ideal.

If Neptune is well-aspected, the parent was probably artistic, psychic, and/or spiritually oriented, and the child probably absorbed much of the parent's viewpoints toward these fields. He or she might even possess the same talents. If Neptune is afflicted, the parent may have been insane, vague, physically ill, or addicted to alcohol or drugs. Nonetheless, the child may always be blind to the parent's faults and believe the parent conformed to an ideal. Anyone involved in a relationship with this sort of person needs to be aware of this tendency toward idealism and to be prepared to deal with it.

Pluto in the Fourth or Tenth House

Pluto in one of the parental houses implies that a parent was secretive, penetrating, and suspicious. The parent may have had a career such as detective work or espionage, or perhaps mining or engineering. If Pluto is well-aspected, the parent may have been a psychically powerful person; one of my clients, the daughter of a skilled magician, has Pluto in the tenth. If Pluto is badly afflicted, however, the parent might have been involved in crime: drugs, prostitution, or even murder. The key phrase for Pluto is "the greater the sinner, the greater the saint," and when this planet is in one of the parental houses there are usually interesting stories attached.

Pluto rules death and surgery, and in some cases Pluto may signify the parent's early death. In others, the parent may have undergone major surgery several times (or be a surgeon). Pluto also rules sex, and if the parent under consideration had a powerful sex drive, this interest in sexuality may have been passed on to the child. In some cases, this can be a boon to romantic partners, but in others, if Pluto is badly afflicted, the individual can be brutal, sadistic, or sexually perverted. It is also possible that the person was sexually molested or manipulated by a sexually provocative parent (or parental figure).

Relationships with such a person can be extremely difficult. The parent may have passed on strange attitudes to this individual, and these ideas can be reflected in relationships. A relationship with someone whose Pluto is well-aspected, however, can be a transformative experience, for Pluto's keyword is regeneration.

6

The Moon, the Sun, and Saturn

The Moon, the Sun, and Saturn are considered to be indicators of the parents. In order to come to a clear understanding of an individual's relationship to his or her parents, and how parental influences have affected that person's adult relationships, it is necessary to look at the signs, houses, and aspects which involve these heavenly bodies.

The Moon

In traditional astrology, the Moon symbolizes the mother. Her sign and house position, as well as her aspects, are said to represent the mother's attitudes toward the individual and the relationship between mother and child.

Modern astrology relates the in-depth psychology of the relationship between mother and child to the Moon. The Moon actually symbolizes the feminine principle in all things, called *shakti* by the Hindus and *yin* by the Chinese. Also, the Moon represents our sense of beginnings, of belonging, of roots, of family. In most parts of the world, it is the mother who, in the early stages of formation of the child's personality, inculcates these ideas into the child's psyche. If the Moon is weak by sign or house, or if badly afflicted in the birth chart, the mother's own sense of belonging was poor, and therefore, she was incapable of passing this security on to her child. In the young child, and even in the adult, this sense of family security is vital to development of self-esteem.

The mother and her self-image relate to a daughter's security in her own womanhood. A strongly-placed and well-aspected Moon implies that the mother felt secure in her femininity and passed that sense of security on to her daughter. An afflicted Moon, however, indicates that the mother felt limited and frustrated by her womanhood and passed these feelings on to her daughter. Interestingly enough, both feminists who have no desire to play the mother role and infertile women who are desperate for children have been known to have weakly-placed or badly-afflicted Moons.

In a man's chart, the Moon represents the mother's impact upon his vision of women, how he reacts to women, and the roles they play in his life. If the Moon is strong and well-aspected, the man liked and respected his mother, and therefore, he likes women and enjoys their company. If the Moon is weak, however, the mother fell short of her son's expectations and did not fulfill his image of the archetypal mother. Such a man is suspicious and distrustful of women, and often prefers to believe the worst of them. His relationships with women throughout life may be crippled, sometimes requiring intense therapy to set them straight.

A weak or afflicted Moon in any chart implies a tense or distant relationship with the mother, and therefore, often indicates a difficult childhood. The person may experience emotional emptiness and a lack of the usual joy and spontaneity inherent in childhood. In extreme cases, the child is physically or emotionally abused, and the emotional pain and trauma can be carried into adulthood in the form of lack of warmth and an inability to express love. Anyone involved in a relationship with a person with an afflicted Moon needs to be especially open emotionally, both as a listener and as a nurturer. In this way, the partner will be reassured and the relationship will be more likely to grow and thrive.

The Sun and Saturn

In any chart, both the Sun and Saturn represent the father, but they symbolize totally different aspects of him. The Sun represents the father as hero, the ideal, archetypal figure, *shiva* or *yang* energy of will and power, the spiritual force that bestows life. The Sun symbolizes the father as a figure to be respected and admired, after whom the child can pattern his or her attitudes and self-image.

In a man's chart, the Sun symbolizes the father as role model. A strong and well-aspected Sun implies that the growing boy's father had high self-esteem and a good sense of his own masculinity, and passed those traits on to his son. A weak or badly-aspected Sun denotes that the father was unsure of both himself and the direction in which he was going at the time of the boy's birth—perhaps he was in a transition period— and therefore, the son has subconsciously identified with these insecurities and probably will carry them into adulthood.

A daughter, on the other hand, will base her image of men on her father. If the Sun is strong by sign and house position, and well-aspected, the woman's father was a powerful, loving figure who liked women and related well to his daughter; therefore, the daughter probably will be at ease with men throughout life. On the other hand, a weak or afflicted Sun indicates that the father felt uncomfortable around women and kept his distance from all of them, including his daughter. The young girl may have resorted to outrageous behavior to attract her father's attention and will probably carry this habit into all her future relationships with men.

Saturn represents the father as authority figure, and therefore, this planet's effect can be very complex. A Saturn that is strong and well-aspected implies a father who exuded authority, but did not abuse it, a father who implanted a sense of discipline into the child without instilling fear or guilt. Saturn weak and afflicted indicates a father who disciplined mainly through fear, often resorting to beatings or other forms of sadism such as teasing. This type of father lacked the gift of communication and often failed to tell the child what was expected, but still resorted to severe punishment when the child failed to fulfill those expectations. Anyone with such a father (and the corresponding Saturn aspects) often suffers from confusion and lack of direction during transition periods in life, at times when a sense of discipline and responsibility are crucial. A potential friend or romantic partner needs to be especially understanding and willing to give support during turning points in this individual's life.

Saturn retrograde indicates that the authority figure in the early home was absent or passive. The father was either taken away by work, death or divorce (or by war), or else was so passive as to be totally subservient to the mother. Or, the father could have been so autocratic that it was impossible for the child to receive any loving guidance from him. Such problems in early childhood seem to manifest later as an almost oppressive inferiority complex, as the child never had proper training in discipline that was tailored to his or her own unique needs. A potential friend or romantic partner may find it necessary often to play the role of loving authority figure to make up for the father's shortcomings—never an easy role to assume.

The Moon through the Signs and Houses

Moon in Aries or in the First House

The mother was an imposing figure, who forced her will on her child through playing on his or her emotions. She probably had an inflated ego and liked to be the center of attention; the child responded as she wanted, making her the focal point of his or her life and doing everything possible to please her. If the child's efforts fell short of the mother's desires, the child may have responded defensively, becoming argumentative or temperamental. However, the overeagerness to please mother never went away; when the mother was unhappy, the child simply tried harder. This pattern of behavior has been carried into the individual's adult relationships.

As a result, such persons tend to be somewhat rash, argumentative, and highly defensive as well as assertive, and usually act without thinking. They may develop the same self-centered egotism that characterized their mothers. On the positive side, they have a passion for life and a love of enterprise and innovation.

If you are involved with this type of person, you may find your partner alternating between an egotistical expectation to be the center of your Universe, and an almost desperate childlike need to reassure him- or herself of your love through impulsive efforts to please you. Try not to put your partner on the defensive, and if differences arise between you, simply talk it out and let it go. Surprisingly, Ariens are more willing to do this than people of other signs are.

Moon in Taurus or in the Second House

The mother may have been possessive of the child, and perhaps tried to live her life through her offspring. She had fixed ideas and was somewhat stubborn, and the child may have felt guilty when his or her ideas differed from mother's. Part of the reason for this guilt may be that the mother also was a very warm and loving person, and the child wanted to make her happy.

Most likely, this person's mother had good taste, and passed on her appreciation for art and beauty, as well as her enjoyment of life, to the child. As a result, such people are usually warm and steadfast and possess an almost instinctive knowledge of the social graces.

If you are involved with this type of person, you probably find your partner supportive, encouraging, and a source of great joy in your life. However, if you are independent and require plenty of freedom, you may find his or her tenacity somewhat stifling. If you decide to end the involvement, you'll learn that this person is hard to shed. Moon-in-Taurus individuals do not give up relationships easily because they have invested so much of themselves in their partners (possibly a reflection of the mother's tendency to live her life through her child). Once this partner is gone, though, you might find that you miss the security and warmth of his or her love, for no one is more devoted and loyal than this type of individual.

Moon in Gemini or in the Third House

This person's mother was probably moody, talkative, changeable, interested (superficially) in many things, and full of wishes and hopes. The only thing predictable about her was her unpredictability. This may have confused the child, though he or she probably found the mother's cheerfulness and curiosity fascinating. The mother undoubtedly passed her gifts of communication and expression on to her child—but she also passed on her moodiness and erratic nature. The child probably tried very hard to keep up with the mother's vacillation and emotional ups and downs, and therefore, in adulthood he or she alternates between enthusiastic optimism and deep despondency.

If you have a number of planets in fixed signs, you may find a relationship with such a person quite difficult. While his or her childlike spontaneity can loosen up a fixed person's stodgy ways, the Gemini-Moon individual's mood swings can be irritating to a fixed-sign person.

Moon in Cancer or in the Fourth House

This person probably has the strongest mother-attachment of all, and if you are involved with a Cancerian Moon person, you may as well accept that you are involved with that person's mother, too. Your partner's mother is probably warm, loving, and very domestic, and her home is a safe and welcome haven for anyone. The mother passed this love of home on to her offspring, and if you live with the Cancer-Moon person, you will find your home is your castle.

Although these people are warm, loving, sensitive and affectionate, (like their mothers), they are also very possessive, and it could be hard for an independent individual to live with one of them. The Moon-in-Cancer person, male or female, likes to mother everyone, and sometimes treats romantic partners more like children who need to be protected than as equals with lives of their own.

Moon in Leo or in the Fifth House

This individual's mother was a queen in her own circle, a very charming woman, probably quite physically attractive, generous, intelligent, and loving. Most likely, she had many friends and admirers. The male child was fascinated by his mother and, as an adult, is only interested in glamorous women. The female child may have felt she was in competition with her mother, and therefore always seeks to improve herself in order to match her mother. (Even if she succeeds, she remains somewhat insecure about her own attractiveness.)

These people are always interested in luxury, glamour, romance, and affairs of the heart. They also may have artistic talent, and might use it to please or compete with their mothers. Men of this Moon type are especially fond of beautiful and charming women, and if you are involved with such a man remember that appearances are especially important to him. Moon-in-Leo women want to be reassured continually that they are fascinating, for they are never totally secure in their own self-worth.

Moon in Virgo or in the Sixth House

The mother was a practical, diligent, and hardworking person, and may have been obsessed with neatness in the home and at work. The Moon-in-Virgo person probably saw his or her mother as a bit of a nag, who insisted on cleanliness. Perhaps he or she fell into the pattern of being "mother's little helper" and may be as diligent as mother when it comes to housekeeping. Such people like their surroundings to be organized and sometimes can be neurotic about it.

Most likely, the mother had good manners and a sense of decorum, and this individual undoubtedly was influenced by her. And, as with all earth signs, the mother was warm and affectionate, therefore, this individual will tend to be so, too. He or she is probably quite fond of animals as well. If you are involved with this type of person, you may find him or her a bit preoccupied with neatness and practicality, but your partner will always be there to provide a sympathetic shoulder when you need it.

Moon in Libra or in the Seventh House

The mother was an outgoing person, who loved parties and social gatherings. Quite likely, she was dependent upon her husband for support and valued her marriage highly. Relationships were so important to her that at times she seemed to live through other people, including her children. She was not adverse to vivid displays of her feelings—positive and loving feelings, or hostile and harmful ones that often were laced with an unhealthy dose of guilt.

Consequently, these individuals feel that they must tailor their feelings and actions to suit others, and often go out of their way to oblige others. They emphasize relationships, just as mother did, but often their interest in relationships includes intense dependency. If you are involved with this type of person, you need to encourage your partner to develop individuality—while still acknowledging his or her devotion to the relationship and reciprocating in kind.

Moon in Scorpio or in the Eighth House

The mother was an intense and passionate person, who would literally fight to the death for her child. However, at the same time, she may have been ruthless in her ambitions and expectations for her children, and not very tolerant of their ideas and desires if they differed from hers. She had a tendency to rule through guilt, often playing the victim, and she usually won her power plays—even when the child was intelligent enough to see through her ploys. Her behavior may have given this individual a toughness and inner strength. Although the child may have grown up with bitterness toward the mother, he or she also admired her fighting spirit. There is a powerful attachment to the mother in spite of everything.

In a relationship, however, this person may unconsciously assume the role his or her mother played, and attempt to manipulate a partner through guilt or other power plays. (Sex is one way that is used quite often.) If you are involved with this sort of person, you may find yourself in constant conflicts. However, your partner's inner passion could be such a potent attraction that it makes up for the difficulties in the relationship.

Moon in Sagittarius or in the Ninth House

The mother was a wanderer, either literally or mentally, and enjoyed a vivid inner life. Strange places and people fascinated her, and she passed on her love of learning about them to the child. She was idealistic and optimistic, although these traits constantly set her up for disillusionment and bitterness, and her changeable nature probably confused the child. These people are constantly restless and desire change, and they can experience great unhappiness if the desired changes don't manifest.

If you are involved with this sort of person, you probably will find him or her quite appealing, entertaining, and knowledgeable about many things. However, these people tend to idealize their partners, and if this is carried to extremes, you both are headed for disappointment when, as a human being, you fall off the pedestal on which he or she placed you.

Moon in Capricorn or in the Tenth House

The mother was probably somewhat reserved and severe, and the emphasis in her life was on practicality and duty rather than on fulfillment of desires. She probably did not believe in much emotional expression, but instead emphasized a sober, patient, and pragmatic outlook on life. As a result, these individuals are probably repressed emotionally. They have a strong sense of duty and responsibility, but sometimes lose sight of the fact that they also have a duty and responsibility to themselves. In other cases, such people tend to overemphasize the duty and responsibility others have toward them and can be not only cold, but selfish as well. If you are involved with this type of person, do not expect an abundance of concern for you; the mother's example taught your partner to be cold and rather unfeeling—unless other factors in the chart offset this coldness.

Moon in Aquarius or in the Eleventh House

The Aquarian Moon signifies a mother who enjoyed carrying the weight of the world on her shoulders. She may have been involved with groups, politics, and/or humanitarian causes. Friends were important to her, and she had high ideals and great plans for the world. Although independent, this mother still was a caring person who loved to help others—although sometimes her need to help others did not include her immediate circle. She probably appeared to care more about the downtrodden masses than her own children; hence the Aquarian-Moon child may have felt he or she was playing second fiddle to the rest of the world.

   As a result, the child may make an effort in adulthood to develop a sympathetic and understanding nature, although the effect of the impersonal mother will have left its mark. In order to vindicate the mother, the child may quash his or her early feelings of being neglected and embrace radical causes or groups dedicated to social change. If you are involved with such a person, it might be best to involve yourself in those groups as well to avoid feeling left behind.

Moon in Pisces or in the Twelfth House

The mother was an artistic, sensitive, impressionable, and/or somewhat psychic person. Although basically optimistic, there was a definite insecurity and feeling of unworthiness buried within her, and she passed these feelings on to her child. She loved her child, but had deep feelings of inferiority and therefore may have either smothered the child or, to shield herself, withdrawn from the child. Deeply introspective, she often seemed to be far away, and the child may have believed that she was withdrawing because of something he or she had done. Therefore, the Pisces-Moon individual developed feelings of inferiority, too.

The mother's more positive tendencies, however, endowed the child with a sense of hope and optimism. Such children grew up believing in the basic goodness of the world and its inhabitants. Unlike Sagittarians, who can become embittered and disillusioned when their ideals are smashed, Pisceans continue to believe the best, even in the face of tragedy.

If you are involved with this sort of person, it is best to enjoy your partner's sensitivity and creativity, and try to help him or her enjoy them as well. In this way your partner may overcome those deep-seated feelings of insecurity.

Saturn through the Signs and Houses

Saturn in Aries or in the First House

This Saturn placement indicates that the father was a leader, an innovator in the child's eyes, and stood apart from everyone else. The child saw the father as one of a kind, a charge-ahead type who wasn't afraid to take chances. Most likely, he also had a big ego and competed with everyone around him, including the child. Because he had power over the child, he may have succeeded in convincing the child that his or her talents, feelings, and ideas weren't important—unless they agreed with dad's.

Therefore, the person with Saturn in Aries or the first house often has difficulties with self-expression. These individuals do not realize that it's okay to be what you are and to express your own views until they reach maturity. Individuals with Saturn in Aries or the first house need reassurance that they are important for themselves, and people involved in close relationships with them often find themselves having to undo the damage father did. If you are involved with such a person, be aware of this, and if you have a child with this planetary position, take care that neither you nor your partner competes with your own child.

Saturn in Taurus or in the Second House

The father was an earthy, affectionate, sensual, and rather lazy person who loved his child, and the relationship between them was probably a good one. However, if the father was materialistic, he either may have tried to buy the child's love with gifts, or else put too much emphasis on money, which taught the child to be miserly.

This planetary position does not necessarily mean that this individual will not make money, as might be surmised, but money will be a priority in the individual's life. He or she may be obsessed with it, be tight with money and possessions, or fear that he or she will never have enough money. If you are involved with such an individual, you might run into arguments over money. My experience is that if you are in a relationship with someone who has this planetary placement, try not to be financially dependent on your partner and keep your money separate.

Saturn in Gemini or in the Third House

In some way, the father inhibited the child's development of communication skills. The father may have been so talkative that the child couldn't get a word in, or, conversely, he may have been so taciturn that the child found it pointless to try to talk to him. The father's viewpoints may have been limited in scope, and the child grew up to be closed-minded, too.

Unless other factors in the chart (such as the Sun, Ascendant, or Mercury also in Gemini or Sagittarius) offset this influence, individuals with this placement in their charts often don't even try to expand their minds until they reach maturity—if they do it at all. Even if they do have other chart factors which offset the Saturn/Gemini reticence, they might not be as comfortable with communications or mental pursuits as people who don't have this Saturnian influence.

If you are a great believer in intellectual expansion and communication, you probably will find a relationship with this sort of person frustrating. However, you might be able to find the intellectual rapport you need in other friends, and thus enjoy other things about your Saturn/Gemini partner.

Saturn in Cancer or in the Fourth House

At some time in this individual's life, the father was absent from the home. There may have been a divorce, or the father may have died or gone away to war. In some cases, the father might not have been physically absent, but he was so ineffectual that he may as well have been. The father probably embraced traditional viewpoints and expected his children to do the same. Perhaps he combined the roles of nurturer and disciplinarian in a strange and confusing way; though he had strong feelings toward his children, he never let them know it, and discouraged them from showing their feelings as well. As a result, such individuals have blocks against any kind of emotional expression, and though they may experience intense emotion, expressing it can be so difficult that doing so makes them physically ill.

If you have this planetary placement in your chart, you need to acknowledge and accept your feelings and know that it is okay for you to express them. If you are involved with such a person, encourage him or her to express feelings, but don't be too disappointed if your partner never does. The inhibitions imposed by the father may be too strong.

Saturn in Leo or in the Fifth House

Although artistic himself, the father may have inhibited the child's self-expression or creativity. He may have belittled the child's efforts so that he or she became unsure and intimidated about expressing talents. The child probably held the father in high esteem and believed him to be an extraordinary person, and was quite proud of him. However, male children especially can find themselves caught up in the "famous father" syndrome, believing that they cannot possibly match father's achievements so why bother to try? Such people need to be made more cognizant of their own abilities and not worry about equaling their fathers. It is quite possible that these individuals will not realize their talents—or make a success of them—until they reach maturity.

Saturn in Virgo or in the Sixth House

The individual may have trouble working for a living. Either the father didn't work, was not always able to work in his own profession, or was forced to perform work that was not of his own choosing.

Though not lazy or unwilling to work, this type of individual feels that certain jobs are beneath him or her and resents it when forced to do such work in order to survive. The person may feel that he or she, like father, is compelled to do unfulfilling work, and needs to find a way to escape the treadmill. If you are involved with such a person, you may have to help him or her find a way to accomplish this. Your own life with that person will be happier if your partner feels more complete.

Saturn in Libra or in the Seventh House

This individual's parents might have been divorced, or they may have been estranged even though they remained married. The father may have expressed a negative attitude toward marriage and/or relationships and therefore, this person is distrustful of them. The individual could have difficulty forming relationships or being happy in the relationships he or she does have—even though marriage and relationships with other people are important to him or her. However, such people are willing to work at their relationships and therefore might make a "career" out of their relationships. They have a tendency, though, to stay in bad relationships long after they should have ended them. If you are involved with such a person, you are relatively secure in the relationship, but if you decide at some time that you would be better off apart, you may have to be the one who breaks it off—the Saturn/Libra person will hang on until the bitter end.

Saturn in Scorpio or in the Eighth House

The father was a magnetic figure and often his effect on others was overpowering. He may have been involved in petty power plays; he enjoyed the command he had over the child and often compelled him or her to perform ridiculous or humiliating acts simply because he could do so. People with this planetary placement generally possess a great deal of inner strength as a result, but they are often reluctant to show it, because their fathers convinced them that they lacked fortitude and because they don't want to be like their fathers. Even if these individuals are able to express their personal power, they still might feel guilt about expressing their sexuality. If you are involved with such a person, expect some sexual reticence—and be prepared to help your partner overcome it.

Saturn in Sagittarius or in the Ninth House

This person's father probably was an intelligent person whose education was blocked in some way. He may have been idealistic as a young man, but later became disillusioned. For this reason, he may have tried to put a damper on the child's ideals and illusions, wanting him or her to be more "realistic." Thus, the child either may have rejected the concept of higher thought or rebelled to the point of making it the focal point of his or her life. (This will depend on other factors in the chart.) Though intelligent, this individual might balk at using his or her intelligence, and probably either rejects or postpones higher education until adulthood. At times, this person can appear scatterbrained. If you are involved with this type of partner, do not expect him or her to be intellectually grounded or ordered. You may have an animated and enlightening discussion with your partner on a particular subject, then find he or she embraces a completely opposite viewpoint the next day.

Saturn in Capricorn or in the Tenth House

The father may have been an ambitious person, not only for himself, but for his child as well. He may have pushed the child towards a high level of accomplishment, perhaps in a field the child would not have chosen personally. While the father's ambition undoubtedly rubbed off on the child, he or she may feel cheated if not allowed to choose his or her own profession. Whatever the career choice, this person probably will strive for success not because he or she wants to be the best in the field, but because he or she desires power and recognition—and to please the father. Although this type of person believes in home, family, and other traditional, conservative values, they are not the first priorities. Power may be this individual's first and only love.

If you are involved with such a person, be prepared to play second fiddle to your partner's career—and possibly to your father-in-law as well. A woman with this planetary placement might not be ambitious for herself, but could desire career success for her spouse and her children. If you are in a relationship with this type of woman, bear in mind that if she does not have a career of her own, she may try to live out her father's ambitions through you. If you share her aspirations, so much the better—but if you do not, you might want to encourage her to seek a profession of her own.

Saturn in Aquarius or in the Eleventh House

The father may have embraced radical causes or ideas to the exclusion of family and friends. New ideas and/or technology were more important to him than personal relationships, and he may have passed this attitude on to his child. The child may have feelings both of attraction and repulsion towards groups, social causes, politics, and ideas, and therefore, as an adult he or she either avoids them entirely or embraces them to the exclusion of all else.

Many of the current "Yuppies" were born when Saturn was last in Aquarius, in the early 1960s, right before the years of protest and "hippie" lifestyles. Hence, we see the children of hippie parents revolting against the anti-establishment philosophy of the sixties and embracing career success and materialism. This image encompasses both of the principles of Saturn in Aquarius: revolt at all costs against parental values and avoidance of radical ideas. If you are involved with this type of person, do not expect him or her to go with you on missions for Greenpeace—unless the parents happened to be fur traders.

Saturn in Pisces or in the Twelfth House

The father was probably an imaginative individual, given to flights of fancy and poetic language, and he may have enjoyed telling stories. Possibly, he had psychic abilities and was drawn to mystical studies. The child, too, is imaginative and creative, and may be drawn to the psychic realm, but he or she might become discouraged, fearing that his or her abilities can never match the father's.

Father also could have been somewhat deceitful, less from malice than from a desire to protect himself and those he loved, but this tendency may have caused the child pain. The child may make an effort to be more practical and honest than the father. Though he or she might try to turn off the creative and psychic inspirations, they must be harnessed rather than ignored.

If you are involved with this sort of person, be prepared to deal with a great deal of guilt. Saturn in this position carries with it the guilt imposed by the father. Also, like Atlas, this individual tries to bear the sins of the world on his or her shoulders. You could become your partner's confessor as well as lover.

Sun-Moon Aspects

The key to understanding Sun-Moon aspects is to remember that the Sun represents the will and the Moon the emotions. In psychological terms, the Sun represents the father and the Moon the mother, therefore, the aspects between the two show how the parents related to each other. Obviously, the parents affect the child's psyche; the father impacts the child's masculine or yang side, the will and ego, the mother influences the feminine or yin side and the emotions. Many deeply-rooted psychological problems have their beginnings in the relationship a person had with his or her parents. From a metaphysical perspective, the father leaves his mark on the child's masculine side (Sun) and the mother on the feminine side (Moon)—regardless of whether the individual is male or female.

Sun Conjunct Moon

This aspect is indicative of a basic feeling of unity between the parents. The will of one parent was compatible with the emotions of the other. The parents' basic attitudes toward life ran parallel, and mother and father functioned well together. This does not necessarily mean that the parents got along, however, especially if the conjunction is afflicted by other planets in the child's birth chart. Sometimes people who are so closely allied frighten each other, and their fears put a strain on their relationship. If the Sun-Moon conjunction is well-aspected, chances are the parents had a good relationship and the child grew up well-adjusted. He or she is likely to be an excellent parent as well. If the conjunction is afflicted, however—especially by Mars, Uranus, or Pluto—the parents probably saw each other as antagonists. The child's relationships, as a result, will be marked by a fear of conflict. This person may turn the fear and hostility which were part of the parents' interactions on his or her own children. Or, perhaps this individual is afraid of losing his or her children.

In a chart comparison, two people with a Sun-Moon conjunction generally have a harmonious relationship; the will of the Sun-person blends with the emotions of the Moon-person. However, as with a natal chart, if the conjunction is afflicted by a planet in either person's natal chart, the basic unity between the two can prove frightening for at least one of the partners and possibly for both of them. The partners might feel a comfortable unity one minute, and the next moment be scared of losing their individuality in the partnership. These people need to realize that even though they are very close, they are still separate and unique individuals, and each needs to acknowledge the separateness of the other.

Sun Sextile Moon

This person's parents probably had an easy-going relationship, interacting with each other when necessary and going their separate ways when it suited them both. This behavior left its mark on the child; he or she has a positive view of male-female relationships and probably will be successful in forming and maintaining them.

The keyword for the sextile, however, is opportunity. Unlike the trine, which brings advantageous circumstances into your life in spite of everything, the good fortune brought by the sextile needs a little work to maintain it. Depending on other factors in the chart, the person with this aspect may have a way of taking relationships for granted.

In a synastry comparison, this aspect may have the same effect upon a relationship. Even though the involvement is basically a sound and satisfying one, there is a chance of the Sun-person taking the Moon-person for granted. (Sometimes it is the other way around, but most often the complacent partner is the Sun-person.) However, the basically benefic nature of the Sun-Moon sextile usually suggests a good relationship.

Sun Square Moon

When this aspect appears in a natal chart it means that the parents were generally at odds with each other; each saw the other as a potential antagonist. Still, the dynamism and challenge created by the square also may have created a powerful attraction that kept them together in spite of their difficulties. The child sees this reflected in his or her own life as a conflict between the masculine and feminine selves, and therefore, this person may unconsciously mistrust members of the opposite sex. The square is perhaps the most difficult aspect to overcome.

In a chart comparison, the two parties involved probably will feel distrust and sometimes hostility toward each other, but at the same time, the challenging dynamics of the square may draw them together and keep them together in spite of their differences. The square creates a tension that is exciting as well as stressful. In this type of relationship, each partner fears that the other is going to leave, and therefore may try to make up for periods of anger with smothering expressions of love. This is the classic "love-hate" relationship. Whether the involvement will last depends on other factors in the charts, but if other aspects hold these two people together, they need to work on developing trust—something that undoubtedly is lacking in the partnership.

Sun Trine Moon

This is a fortunate aspect indeed to have in the natal chart, for the parents probably had a wonderful partnership and the child's attitudes toward relationships are favorable. This is not to say that all his or her relationships will be perfect— other factors in the chart also must be considered— but it does mean that love will come easily to the person throughout life. Such individuals possess an easy-going nature that makes them highly attractive to others. Love relationships will probably be fortuitous and bring many benefits, both emotional and material.

In a chart comparison, this aspect hints at a strong and loving attraction between the two people and suggests that, for the most part, the relationship between them will progress smoothly. Unless other powerfully disruptive aspects exist between them, the attachment probably will be long and positive, characterized by a harmonious blend of will and emotions. This is a partnership that will carry the two individuals through both good times and bad.

Sun Quincunx Moon

Ouch! I compare the quincunx to a fingernail scraping across a blackboard. The two planets involved in this aspect are in signs that have no affinity for each other, and therefore, there is little chance that the will and emotions will ever blend. This person's parents probably had no relationship at all; they might have divorced, or simply may have lived under the same roof while leading separate lives. Therefore, the child will probably be uncomfortable with intimate relationships. If you have this aspect in your chart, unless other factors offset it, you probably see marriage as a social convenience or a necessity for producing children, but even if you are married you really live alone.

It is difficult to imagine that two people with a Sun-Moon quincunx in their synastry chart comparison would ever form an intimate relationship (in my seventeen years as an astrologer, I have never seen one), but if they do, it would seem that each party enters into the alliance for reasons of his or her own, reasons that are unrelated to the relationship itself. The will of the Sun-person and the emotions of the Moon-person do not blend, and so that part of their life together is shut off. If there is another aspect between the Sun-person's Moon and the Moon-person's Sun, the relationship will have another dynamic, but there always will be periods when the two individuals go their separate ways.

Sun Opposition Moon

This may sound like a terrible aspect to have in the natal chart, and in some cases it may be, but often, surprisingly enough, it can prove advantageous. Depending on other aspects to the opposition, particularly if Venus or Jupiter trines one and sextiles the other, the parents may have complemented each other even if they had very different natures. As a result, the child probably will be attracted throughout life to people who are his or her opposites. Such a person, however, will be able to turn these relationships into mutually beneficial partnerships where the natures of the two people involved serve to balance each other.

If Saturn, Uranus, or Pluto squares the opposition, however, the parents probably never got along. Consequently, this person will still be drawn to people of opposing natures, but instead of complementing each other the two personalities will clash. If you have this aspect in your chart, you undoubtedly will have to learn to trust your partner, regardless of how different the two of you are, and make use of the traits he or she has that you don't, rather than allowing your differences to create conflict and unhappiness.

In a synastry chart comparison, this aspect will have basically the same effect upon a relationship as it does natally upon a person's character. If the other aspects in the comparison strengthen the interaction, the will of the Sun-person and the emotions of the Moon-person will balance each other, and the relationship can be a mutually beneficial one. If other aspects in the comparison are adverse, however, there can be a powerful attraction between the two individuals, but the relationship will be fraught with conflict, and probably it will not endure. If you are involved in this type of a relationship and wish to make it last, it would be best to try to understand the differences between your partner and yourself, and make the most of them rather than allowing them to be constant sources of conflict.

Sun-Saturn Aspects

The Sun in a person's chart represents the father as hero and role model—the ideal father—and Saturn represents the father as authority figure and disciplinarian. In a natal chart, if there is no aspect between the two bodies, the relationship between the two different sides of father can be judged by the nature of the signs in which the Sun and Saturn are placed. If they are in aspect, the aspect will describe how the two different father images interacted, and therefore, how they affected the child's life.

The Sun-Saturn relationship, if any, marks both men and women's attitudes toward men. In a man's chart, the Sun-Saturn aspect affects not only his relationships with other men, but with himself as well. In a woman's chart, the Sun-Saturn aspect will influence her involvements with all men: her brothers, teachers, male co-workers, friends, and lovers.

In a synastry chart comparison, a Sun-Saturn aspect shows how the will of one person (Sun) interacts with the traditional values (Saturn) of the other. If the aspect is a harmonious one, the two blend well and the relationship probably will be a beneficial and lasting one. If the aspect is stressful, however, the Sun-person will probably see his or her self-expression as being blocked by the Saturn person. Occasionally this tendency is reversed, meaning that the Saturn-person feels stifled by the Sun-person, but usually the first effect occurs.

Sun Conjunct Saturn

In a natal chart, this indicates that the individual saw the father's roles as hero and authority figure as unified. The father was probably a kingly person and a natural leader—particularly if the conjunction occurs in Leo. Of course, the person's idea of the father is colored by the sign in which the conjunction occurs. This not only describes how the father actually was, but how the child saw the father. If the father's natal chart reveals an entirely different type of person, his child may be living with a false impression. This usually means that the individual also has an erroneous image of men in general, and if the aspect is in a man's chart, his image of himself could be distorted, too.

If the conjunction is well-aspected by other planets in the chart, the person's image of the father was a good one, and he or she probably has a positive attitude towards men. If the aspect appears in a man's chart, it suggests he has a good self-image. If the conjunction is afflicted by other planets, however, the person saw the father as a limiting influence, and therefore, views men in general as frightening figures. Men with this combination might fear their own masculine side.

In a chart comparison, the Sun-Saturn conjunction often means that the Sun-person sees the Saturn-person as stifling his or her self-expression, and therefore, the relationship may never get off the ground. Sun-Saturn ties, however, are among the hardest to break because they are karmic in nature, and if the two people with the Sun-Saturn conjunction do form a relationship, it is generally one that will endure, whether it brings pleasure or hardship to the people involved. Aspects from other planets to the conjunction will show whether or not the two individuals wish to end the relationship. If the Sun-Saturn conjunction is well-aspected by other planets, chances are the relationship will last a long time; if it is poorly-aspected, the partners probably won't break up, but may wish that they could.

Sun Sextile Saturn

This individual's images of father as hero and father as authoritarian seem to blend easily, and he or she probably likes men and trusts them. If this aspect appears in a man's chart, his self-image is good and he probably attracts the respect and esteem of male friends and co-workers. In a woman's chart, it indicates that she likes men and enjoys their company, and may have more male friends than female ones. Whether this affinity with men carries over into romantic relationships depends on other factors in her chart.

In a chart comparison, this aspect offers an opportunity for the relationship to develop into a beneficial and lasting one, but whether or not it will depends on the aspects between other planets in the comparison.

Sun Square Saturn

This person often finds men frightening and untrustworthy; the father figure may have alternated between being a generous, adoring parent and a stern, fearsome Jehovah. Therefore, throughout the life of this individual, relationships with men will be marked by distrust. He or she will approach men warily, and may never trust male teachers or employers. Only after male friends or lovers have proven themselves will this individual feel comfortable with them.

If this aspect shows up in a man's chart, it suggests that throughout life he will experience conflicts between what he wants to be and what he thinks he should be. If the Sun is stronger by sign, house position, and other aspects, he will probably allow himself to have his way, though he might feel guilty about it. If this aspect appears in a woman's chart, it indicates that she probably will not allow herself happiness with a man until late in life.

If this aspect occurs in a chart comparison, the Sun-person will constantly feel blocked by the Saturn-person. It will be hard to resolve this conflict without intense effort from both parties. If you are considering entering into a relationship with a person whose Sun squares your Saturn or vice versa, look carefully at the relationship before committing to it seriously and make sure it is what you want. Once you enter into a Sun-Saturn relationship, you may find it very hard to get out.

Sun Trine Saturn

This is a solid, stabilizing aspect in a natal chart. The father was probably a fine, upstanding person, who was both hero and disciplinarian. As a result, this individual's relationships with men throughout life will be beneficial. If the aspect is in a man's chart, it suggests that his self-image is probably a positive one. In a woman's chart, this aspect indicates that relationships with men come easily and probably will be advantageous for her. Saturn-Sun aspects also can mean that the individual is attracted to older men.

In a chart comparison, this aspect signifies a relationship that is solid and enduring. This is particularly true not only of love relationships, but of business partnerships as well. The two individuals can be of help to each other and can temper each other's excesses.

Sun Quincunx Saturn

This person's father may have seemed like Jekyll and Hyde to the child, as though he were two entirely different people. (If the father's chart was dominated by Gemini, Sagittarius, or Pisces, the image is probably correct!) Unlike the square aspect, however, the quincunx does not produce the dynamic attraction between two individuals, so this person probably learned at an early age to stay out of the father's way.

This attitude will be reflected in his or her later relationships with men. If the aspect appears in the chart of a man, it indicates that his self-image is confused and uncertain. He is probably a loner with few friends, who keeps a safe distance from business associates. In a woman's chart, this aspect can mean that her romantic life is crippled. Some sort of therapy, counseling, or self-help seminars may be a good idea for people with this aspect in their charts.

In a chart comparison, this aspect brings confusion. The Sun-person may see the Saturn-person as an inhibiting factor, and the Saturn-person may see the Sun-person as too self-willed, when neither is actually true. The will of the Sun-person and the discipline of the Saturn-person do not mesh at all; therefore, these two individuals go in different directions and often lose sight of each other. The quincunx usually shows a lack of direction, and when it is between the Sun and Saturn the self-image is involved. In a relationship, neither partner may either see or accept the other as he or she actually is.

Sun Opposition Saturn

This aspect indicates an opposition between the two aspects of father, and the individual's perception of father is definitely colored by the signs in which the two planets are positioned. A person with the Sun in Taurus and Saturn in Scorpio, for example, may watch in terror as the father who was generous and loving only a moment ago turns into a sadistic, avenging disciplinarian.

If this aspect is in the chart of a man, it shows that he has a contradictory self-image, and often will express himself by alternately manifesting the contradictory characteristics of the Sun-sign and the Saturn-sign. If the aspect appears in a woman's chart, it indicates that she will seek men just like her father, but probably will find few who express both sides of the father's contradictory nature. For this reason, all the men she meets will fall short of her expectations, particularly if Neptune also aspects her natal Sun-Saturn opposition. Most likely, she will see the men in her life as inhibiting her desires.

In a chart comparison, this is a difficult aspect to handle. It can prevent the relationship from getting started. However, once the relationship has begun, it is hard to end it—perhaps more difficult than with any of the other Sun-Saturn aspects. The Sun-person sees the Saturn-person alternately as a drag and as an inspiration, and, it seems, "never the twain shall meet." Understanding and accepting the partner's individuality is the key to balancing this aspect.

Moon-Saturn Aspects

In analyzing Moon-Saturn aspects, we are considering the relationship between mother as nurturer and father as head of the household. However, with certain individuals these positions could be reversed; the father could be the nurturer and the mother the head of the household. The Moon, as ruler of the sign Cancer and the fourth house, also represents an individual's attitudes toward the home, while Saturn, as ruler of the sign Capricorn and the tenth house, represents the person's ideas about society. Thus, Moon-Saturn aspects show the interaction between home and state, private and public life.

Moon Conjunct Saturn

The mother and father probably had similar ethnic, social, educational, political, and religious values, and both subscribed to traditional attitudes about the structure of the home environment. If the person's birth chart also contains an aspect between this conjunction and the Sun, it will show how the parents' attitudes affected the child itself. If there is no aspect between the Moon-Saturn conjunction and the person's Sun, he or she probably paid little attention to the attitudes of the parents and went his or her own way. If there is a harmonious aspect between the conjunction and the Sun, the parents' attitudes and the way they ran the home benefitted the child, and he or she probably adopted the same or similar viewpoints. If the aspect is a stressful one, however, the parents undoubtedly saw the child as a rebel, and may have punished him or her by withholding love. This may have had the effect later in life of causing the individual to keep a tight rein on his or her feelings in order to avoid being hurt.

In a chart comparison, the Moon-person is probably the more emotional of the two partners; the Saturn-person expresses a marked reserve, and the Moon-person may see the Saturn-person as cold and emotionally repressed. Conversely, the Saturn-person may see the Moon-person as overly emotional and may attempt to control the Moon-person (like the father-disciplinarian) by inhibiting the partner's expression of feelings to others.

Moon Sextile Saturn

The father and mother generally agreed on the running of the home. They may have had a few attitudes that differed, but even those were not serious and the parents got along well. The child, therefore, learned to express emotions with some restraint and, though he or she may seem blocked emotionally on occasion, for the most part the emotional life is quite healthy.

In a chart comparison, the emotional expression between the two partners is probably open and healthy, and their domestic values—whatever they may be—are compatible. The relationship will probably be a lasting one; however, the changeable, restless Moon is not as strong an indicator of longevity as the Sun.

Moon Square Saturn

In my own experience I have found that frequently people who have this aspect in their charts saw their parents as reversing the roles of nurturer and household head. In these cases, the father usually is represented by the Moon and the mother by Saturn. This is only my observation, however, and should not be judged as an absolute by any means. It is likely this person was closer to one parent than the other, and the parent that was left out may have felt abused in some way. Therefore, this individual probably nourishes subconscious guilt for neglecting one parent, and may carry this over into adult relationships. Such people might overcompensate for the neglect of that parent by being especially attentive to members of the same sex as that parent, or, he or she could justify that neglect by finding fault with members of the same sex as that parent.

If this aspect appears in a man's chart and the Moon-parent was the father, a masculine/feminine identity conflict is indicated. If the aspect is in a woman's chart and the Moon-parent was the father, a "Daddy's girl" syndrome is implied, and in her adult life she compares all men she meets to her father—often to their disadvantage.

In a chart comparison, the two partners' home v. career values clash. The Moon-partner sees the Saturn-partner as cold and unfeeling. The Saturn-person, on the other hand, too often considers the Moon-person's emotional expression as excessive. Either situation may or may not be true. The relationship could be an on-and-off type, but not in the sense that a Uranian relationship is. The Moon-square-Saturn attachment often follows a pattern of emotional conflict (Moon) followed by a breakup, but the bond (Saturn) is too strong to break, and the couple ends the conflict with a tearful reunion (Moon). This merry-go-round ride can last for years, limiting the growth of both partners. Whether the relationship has the potential to settle down and become a mutually supportive unit depends on other factors in the chart.

Moon Trine Saturn

The parents' values dovetailed and the home probably ran smoothly. The parents loved each other and taught healthy emotional expressiveness to the child by their example. In adulthood, this person usually is attracted to people who share his or her values (depending upon other factors in the chart) and generally repeats the parents' pattern of a smoothly-running home.

In a chart comparison, this aspect more than any other signifies a beneficial exchange of emotional expression between the two partners, as well as shared social and cultural values. The trine shows promise of a lasting and mutually positive attachment.

Moon Quincunx Saturn

The parents had values that did not merge in any way, and the home was probably filled with confusion. Unless other factors in the chart offset the tendency, this individual probably does not display emotion at all—neither healthy emotional expression, (as with the sextile and trine) nor repressed or excessive emotion (as with the square and opposition). He or she seems difficult to reach emotionally and has little capacity to understand the feelings of others.

In a chart comparison, this aspect signifies people from basically incompatible home atmospheres, and the involvement may suffer from conflicts between basic domestic values. Other factors in the comparison, however, will have to tell if the relationship has a chance to succeed in spite of this fundamental difference.

Moon Opposition Saturn

The parents may have had an emotional impasse between them, and, particularly if Mars also aspects the opposition, there was probably an intense amount of conflict in the home. This individual, therefore, chooses to keep an emotional distance from other people, especially romantic partners. Such reserve can cause conflict not only within the person, but in relationships as well. The individual may deliberately block expression of any feeling at all, thereby frustrating partners.

In a chart comparison, this aspect generally indicates that the two people came from different backgrounds, but if the planets in the opposition are otherwise well-aspected, the two can use their differences to enrich their growth as individuals and as a couple. If the Moon and Saturn are afflicted by other planets, however, the partners may be unable to resolve their differences and thus inhibit the relationship from either growing or enduring.

Part Three

Romance and Marriage

7

Romance and Marriage

Regardless of how much we study and analyze it, romantic love remains a mystery. Just what is it that attracts two people to each other in such an intense, passionate way, what we call romantic love? What else can catapult us to the heights of ecstasy or hurl us into the depths of despair more quickly and completely than romantic love? Who among us has not dreamt of being swept off our feet by a handsome stranger or beautiful maiden, and living happily ever after in a haze of romantic bliss?

Most of us do fall in love at least once in our lifetimes, and usually more than once. Regardless of the staggering divorce rate, the dream of perfect romance seems to be alive and well. Just as medieval nobles and peasants alike once listened to minstrels sing about the romantic loves of Lancelot and Guinevere, Tristan and Iseult, we are captivated by modern romantic myths: the on- and off-screen romances of Bogart and Bacall, Tracy and Hepburn, or Burton and Taylor. Television soap operas center on romantic intrigue. Though few of us have escaped the heart-rending pain of a failed romance, we do not seem to be jaded. In spite of disillusionment and divorce, most of us still believe we will eventually find happiness through love. Somewhere out there is Sir Galahad or Iseult the Fair, waiting for us and us alone. Our lives will never be complete, we think, until we find that one perfect partner.

This idea, of course, is a myth. Although every psychologist seems to have a different theory about the nature and significance of romantic love, most agree that the dream of finding the perfect partner and lifelong ecstasy is a fantasy. The best possible relationship between a man and a woman, they maintain, is a commitment based more on mutual goals and interests than on passionate attraction, in which both parties not only accept each others' human failings, but at times even find them endearing. However, here psychologists appear to part company. Most of them disagree about why romantic love exists in the first place, and about its history and significance in the course of human evolution.

Some psychologists, perhaps the most skeptical, maintain that love is merely an extension of libido, that romance is nothing more than a justification for indulging the sex drive, and ultimately perpetuating the species. Others relate this feeling to an unconscious desire to re-create the primal physical union with the mother. Still others believe that romantic love is a more earthly manifestation of the same desires that lead to religious experience.

Metaphysical research finds that, after the primal creative force, the force of polarity (the balance of yin and yang) is the strongest in the Universe. Nuclear energy, for instance, is based on the bonding of positive and negative electromagnetic forces. Protons (positively charged atomic particles) cannot exist without the corresponding negatively charged particles, electrons. Physicists now are postulating that *matter* (composed of positively charged energy) is balanced in other dimensions by *antimatter* (composed of negatively charged energy). The equilibrium of the entire Universe, it would seem, rests on a somewhat precarious balance between the positive (yang, active, masculine) and the negative (yin, passive, feminine).

Indeed, the force which attracts the sexes to each other must represent a stronger drive than the mere propagation of the species. There are life forms on Earth which reproduce asexually, and therefore it seems that the idea of sex for the sole purpose of reproduction is an oversimplification. Some biologists maintain that the purpose of sexual reproduction is to mix the genes and thereby create hardier forms of life. Yet the amoeba, which reproduces by the simple method of cell division, so that the genetic code of the primal parent is kept intact for billions of years, is one of the oldest forms of life on Earth. It endures while other "more advanced" forms of life become extinct.

The development of romantic love is traced in the myths of many cultures, such as those about Paris and Helen of Troy, or Cupid and Psyche. In the Bible, the Song of Solomon is still hailed as one of the most passionate love poems ever written. Even pragmatic Plato refers in his writings to romantic love, stating, "What is Eros? What power has Eros? To interpret and communicate to the gods that which is human and to man what is divine. He fills the space between gods and man so as to bind together by his power the whole Universe."[1]

But is the feeling described in these writings what we now call "romantic love"? Again, psychologists differ. Celebrated psychologist

Nathaniel Branden would probably say that it was at least an early form of that emotion. In *The Psychology of Romantic Love,* Dr. Branden defines romantic love as "a passionate spiritual-emotional-sexual attachment between a man and a woman that reflects a high regard for the value of each other's person"[2] and there is no doubt that Homer, Solomon and other writers wished to portray this type of feeling.

Jungian theorist Robert A. Johnson, however, would probably disagree that this sort of involvement actually constitutes romantic love. In *We: The Psychology of Romantic Love* Dr. Johnson differentiates between "romantic love" and simply "love."[3] The type of emotion defined by Dr. Branden appears to be what Dr. Johnson would identify more with "love" than "romantic love."

I tend to associate "love" with the popular idea of the "Girl Next Door." According to this modern stereotype, a young boy grows up with a particular girl as a playmate, and then suddenly, in the years after they both reach puberty, he notices that the pigtails and braces are gone, and that the girl is becoming tall and shapely, exuding an aura that she didn't project before. The boy has always "loved" his childhood companion, and loves her still; he enjoys her company immensely and shares with her the values and viewpoints of their common background. But with the coming of adulthood, the relationship has taken on an added dimension: sexual attraction.

Love, as defined by Dr. Johnson, also appears to me to describe the feeling which men and women develop for each other after several years of marriage. The initial romantic mystique has disappeared; the partners know each other too well for any illusions to have survived. Yet if the relationship has a firm foundation underlying the initial romantic passion, it can continue to develop without the need for the insecurity, uncertainty, and alternating ecstasy and pain which we associate with romantic love. Most psychologists agree that it is at this stage in a relationship that the true commitment begins and the couple can really work on developing a life together.

Still, in our confused society, when the romantic mystique disappears the marriage often dissolves. When the illusions vanish, many people believe that they no longer love each other and decide to part—even though the relationship is still strong enough for them to want to remain "friends"! The mythical ideal of Sir Galahad or Iseult the Fair is hard to overcome for most Westerners, and the ideal is reinforced constantly by movies, romance novels and popular songs. According to popular guru Werner Erhard, even some happily married people never give up the idea of finding Prince Charming or Sleeping Beauty, and they continue to look for those figures even after a firm commitment to a wife or husband has been established.[4]

In Japan, divorce only occurs when a relationship becomes intolerable, and when a couple does divorce, the bond is generally severed. The Japanese, therefore, find it hard to understand why a couple would want to split up and yet remain "friends." "If we could still be friends," one Japanese woman puzzled, "then why would we want to get divorced?"[5]

Years ago, I read an article in a popular women's magazine which proposed that the marriage ceremony be changed to reflect the rising divorce rate. "As long as we both shall live," the article maintained, should be replaced by "as long as we both shall love." This tends to make one wonder: Does commitment really mean anything anymore?

As a twentieth-century woman with one divorce behind me, I would never recommend that a couple stay together if they are hopelessly going in different directions; but, if two people are willing to split up as soon as the fantasy begins to dim, then why marry at all? Here, according to Dr. Johnson, the ideal of commitment often clashes with that myth we call romantic love.

According to Dr. Johnson's definitions, "love" between man and woman has existed since the first stirrings of compassion. The enigmatic congeries of emotion, passion and fantasy which we call "romantic love," however, did not exist until the eleventh or twelfth century.

Throughout prehistoric and ancient times, the feminine principle was acknowledged as a valuable and essential part of human life. With the rise of the Greek and Roman Empires, however, reverence for the feminine began to decline. The continuous wars caused people to overemphasize the importance of the "masculine" traits: aggressiveness, pragmatism, and the drive for power. By the early Middle Ages, respect for the feminine principle—that which is gentle, yielding, and sensitive—had all but vanished. Women were regarded as a necessary encumbrance, and in some religious sects they were even regarded as evil, the embodiment of temptation. These sects taught that women were to be scrupulously avoided by men, except for the expressed purpose of begetting more men.

However, the need in the Universe for balance of the forces of yin and yang is too essential; the feminine had to make a comeback. There appeared in the courts of Europe (possibly instigated by that queen of queens, the clever and beautiful Eleanor of Aquitaine) a new etiquette: the ideal of courtly love. Suddenly women were revered once again, regarded as the embodiment of perfection, as objects of worship.

The accepted practice was for a young knight to find himself a lady to love, honor, and cherish. He was not to have a sexual relationship with her, nor was he to grow too emotionally or mentally close to her. He was to consider it an honor to be allowed to worship her from afar.

Each knight was cautioned not even to consider marrying the woman he loved. In fact, in most cases the knight's chosen "lady" was married to another man. The courtly ideal maintained that sexual intimacy precluded development of the highest and truest type of spiritual love, and therefore courtly lovers, although they were expected to experience intense, undying passion for each other, were never to consummate that passion. Instead, they were to swear undying love and devotion, and to worship each other until death. The knight, especially, was sworn to spend his life undertaking quests and accomplishing glorious deeds, all for the sake of his ladylove. According to Dr. Johnson, this sudden glorification of the "lady" was a direct reaction to the contempt for the feminine principle which had been commonplace during the Classical and Dark Ages.

The practice of courtly love worked well for awhile, so long as the ideal of romantic love was kept separate from the institution of marriage. Marriage, in medieval times, was often (though not always) a business or political arrangement between families. If husband and wife were attracted to each other and eventually developed a mutual affection, that was regarded as mere "icing on the cake." Therefore, for a husband or wife to develop a passionate attachment apart from the marriage was accepted, though not always openly acknowledged.

In the centuries following, the idea of marrying for love became more attractive to Europeans, and eventually the practice became widespread, among the nobility as well as the peasantry. The ideals of courtly love mixed with the notions surrounding marriage. Eventually, however, this development proved something of a disaster.

In *We* Dr. Johnson asks candidly if the institution of courtly love, which denies sexuality and other forms of intimacy, precludes mental and emotional closeness, and encourages love and passion outside the marital bond, can really provide a firm foundation for a lifetime commitment between two people. The answer, of course, appears to be a resounding "No!" Yet the ideas which constituted courtly love form the basis for all our attitudes and practices toward marriage today![6]

In the days when people were old at thirty and dead by forty, and spent most of their lives slaving at back-breaking labor just to survive, mostly everyone was too busy to think about whether or not their relationships were working. People simply made the best of what they had. Today, however, people are placing more emphasis on their relationships. We demand more of our partners and expect them to fulfill our needs and desires—if this doesn't happen, most likely the relationship will end. Yet despite the prevalence of divorce, disappointment in love affairs, and sexually-transmitted diseases, we aren't willing to abandon the search for romance and the perfect lover.

In *The Road Less Travelled,* M. Scott Peck, M.D., maintains that it is not the feeling of mystical union between partners that makes a romantic involvement last a lifetime, but rather the separateness between them.[7] For a marriage to work, Dr. Peck maintains, each partner should have a life and interests of his or her own, and the individuals should grow as human beings both separately and together. In this way, they can provide constant stimulation for each other and "keep the romance going" in their relationship.

Barbara De Angelis, Ph.D., author of *How to Make Love All the Time* and founder of the successful "Making Love Work" seminars, emphasizes open communication and emotional expression in relationships between men and women. Like Dr. Peck, she recommends giving a partner plenty of space and respecting his or her individuality—*and* taking special pains to avoid routine in order to "keep the romance going."

How can we reconcile our desires for commitment to another person and our deeply-ingrained romantic ideals? Modern spiritual teachers suggest that the answer lies in metaphysical and spiritual principles. As mentioned above, Dr. Johnson maintains that the heights of romantic ecstasy are actually a more earthly manifestation of religious experience. Carl Jung maintained that each of us wishes to come to terms with the opposite sex side of ourselves. He called this male part in a woman the *animus* and the female part in a man the *anima*.

We seek the God or Goddess in the form of another person, when actually both God and Goddess dwell within us.[8] Only when we achieve union with the inner god or goddess can we have successful relationships with human beings of the opposite sex. When we have achieved the mystical union, experienced the ecstasy—not with another human being, but with our own Divinity—it is easier for us to accept our partners' human failings and not to feel betrayed if they do not continue to embody our inner ideals. Popular guru Ram Dass writes in *Grist for the Mill* that the only valid reason for two people to commit to each other is that they feel they can best find God together.[9]

All these suggestions from all these different experts, however valid, will not work for everyone, though. Each of us is here to learn particular lessons from our relationships. You will never be able to convince a person whose birth chart is dominated by Pisces that he or she should not pursue romantic ideals in relationships, for romantic ideals are a part of the Piscean's very being. A Scorpio or Taurus person will never believe that sex is a minor part of a marital commitment, no matter what some theorists say. And no one will convince a Capricorn that marriage for status or social gain is unromantic and therefore undesirable; the saying "It's just as easy to fall in love with a rich man as a poor one" was probably coined by a Capricorn woman.

Passionate, romantic attraction, the "sighting of a stranger across a crowded room," is usually due to close Venus-Mars, Venus-Uranus, or Venus-Pluto (and sometimes Venus-Neptune) aspects between the birth charts of two individuals. But in order for this relationship to last, the initial attraction must be backed up by Saturnian aspects. If Saturn in person A's chart, for instance, is in a favorable aspect to the Sun, Moon, or Venus of person B, the relationship will last and, depending on other aspects and the basic nature of each individual, it probably will be a re-warding one. If A's Saturn is in stressful aspect to the planets in B's chart, however, the relationship will indeed last—but both parties might wish it hadn't!

In the course of all love relationships that end in commitment, ro-mantic passion does eventually dissipate. If there is nothing to back up the passion, and no effort is made to maintain it, the relationship is likely to break up. However, if you understand your partner's basic nature, your relationship is less likely to suffer from an unhappy ending.

One way to get a better idea of your partner's real nature is through astrology. In the following section I explain the basic love nature of "pure" zodiacal types, but please bear in mind that very few people are "pure" zodiacal types. Most people are a blend of several different influences, therefore, each individual's attitudes and behavior will be colored some-what by other factors in the chart. Also, please remember that this is *not* a Sun-sign astrology text. When I refer to "the Aries lover," for example, I don't mean only those people who were born between March 20 and April 20 of any given year. An Aries lover could have Aries rising, the Moon in Aries, several planets in Aries—even a prominent Mars—in his or her natal chart. And if your Aries lover has the Moon and Mars in Aries, but the Sun in Aquarius, for example, I suggest that you read the sections on both Aries and Aquarius. Chances are your lover combines the charac-teristics of both signs.

Chapter 8 deals with the animus and the anima. This describes the inner woman within each man and the inner man within each woman, as shown by the positions of the Sun, Moon, Venus, and Mars. Reading it will help you understand what you and your lover(s) subconsciously seek in a partner.

Chapter 9, "Astrology and Sex," gives basic analyses, both individu-ally and synastrically, of Venus-Mars, Venus-Uranus, and Venus-Pluto aspects, which reveal the basic sexual nature. Chapter 10, "The Neptune Connection," deals with each individual's susceptibility to and need for the romantic ideal. I have included case histories, carefully chosen to illus-trate different types of romantic and marital relationships.

My hope is that the following will give you, the reader, a better under-standing of your own needs and those of your partner(s) or potential part-ner(s), and to help you judge objectively whether a new romance could become a lasting, rewarding commitment, or should simply be treated as a "good time."

The Aries Lover

If you are romantically involved with an Arien type, you may find that he or she prefers relationships that have some excitement in them. Ariens are looking for thrills and new experiences and seek lovers who share their desire for anything new and different. If excitement is not a regular part of the Arien's lifestyle, he or she will tend to channel frustrated energy into conflict and argument, and relationships will be somewhat stormy. Too many times Ariens (who in many ways are still children) blame their lovers for the lack of excitement in their lives instead of making their own thrills for themselves.

Ariens are great starters, but are not too good at setting goals and working towards them. Therefore, their dreamed-of adventures may never take place—not from lack of desire, but from lack of planning. If you are romantically involved with an Arien and you want to reduce the stress and conflict in your relationship, try to discover exactly what sort of thrills and excitement your lover seeks, and make it possible for such events to occur.

Two clients of mine who were passionately involved were both Ariens, born within a few days of each other. The attraction between them was obvious because all their planets were conjoined and their Moons were in a sextile. However, their life together was a constant battle. Her Moon was in Capricorn, so her idea of excitement involved more traditional activities: going to the theatre, parties, get-togethers with friends. His Moon was in Pisces, therefore his idea of new experiences centered around creative pursuits: writing plays and composing music, activities which required a great deal of solitude. Both individuals, as typical Ariens, were somewhat self-centered and each expected the other to adopt his or her interest rather than working toward a mutual exchange. Each blamed the other for being "selfish" and "unwilling to compromise."

Since the need for excitement is key to the Arien nature, the success of your relationship with an Arien partner might depend on your ability to share his or her desire for constant stimulation. The rest of the chart will tell you where your partner is most likely to seek stimulation. For instance, if Sagittarius also is prominent in the chart, he will probably pursue excitement through travel. If Taurus or Scorpio is emphasized, she probably will find stimulation through new and exciting methods of making money.

Don't expect much nurturing and emotional support from the Arien. Ariens are too involved with themselves; they are independent and will expect you to be the same. They do not want to be "tied down," so to speak, and seek extensive freedom in relationships. However, perhaps because of their self-centeredness, they are not always prepared to grant their partners the same freedom. They may not always be there when you need them, but might expect you to be continuously available.

Yet in spite of this underlying self absorption, many Ariens do possess a certain desire to be fair. The reason for this is the unconscious influence of the sign opposite Aries: Libra. This Libran shadow affects the personalities of all Ariens. Therefore, if the unfairness of their expectations is explained to them, they may make allowances and, at least intellectually, accept your need for freedom, though they probably will never accept it in their heart of hearts.

Unless there is also a strong influence from a loving and sensual sign such as Taurus, Cancer, or Leo, the Arien does not make the best sexual partner. The Arien is too concerned with his or her own pleasure to think much about the desires of the partner. Again, in this age of how-to manuals and articles on sexual performance in every magazine, there may be a certain *intellectual* condescension to the necessity of pleasing a partner. Your lover may even act upon this belief. But, deep down, the Arien has little interest in anyone else's satisfaction. In the manner of the baby or young child, the Arien sees others as extensions of him- or herself, rather than separate individuals. Therefore the underlying assumption is that his or her pleasure is your pleasure too, and, except intellectually, the Arien is not always aware that the other person has needs that are separate from his or her own. If you are a sensual, affectionate person and involved with an Arien, you can appeal to the intellectual Libran side of the Arien nature and try to communicate your needs to your partner. How he or she will respond depends on other influences in the natal chart.

In the initial stages of involvement with an Arien man, the need for freedom within a relationship may be frustrating to a woman, especially if she is of a more constant and faithful sign such as Taurus, Cancer, Scorpio, or Capricorn. The Arien male, perhaps more than men of other signs, needs to "sow his wild oats" and to see and experience many different partners. Therefore, he will not give up "playing the field" willingly. If you are in the early stages of a relationship with an Arien male, do not be discouraged if he does not throw himself totally into his relationship with you all at once. Once an Arien commits himself to a relationship (again depending on other factors in his chart) the influence of marriage-oriented Libra may come into play and the Arien male could embrace fidelity as fully as any Taurean. In some instances, the impulsiveness inherent in Ariens of both sexes leads them to plunge into commitments before they are fully aware of the circumstances of such involvements. Before you make a romantic commitment with an Arien, you might want to exercise enough caution for two.

Arien women, possibly because of societal conditioning, may not be as promiscuous as their male counterparts. However, they have the same need for constant stimulation, and therefore, they may engage in constant flirtations with a variety of men, even after a commitment to one partner has been made. Both sexes often have an attitude of "the grass may be greener" and subconsciously continue to look for new partners even after marriage. Whether or not they act on this attitude depends upon other factors in their natal charts.

A romance with an Arien can be exciting, stimulating, and full of new ideas and experiences. If you are a person who values such a lifestyle, the Arien may be an excellent partner for you. The best partner for an Arien, however, is not someone who is also self-oriented. Like the two Arien people mentioned previously, a relationship between two such individuals may resemble the proverbial confrontation between the irresistible force and the immovable object: two people who are basically incapable of separating their own needs and desires from others'. The Arien generally requires a partner who is patient, understanding, and capable of making some degree of self-sacrifice without feeling used or imposed upon, someone who is capable of dealing with the Arien as if he or she were a child. Don't forget that Aries is the "I am" sign of the zodiac, and part of the purpose of the Arien's current incarnation is to get to know his or her human self, needs, and desires. One of the functions of the Arien's partner is to help him or her attain this spiritual goal.

The Taurus Lover

If you are looking for affection, loyalty, and constancy from a lover, you may find all you need in the Taurean. Taureans can be trusted to keep the home fires burning, to create beauty in their surroundings, and to cultivate an atmosphere of stability and enduring love. Their warmth and sense of fidelity are unrivaled by most other signs. People who have Taurus figuring strongly in their birth charts are generous with all their resources—emotional, spiritual, and material—and they are more than willing to shower these on their partners. However, their gifts are not given without strings, and Taureans have a tendency to try to buy love.

The Taurean can be quite possessive, sometimes without realizing it consciously. Because Taureans are inclined to assign "ownership" to just about everything, they often view their partners as possessions, too. The Taurean needs security in love, and may seek reassurance constantly from his or her partner; because such reassurance is so important to Taureans, they probably give it in large doses to their partners, too. Fire or air-sign partners may find this stifling, though, and avoid the Taurus lover.

Remember, Taurus is the "I have" sign of the zodiac. Persons born under its influence have karmic lessons to learn regarding possessiveness, and therefore, except in circumstances where the "clinginess" becomes obsessive, partners might be encouraged to make allowances.

Though Taurus lovers are not always the most exciting or stimulating companions—indeed, people whose charts are dominated by fire and/or air signs might find them downright dull—their stolidity can provide a dependable base for less practical individuals. The security and warmth of Taurean love can give the fragile egos of Ariens, Geminians, or Sagittarians the constant boosting they need.

If you are involved with a Taurean and wish to take advantage of the loyalty and security that his or her love provides, you should also be prepared to accept (within reason) the Taurean's deep-seated need for security. This might require you to give more lip service to your love and devotion than would be necessary with partners of the other signs.

Paradoxically, however, once a relationship is established, Taureans can appear to be too complacent. Unless other influences in the chart indicate otherwise, the Taurean is rarely jealous. This may prove frustrating to the partner who believes that he or she is being taken for granted. However, Taureans are not actually complacent; it is just that once a commitment has been made, they feel secure in your love for them and assume that you feel the same way. If you let him or her know that you feel you are being taken for granted, your Taurean partner undoubtedly will be glad to provide you with the reassurance you need!

Too often, Taurean romances, particularly with fire- or air-sign partners, can turn into cat-and-mouse games. The usual course of events involves the partner's playing hard-to-get ("I don't love you anymore") in order to express a need for freedom. The Taurean then may turn the tables to get even and appear to pull away ("So what if you don't love me? I don't give a damn!"). The partner, if not put off entirely, may return in a panic, desperately seeking reassurance again. Such games might be inevitable in the initial stages of a romance, but are unhealthy and destructive once a commitment has been established. It would be better for the fire/air partners to communicate honestly and attempt to reach a workable balance.

Sexually, the Taurean lover is warm and passionate. Unlike the Scorpion who sees sex as a method of exercising power over the partner, Taureans regard sex as an expression of affection. Their attitude is usually "I'll try anything once!" if they feel it will give them and their partners pleasure. For Taureans, sex is an extremely important part of a relationship, and they are not likely to place a partner's satisfaction over their own. If the Taurean's sex life is not physically satisfying, his or her frustration may develop into bitterness and resentment toward the partner. A "tease" is not a good partner for the Taurean, nor is a person who is only concerned with his or her own pleasure. However, Taureans often are reluctant to discuss sexual problems and their partners may have to take the first step to resolve problems in this area.

Taurean devotion often may seem a blessing, but if a relationship sours, a Taurean partner can become a burden. The persevering and obstinate Taurus lover rarely writes off a relationship until there is absolutely no hope whatsoever of its success. However stressful the relationship might have been, it has given the Taurean a sense of security which he or she is unwilling to release. The Taurean's partner may want to end the relationship, but finds it almost impossible. In spite of problems, the Taurean clings to the old affection, and the partner, not wanting to cause more hurt than necessary, often lacks the determination to make a final break. Such individuals need to realize that they are not serving their Taurean mates by prolonging the relationship. Though Taureans are hurt under these circumstances—often they cannot understand why their loyalty and warmth were rejected—they still are more practical and thick-skinned than people of other signs. They rarely indulge in the hysteria typical of water signs or the anger for which fire-sign people are known.

Once the relationship has ended, a Taurean will rarely try to re-establish it. Taurus lovers are well-known for their stubbornness, but they are also proud. Therefore, if you have ended a romance with a Taurean and are now having second thoughts, don't wait for your former lover to make the first move—you might wait a long time. Swallow your own pride; the loyalty and enduring love of the Taurean is probably still there, and well worth your effort.

The Gemini Lover

A Gemini lover can be a delight, especially in the initial stages of a relationship. Gemini's intelligence, youthfulness, and childlike curiosity can prove irresistible; these characteristics can restore enthusiasm in someone who is jaded about love and world-weary. The Geminian lover's versatility and diverse interests can be a source of constant stimulation.

As the relationship progresses, however, the Geminian vacillation and unpredictability can drive a more consistent partner crazy. I have found that the most successful relationships involving Geminis have been with other Geminis.

Gemini is a friendly, sociable, and communicative sign. It is essential to the Geminian to have a lover who also is a friend. Physical attraction, security, money, or status aren't always top priorities with Gemini. Geminians want partners with whom they can talk, go out, share activities, who are full of ideas and interests and who will teach them.

The exact nature of a Gemini lover is elusive. Gemini is a mutable sign—impressionable and adaptable. It bears the neutrality of its planetary ruler, Mercury, and the intrinsic dualism of its symbol, the twins; thus it is almost impossible to pin down the Gemini lover. Gemini is an air sign and tends to intellectualize everything, including love, and the Gemini lover's feelings do not run very deep. Gemini is the "I think" sign of the zodiac, and for these people feelings are secondary to ideas.

If you are involved in a romantic relationship with a Geminian, do not expect intense passion or deep feelings. Nor should you look for constancy, fidelity, or a long-standing relationship—Gemini is just too changeable for that. Since traditionally this sign is considered gender neutral, the Geminian probably would express little interest in sex and tend to have an intellectualized attitude about it. Studies have shown, however, that some people work out their nervousness, tensions, and anxieties through sexual activity, and certainly Geminians are nervous and high-strung. Or, perhaps Gemini's natural curiosity leads them to experiment with lots of sexual partners. I make this supposition because I have had many Geminian clients who are quite sexually active, but who paradoxically seem to have little genuine interest in lovemaking.

One young woman I knew, who was a virgin, was stricken with a serious heart ailment (from which she later recovered). For a time she feared she was going to die, and she did not want to leave the body without experiencing sex. She took the first available partner, then appeared to lose interest both in her partner and sex.

In my practice—and I study hundreds of charts a year—I find Geminian romances are not always purely intellectual. In nearly all of my cases, I have observed that in matters of the heart, the Gemini person reverberates to other factors in the chart when it comes to sex or affection. For example, many Geminians also have a strong Taurean or Cancerian influence in their charts (often Venus is in Taurus or Cancer). Therefore, in relationships they seem markedly Taurean or Cancerian in their attitudes and behavior. That is to say, they are sensitive, loving, protective, sensual, and affectionate—nothing like the asexual, inconstant, pure Geminian type you might expect.

The one "pure" case in my files is a young woman who has her Sun and Ascendant in Gemini and her Moon in Sagittarius. Bright, talkative and amusing, she loved to flirt and moved from casual date to casual date. But when she finally fell in love she became more like someone with Venus in Taurus: warm, loving, loyal, generous, and supportive of her partner. Another double Gemini client with Moon in Capricorn was cold, reserved, and aloof; he liked to keep a comfortable distance between himself and his wife. He was generally disinterested in sex and his performance was rather mechanical, without much affection. Though he intellectualize his marriage, his emotional attitude suggested the extreme lack of feeling associated with Saturn and Capricorn.

Consequently, if you are involved with a Geminian partner, consider other factors in the chart carefully in order to understand your lover's romantic needs and desires. The romantic appeal of the Geminian may be based on intelligence, but your lover's behavior and attitudes are probably somewhat less cerebral. In all individuals, romantic needs and desires are a reflection of the synthesis of many factors. Gemini's adaptable nature usually bows to other influences.

The Cancer Lover

Cancer is associated with the home, mother, family, and traditional values. Therefore, if you are involved with a Cancerian, you probably have found that your partner is oriented strongly toward marriage and family, and that a stable home environment is important to him or her. I find that for the most part Cancerians are not totally comfortable just living with a lover; most prefer marriage.

The Cancer individual is warm, sensitive, and loving by nature, and greatly enjoys protecting the partner. When in a relationship, Cancerians are totally committed; only under extremely painful conditions are they likely to seek divorce or end a long-standing relationship—and when they do, it is only after they have given the partnership every possible chance.

Cancerians need plenty of physical closeness, and therefore, kissing, hugging, and touching are an important part of their relationships. Most Cancerians are highly sexual, though unless Taurus or Scorpio is prominent in the chart, cuddling and closeness probably are more important to them than the sex act itself.

One of the first considerations in a Cancerian's relationship is establishing a home. Most people who have Cancer strongly figuring in their charts enjoy good food, and both males and females are skilled cooks. To Cancer, however, food is more important as a subconscious symbol of mother's love than for its own sake (as is the case with Taureans). Though not artistic in the sense that the Taurus, Leo, or Pisces person is, the Cancer individual often possesses skills such as knitting, sewing, and interior decoration, and enjoys putting these talents to use in his or her home.

Cancerians are not adventurous by nature. Unless other factors in the chart imply otherwise, they prefer staying home or visiting with a few close friends to traveling or social activities. Therefore, a person who craves excitement, such as someone with Aries, Leo, Aquarius, or Sagittarius prominently placed in the birth chart, does not always make a good partner for the Cancerian. Although the warmth and sensitivity may be appealing in the early stages of the relationship, eventually the more adventurous partner will find the Cancerian stodgy and boring, and may move on to other, more exciting involvements.

Cancerian men generally have strong, solid relationships with their mothers, and therefore, they often love and respect all women. For this reason, they can make supportive and loving husbands. However, because of their strong preference for life at home, Cancerian men often are not much interested in having high-pressured careers (unless, of course, other influences in the chart counteract this tendency). Sometimes they may enjoy their jobs and make the workplace a second home, and coworkers a second family, but for the most part, when the clock says five they're out the door (or long to be). Nor is the Cancerian male overly concerned with making large amounts of money; if he has enough to provide himself and his family with a comfortable home and a few luxuries, he is generally content.

The Cancer male usually is the most devoted of husbands. These men can be quite solicitous of their lovers and, at least in the initial stages of the relationship, they spoil them. In my practice, I have observed that Cancerian men are the least likely of all signs to engage in extramarital affairs or seek divorce; they idealize their women, yet at the same time are tolerant of their human foibles. It is my experience that Cancer men are more forgiving than all other signs. Regardless of how badly his partner has treated him, the Cancer male will always take her back. Sometimes it takes years for the Cancerian to give up on a former relationship and seek happiness elsewhere.

A woman can feel quite secure with a Cancerian partner, *if* she is prepared to accept the omnipresence of another woman in his life: his mother. Though some "liberated" mothers might discourage this clinging tendency in their adult Cancerian sons, in most cases the mothers enjoy their sons' dependence. This attachment is something the wife or lover of a Cancerian man simply cannot fight. If the Cancerian factor in the man's chart is badly afflicted, the relationship with the mother could be fraught with tension and conflict; however, the attachment will be nonetheless binding. Such a situation can be difficult for a wife or lover, and requires a great deal of understanding and patience on her part. Expressing discontent with the intensity of the mother-son relationship will not put you in a better position; it will only make your mate miserable.

How can a Cancer man choose between wife and mother? He is not meant to; most likely, there is a powerful karmic bond between mother and son which is to be resolved in the current incarnation. The best course for the Cancer male's partner to take is to become close to his mother herself, if at all possible. Hopefully the mother-in-law will regard the wife as a friend instead of a rival.

The Cancer woman, although she loves and respects her mother, does not always develop such a strong attachment as the Cancer man does. Rather, she herself becomes the mother, and behaves most maternally toward her partner. Most men enjoy this treatment in the early stages of the relationship; some continue to do so even after the relationship has matured. Others, however, find the possessiveness inherent in Cancer stifling. Unlike the Cancer male, the Cancerian woman is usually insanely jealous, surpassed only by the Scorpio woman. The Scorpion feels jealous and angry, and has no qualms about expressing either emotion. The Cancerian woman, however, feels jealous and hurt, but rarely expresses her feelings in an open, direct manner.

Martian or Uranian types generally do not make good partners for Cancerian women. I had a friend and client once, a man with his Sun in Aries and Mars in the first house, who had a brief romance with a Cancerian woman who had Scorpio rising. In spite of a powerful attraction, the relationship was over in a month. Her jealousy and possessiveness conflicted with his need for freedom.

Children are important to the Cancerian woman, and her husband might find himself playing second fiddle to them. To some men this is normal and admirable; others feel hurt and left out. If you are involved with a Cancerian woman, you need to realize that the maternal instinct is part of the lesson she has to learn in this life. Her love for her children does not necessarily detract from her love for you.

Because Cancer is the "I feel" sign of the zodiac, Cancerians experience their emotions more profoundly than most other signs do. From childhood, the Cancerian has internalized too many negative experiences, often blowing them all out of proportion. A minor annoyance for a Taurus, Leo or Capricorn can be traumatic for the Cancer person. Therefore, if you are romantically involved with a Cancer partner, be prepared to face his or her deep-seated insecurities which may seem to have no logical foundation.

Part of your karma may be to build up your lover's self-confidence and help him or her overcome these insecurities. You also may need to reassure your partner that it is all right to be emotionally vulnerable, to feel pain, and to remain sensitive in an insensitive society. Hopefully, adopting such viewpoints can help the Cancerian male to lessen his dependency on (though not his affection for) his mother, and enable the Cancer woman to overcome much of her possessiveness and jealousy.

If you are involved with a Cancer partner, you can expect a warm and loving marriage and a secure home life. And if you are not an adventurous type with a strong desire for freedom, the Cancerian may be just what you need.

The Leo Lover

The Leo lover is charming and charismatic, often physically beautiful, and he or she attracts throngs of followers. Many of these admirers, swept away by the glamour, warmth, and enthusiasm of the Leo individual, may become lovers, or potential lovers. Of all signs of the zodiac, the Leonine lover is the most generous with his or her love.

The Leo male may appear promiscuous by nature, and generally has many sexual partners. For the most part, however, the Leo man is not a "love 'em and leave 'em" type. As long as he is involved with a woman (whether it be a one-night stand or a long-term commitment) he genuinely believes he loves her—and probably he does. He is flattered by her attention, and whether or not he feels a deep and abiding bond with a particular woman, if she wants him he is all too willing to give her what she wants, at least for awhile. When another woman comes along who wants him as much or more, he is likely to turn his affections to her as well. This does not mean that he has ceased to love the first woman. If confronted, he will undoubtedly protest, "But I love you both!" and this is the absolute, unvarnished truth. He simply loves women, period. Perhaps the most perfect historical example of the Leo lover was the Emperor Napoleon, who had many women in his life but never really stopped loving and needing Josephine.

Even when a Leo male falls passionately, head-over-heels in love (as opposed to the admittedly superficial type of love he feels for his casual partners) and makes a commitment, his eye will continue to rove and he will still be attracted to many women. Whether or not he follows up on the attraction depends on other factors in his chart. If Taurus, Cancer, Virgo, or Pisces is prominent in the chart, he probably will limit his activities to looking and appreciating; if Scorpio is prominent, however, there is a strong possibility that he may have affairs—even though emotionally he is committed to his mate and has no intention of ever leaving her.

If you are married to a Leo man, be prepared to share his attentions, if not his body, with other women. This will require open-mindedness, patience, and a sense of humor. One of my clients, married to a Leo-Sun man who is constantly pursued by women, told me, "I feel flattered that out of all those women who wanted him, he chose me."

In the early stages of a romance, however, any woman involved with a Leo male should not assume that he is seeking marriage or commitment. He may be, but, unlike the Cancer or Pisces man, the pure Leo type is not oriented toward monogamy. If you are beginning a relationship with a Leo male, remain wary until you know him better, for although he may love you he does not necessarily associate that feeling with permanence.

If, one night, you find him flirting happily with a group of women, don't think that he no longer loves you, or that he is looking to become involved with someone else. Leos thrive on attention, and they usually reciprocate, like a king bestowing royal largess on his subjects.

Unless you have no interest in marriage or commitment, I would never recommend getting involved with a married Leo man. Even though Leos appear to be overly generous with their love, once married, they tend to stay married. (Leo is, after all, a fixed sign.) In most of the divorces I have observed involving Leo men, it was the wife who wanted out.

If you want to keep your Leo partner's interest in other females at a minimum, give him plenty of adulation and ego-boosting. The more he gets at home, the less likely he is to seek it elsewhere. He also needs to feel that he is the king of his household, whether or not it's true. I once asked a Leo man what he liked most about his wife of twenty years, and he said frankly, "She is in total awe of me."

The Leonine ego is often a cover-up for massive insecurities, and, unlike the Cancer man, who tries to overcome these insecurities through attachment, the Leo person convinces himself (or herself) superficially that he (or she) is the greatest thing that ever happened to the world. Leos are kind, generous, and charming, but often their infantile conceit can be insufferable. (This is especially apparent in Leo men.) If the Leo man's lover can manage to find this egocentricity amusing rather than irritating she will be much happier, for this trait is intrinsic to Leo and will not go away. Leo is the "I will" sign of the zodiac, and one of the karmic lessons associated with Leo is learning to play the role of the king of beasts.

Unless other influences in the chart indicate otherwise, the Leo woman is not as overly promiscuous as the Leo man. She may be flirtatious, enjoy the company of men, and often find herself surrounded by admirers, but unlike her male counterpart, she is not generous with her favors. The love of one man is important to her, and she generally prefers to save her body for the one man whom she considers worthy of it. She is the queen in her court, and knows that men are more likely to appreciate her if she makes them feel unique and important, honored above all other men.

After marriage, the Leo woman is devoted to making the man in her life feel like the king she believes him to be. Problems in her relationships generally are the result of her queenly and somewhat domineering nature, not because she is threatened by rivals. The Leo woman is strong and assertive, and not afraid to demonstrate her capabilities. Her "take-charge" manner can be threatening to some men; others are proud to have such a strong woman for a partner.

If you are involved with a Leo woman and are intimidated by her overbearing behavior, some honest communication with your partner would surely help. Leo women are anxious to please, and to make their men feel special. Your Leo lover's need to take charge of situations will not go away, but if she knows it offends you she will be less overt about it, and allow you at least to believe you are the driving force in the relationship! (I personally believe it would be better to accept her as your equal, but this may not be an easy thing for you to do, especially if you too are a Leo!)

Sexually, Leos are some of the best lovers. Not only do they enjoy giving their partners pleasure, they genuinely are "in love" with their sexual partners—at least momentarily—and want to express that love with physical affection and emotional support.

Relationships with Leos can be warm and loving, and a real ego-boosting experience as well. Leos may have powerful egos themselves, but they are also quite good at enhancing the confidence of others and making them feel loved and appreciated.

The Virgo Lover

I find that the popular image of the chaste Virgoan who emulates the Virgin Mary is a myth. The Virgoan lover is very choosy, and I know few promiscuous Virgoans, unless the promiscuity results from other factors in the chart. Remember, Virgo is an earth sign, and earth sign people are usually comfortable with their physical nature, which includes sex. Therefore, I find that most Virgoans, though picky about their partners, enjoy the physical side of love. They use their detail-consciousness to figure out just what will give their partners the most satisfaction, down to the smallest gesture.

Virgo is neither possessive like Taurus or Cancer, nor flamboyant like Leo. For the most part these people are pleasant, well-mannered, and intelligent, always willing to pitch in and help. However, sometimes they can be their own worst critics and are too hard on themselves. If you are in love with a Virgo person and think that person is terrific, you probably will wonder why your lover puts him- or herself down constantly. Such self-abnegation can be a source of constant frustration for you, and you might agonize over why your partner does not believe he or she is as wonderful as you do.

Surprisingly enough, your attempts to build your mate's self-esteem can hurt rather than help the relationship. Virgo is by nature a self-effacing sign, and you can't change your partner's attitude. By maintaining that you think he or she is perfect, you may cause your lover to wonder if there is something wrong with you. The best way to handle this basic Virgoan trait is to let your partner know you love him or her, but be supportive of attempts to improve him- or herself. Each success the Virgo individual attains increases self-esteem; if you are part of these victories the bond between you and your partner will be stronger.

The Virgoan search for perfection can prove counterproductive to the development of a romantic relationship in other ways, too, for Virgoans seek perfection in their mates as well as in themselves. Often it may seem as if they are picking you apart and dwelling on your faults, and during quarrels they have a way of remembering every mistake and shortcoming you have demonstrated in the past ten years! If your self-esteem is shaky in any way (and whose isn't?) this can cause you great pain. When one of my clients ended a two-year relationship with a Virgoan man, she told him she was "tired of being made to feel inadequate, because I'm not inadequate."

Needless to say, if you are a Virgoan, this tendency to be critical probably needs to be curbed. You may see your little criticisms as constructive, a way of helping your partner to improve, but unless your partner is a strong Aries or Leo (who will think he or she is great no matter what anyone else says) your words will hurt. For many people, criticism from lovers implies that their mates no longer love them—and that can only damage the relationship.

The search for perfection in a partner can lead Virgoans to abandon potentially good relationships or hesitate to commit to them. Instead, they keep seeking some ghostly ideal that doesn't exist. No one expects you to abandon your quest to be the best you can be and expect the same from those who love you—but this drive needs to be kept in perspective.

If you are involved with a Virgoan, bear in mind that your partner would not be with you if he or she did not consider you unique and special. Even though Virgoan mates may appear to expect total perfection, they undoubtedly believe the lovers they choose come close to their ideal, or they wouldn't be around. Remember that Virgo is the "I analyze" sign of the zodiac, and that the Virgoan is here on Earth for the purpose of developing critical and analytical capacities.

You can put that analytical tendency to work for you. Mercury rules Virgo, therefore, the Virgoan enjoys honest communication. Have a good long talk with your partner and express your feelings about being "picked apart." Your mate may try to analyze why you feel the way you do—and how he or she can best relate to you! Unless their natal charts are badly afflicted. Virgoans do not really want to hurt anyone. On the contrary, they are naturally inclined toward kindness and good manners. The tendency to criticize is almost unconscious with Virgoans, and if the hurtfulness of it is brought to their attention, they probably will attempt to curb this trait, or at least try to be more tactful.

Once a relationship has been established, living with a Virgo person poses a different set of problems. I have lived with several, and I have noted a vast difference in the attitudes of Virgoan men and Virgoan women. Here I wish to bomb the popular image of the perfectionist Virgoan, obsessed with keeping a house clean and neat. In the case of Virgoan housewives, this image may be accurate. Virgoan women who work outside the home, however, throw so much energy into their jobs that at home they want to rest. Housework is the last thing on their minds, although they may bewail the messiness and wish they had the time or inclination to keep it neat and tidy. This generally doesn't pose problems in their relationships—unless their partners also are Virgos.

Virgo men are a totally different story. We have all heard the saying, "I can't stand other people's mess, but mine is all right." This old bromide seems to illustrate perfectly the attitude of the Virgoan male. Like the Virgoan working woman, he may be uncomfortably aware of the disorder, but doesn't take the time to clean up after himself. If the Virgoan factor in his chart is badly afflicted, the Virgo man may leave clothes scattered on the floor and dishes piled in the sink, apparently oblivious to this clutter. But, if you leave anything out of place, you become a hopeless slattern. If you try to point out that he makes bigger messes than you, he will deny it vehemently. He is not lying to you—he genuinely believes what he is saying. My experience is that this disconcerting tendency isn't something you can change easily; you may just have to learn to live with it.

Although Virgoan love is quieter and less salient than that of the emotional Cancer or the flamboyant Leo, it can be strong and abiding, and comforting in times of crisis. A Virgoan partner can be a staunch, loyal, and exceedingly helpful mate.

The Libra Lover

Libra is associated with love, particularly the kind of love that leads to marriage. Libra is also the sign of balance, harmony, and social interaction, therefore, the person with a Libran emphasis in his or her birth chart is generally gracious, well-mannered, and anxious to please everyone. Finally, Libra is an air sign, so the Libran is generally intellectually-oriented and talkative. People with Libra strongly figuring in their charts love a good discussion or debate, and because they can see both sides of any issue, they can argue either side effectively.

Quite frequently, Librans are physically attractive and charming, and they are almost always tactful and considerate. Kind and solicitous, they are willing to help and never forget that the other guy has feelings, too. They can, however, be moody; frustrations and setbacks in their lives can cause the Libran scales to become unbalanced, and it may take a great deal of understanding to help the Libran partner regain his or her equilibrium once again.

Libran lovers want you to whisper words of love in their ears, and they don't hesitate to express their love for you. The Taurean lover shows affection through physical forms of expression, but Librans, like other air-sign people, like to talk about their love. Libran men are somewhat more flowery in their love-expressions than Libran women, and they tend to subscribe to the concept of "courtly love." They may write poems to their lovers or bring them wine and roses, and can be quite the romantics.

Librans are very much concerned with what people think and what is the "proper thing to do." Because of this regard for society's mores, Librans, like Cancerians, generally aren't comfortable with a "living together" type of arrangement and much prefer to legalize their love through marriage. I find, however, that a Libran who has experienced divorce may try living with a potential partner before taking another chance on marriage; Libra's respect for the institution of marriage makes and him or her want to be absolutely sure of the firmness of the commitment so as to avoid another mistake.

Unlike the other air signs, Librans are not "free spirits" who like such unconventional arrangements as "open marriage." If other features in their charts—other air-sign influences or strongly sensual factors—incline them to extra-marital affairs, their primary commitment to their marital partners remains firm. I once had a male client with a Libran Sun, a Scorpio Moon, and Leo rising who had an agreement with his wife that both could see whomever they wanted. When I met them, they had been married for ten years, and the last time I heard from them, four years later, they were still together.

Librans see sex primarily as an expression of love. If they have influence from Leo or Scorpio (many Librans have Venus in Leo or Scorpio) they are exciting and sensual lovers, always ready and willing to please. They will do whatever they think is appropriate; if a certain action gives a partner pleasure, the Libran will gladly perform it, but, later, in another relationship with someone who doesn't like that particular gesture, the Libran will tactfully avoid it. Unlike the Aries lover, who is most concerned with his or her own pleasure, the Libran is most concerned with the partner's satisfaction. Hopefully their mates will be sensitive to this and reciprocate, for the Libran is not likely to ask.

One of the main problems with Libran lovers is their sometimes overwhelming concern with what people think. If you are an unconventional type who loves to flaunt society's standards, it would be a good idea to consider this tendency in your Libran lover before you make a commitment. Librans are rational and changeable, therefore, their concern with society's opinions is not so firmly engraved is the case with some other signs. Other factors in the chart should be considered, too. Is Uranus or Aquarius also prominent? If so, your Libran friend is probably much less conventional than most Librans. Is Neptune, Sagittarius, or Pisces dominant? If so, your partner's idealism probably outweighs his or her need to be traditional. However, if Virgo or Capricorn is emphasized, conservatism probably is pronounced, and you should think carefully about this relationship.

Conversely, if you are conventional by nature, you should consider that in the early stages of any relationship, and in business and social situations, the Libran always appears to do what is socially correct. What he or she is likely to do in personal and private life might be something entirely different. Once again, this can be ascertained by looking at other factors in your partner's chart.

Another potential problem with Libran lovers is their intense moodiness, especially if the Libran influence in the chart is badly afflicted. Progressions or transits can cause the Libran to sink into the blackest of depressions. The reason for this may be a lack of self-esteem; Librans fear others will have the same low opinion that they have of themselves. If you are involved with a Libran partner, try to give your partner plenty of support and encouragement to bolster his or her confidence and reduce susceptibility to insecurities. If Mars is prominent in the chart or involved in the affliction, the Libran can be quarrelsome—sometimes just for the sake of being difficult. If you can let your Libran mate know that *you* think he or she is wonderful—and why—you may avoid this problem.

Librans are oriented toward love and relating, and this is a central focus in their lives. If you are looking for commitment, the Libran will give it to you—and the relationship is likely to last a long, long time.

The Scorpio Lover

Usually Scorpio is regarded as the sex sign of the zodiac, and for the most part it is. Scorpio's main concern, however, is power—and sex is only one expression of power. In fact, most Scorpions enjoy the power inherent in sex, and if the Scorpion factor in the person's chart is afflicted, he or she may use sex to control partners. One Scorpio client of mine told me he liked knowing he had the power to make his lover moan.

While the Scorpion can be a great bed partner, his or her motives may be other than the partner thinks. The Scorpion can be an intense, devoted, and loyal lover, particularly if Venus or Neptune is part of the Scorpionic influence—but, these people also can be manipulative, particularly if they sense that their partners are dependent on them. If the Scorpio factor is afflicted, they may use the relationship as a tool to get what they want, and overly devoted partners can fall prey to their power plays. This can cause the Scorpio partner to lose respect for the mate, and thus damage the relationship.

If you are involved with a Scorpio, you will want to remain alert to this tendency toward manipulativeness and take care to stand up for yourself. Scorpios are more vulnerable than they would have you believe—and they are more concerned with relationships than they themselves realize.

In fact, they are so concerned with their relationships that they can be insanely jealous, often for no apparent reason. Suspicious and nosy, a Scorpio may be difficult to live with if you have a strong need for privacy. Yet Scorpios are quite secretive, and often hide parts of themselves. It is not easy to lie to Scorpions; they are not only master psychologists, but are quite psychic and may be able to sense when you are not being entirely truthful with them. The best way to handle this, apparently, is simply to allow them their secrets—and learn to keep a few yourself!

Communication can be a problem with Scorpio lovers, since they are not inclined to share their innermost thoughts with their partners. On the outside, they may seem merely to be a little preoccupied, but inside anger, confusion, resentment, unsatisfied passion, and other deep emotions are smoldering— feelings of which they may not even be aware. A progression or transit can trigger an emotional explosion; therefore, it is best to encourage your Scorpion partner to express his or her feelings and get them out in the open in order to avoid a holocaust.

This may or may not work, depending on how heavy the Scorpion influence is and what else is in the person's birth chart. If a gregarious sign such as Leo, Gemini, or Sagittarius is prominent in the chart, your partner may not require much encouragement to communicate; if the Scorpion influence involves a combination of Sun, Moon, Ascendant, and/ or several planets, however, your partner may never open up, no matter how much encouragement you give. You may have to learn to live with his or her pent-up feelings, and if you are particularly sensitive, this might not be easy.

Scorpions often crave solitude, and they may take off from time to time by themselves just to be alone. Partners who are not aware of this tendency may feel hurt and confused, wondering if they did something to make their Scorpion partners leave. Although some event could have triggered the departure, generally the introspective Scorpio person simply needs some isolation. The mate of a Scorpion had best be prepared for this and might learn to enjoy solitude as well. The Scorpio usually will come back; remember, Scorpions' relationships are much more important than they care to admit.

Scorpions tend to be money-oriented, and, if other influences in the chart reinforce this, they may be hard workers and keen investors. They also can be misers, unwilling to spend money on what they consider luxuries. Sometimes the Scorpion looks for a mate with money, or at least a good job or an adequate source of income. I find that Leo-Scorpio combinations love to be supported. They are less concerned with making a living than with devoting themselves to creative projects that they hope will make them a lot of money, therefore, they tend to gravitate toward partners who will carry the financial burden until their efforts bear fruit. This is true of both men and women.

If Neptune is prominent in the Scorpio-Leo person's chart, these projects might remain castles in the air. Only with extreme reluctance do these people try to make their living at nine-to-five jobs. This is fine if they are involved with partners who believe in their projects and are willing to contribute—but if the partner is conservative and practical, this situation could cause great stress in the relationship.

The Scorpio lover is an enigma, and will probably always be so; mystery and secrecy have always been typical of this sign. Perhaps it is the mystery that makes Scorpions so intriguing and gives them their appeal.

The Sagittarius Lover

The keyword for the Sagittarian lover is *enthusiasm.* If a Sagittarian falls in love with you, he or she embraces the relationship totally and completely, with few reservations. Your Sagittarian partner will want to give you everything, do everything for you, and plan a life full of adventures together. Eventually, however, you will have to confront the Sagittarian's tendency to overidealize everything.

Sagittarian lovers have a way of believing that each new lover is *the one,* yet they may go through three or four overidealized "romances" in the course of a month. I had one female Sagittarian client who met a different man every week. Within a day or so of their initial meeting, she was positive that each was Prince Charming, and she wanted me to do chart comparisons and composite charts for every new relationship she embraced. When every relationship fizzled out after a few days it became rather tedious! Remember that the planetary ruler for Sagittarius is Jupiter, and that Jupiter's keyword is abundance. Sagittarians may go through many relationships before they finally settle down to one—and some may never settle down. Particularly if a sensual sign such as Taurus, Leo, or Scorpio is prominent in the chart, the Sagittarian may have several romances going at once.

Part of this is due to Sagittarian idealism. Sagittarians don't seem to be able to accept that there are no Prince Charmings or Fairy Princesses out there, and so they search eternally for Sir Galahad or Iseult the Fair. Since Sagittarius is a sign associated with wisdom and understanding, it doesn't take long for the Sagittarian to realize that a new prospective partner does not live up to the ideal. Instead of accepting the new lover as a human being, the Sagittarian will move on, continuously hoping to fulfill his or her ideal.

If you are considering an involvement with a Sagittarian, you might try tactfully to help him or her acknowledge your basic humanness. Hopefully your lover will see your human "flaws" as endearing traits, just as lovable as the sought-after perfection. The ability of the Sagittarian to do this depends on other influences in the chart. If practical signs such as Taurus, Virgo, or Capricorn are also prominent, it shouldn't be too difficult. However, if Neptune or Pisces is dominant, my guess is you have two choices: Either do your best to live up to your lover's ideals, or accept that the relationship may not last and enjoy it while you can.

A relationship with a Sagittarian can be quite enjoyable. People whose charts feature this sign prominently are good-natured, jovial, happy-go-lucky, and full of zest for life. For as long as they are with their partners, they pour a tremendous amount of energy into the relationship, and the result can be quite pleasurable. If there is a strong Taurean or Cancerian influence in the chart, too, these people can be overly possessive. Therefore, persons with powerful Martian or Uranian concentrations in their charts generally do not gravitate toward serious relationships with Sagittarians. However, if you don't find such possessiveness too stifling, you may enjoy having someone channel so much energy and enthusiasm into a relationship with you.

Sexually, Sagittarians are enthusiastic and exciting, and especially if Taurus, Cancer, Leo, or Scorpio is also prominent, they can make excellent lovers.

As a rule, these individuals are witty and intelligent, although their thoughts often appear scattered and unconnected so that sometimes it seems as if they don't know what they are talking about. Talkative by nature, they enjoy discussing their feelings and opinions with you, and such openness could contribute to the quality of your relationship. However, in serious discussions, their lack of concentration can prove frustrating. Your partner may drift away from the subject and go off on tangents which have little or nothing to do with your conversation.

Life with a Sagittarian can be exciting and full of adventure. If you are seeking some adventure, a relationship with a Sagittarian may prove intensely rewarding. You should consider your own basic needs for stability, however, for this isn't likely to be an issue for the Sagittarian. If you have strong security needs and nothing in your Sagittarian mate's chart indicates similar needs, you may not want to make a final commitment to that person. But, as long as you are together, you are sure to have plenty of fun, excitement, and stimulation.

The Capricorn Lover

Generally, the sign Capricorn is not associated with love. In fact, Capricorns often are thought to be cold, emotionless, and reserved—and in many cases this can be true. However, there are few pure Capricorn types. The intensity of any individual's emotional needs are always the result of many influences in the chart, and therefore, please bear this in mind when considering the effects outlined in the following paragraphs.

Regardless of other factors in the chart, however, in the early stages of any relationship Capricorns are going to be cautious. They will express interest discreetly, then keep some distance between themselves and their new acquaintances. Over time, this distance probably will erode, though the length of time it takes will depend on other horoscopal factors. If fire or air signs are dominant, too, the relationship will probably develop much more quickly than if earth or water signs are prominent.

If Capricorn is the strongest factor in the chart, the individual will probably continue throughout life to remain a certain distance from all loved ones. These people rarely talk about their feelings or their needs and desires in a relationship. Unlike the Scorpion lover, who does not talk about feelings because he or she desires privacy, the Capricorn lover often is unaware of his or her emotional needs. How successful communication or therapy could be at putting the Capricorn in touch with deep-seated feelings depends, again, on other factors in the chart.

The sex drive of Capricorns also depends on other factors in the chart. Often Capricorns are cold and sexually aloof, not so much because they lack physical drive but because they are out of touch with their feelings. This trait is intensified if air signs are prominent in the chart, since air is intellectual, not sensual. If Arien influences are involved, the fiery nature of Aries can help counteract the coldness of Capricorn; however, there is a likelihood that the individual then will be concerned mainly with his or her own pleasure. However, if a feeling sign such as Taurus, Cancer, Leo, or Scorpio is prominent in the chart, he or she can be a tender and sensual lover. Capricorn, after all, is an earth sign and sometimes the Capricorn partner only needs a nudge to make him or her feel more at home with the physical body.

More than most of the other signs, Capricorn is concerned with status, therefore, these people often seek partners who can contribute to their social status in some way. They might look for someone who has money, business or intellectual prominence, or comes from a good family. A client of mine who has strong Capricorn factors in his chart became involved with a woman whose sister is a celebrated public figure; the sister's fame was a big plus in the relationship.

Capricorn is associated with conservatism, and most Capricornians prefer a traditional family structure; they usually are more comfortable with marriage than simply living with a lover. Capricorn men frequently find the image of the prosperous husband/father and the devoted, supportive wife/mother very appealing. Remember, this sign is associated with ambition, and traditionally Capricorn women have been ambitious for their mates. In this era of changing values, however, the Capricorn woman may be ambitious for herself as well, which might pose problems for some partners. Because we are attracted to qualities which we desire in ourselves, a Capricorn man may be drawn to women who are ambitious, successful, and independent. As the relationship progresses, however, such a woman may learn, paradoxically, that her mate expects her to put aside her own career and concentrate on his.

Men who are more laid back and less ambitious professionally usually don't make good partners for Capricorn women. The Capricorn woman who drives herself hard but wishes for more leisure time may be attracted to someone who is more happy-go-lucky than she. Once she makes a commitment to him, though, she probably will want him to build a stable and secure career.

If status, stability, and security are what you desire in a partner, someone with Capricorn emphasis may be perfect for you. However, if you want excitement, or if your lifestyle and attitudes are avant garde, you probably would be wise to look elsewhere.

The Aquarius Lover

Like the Sagittarian, the Aquarian is inclined toward an adventurous and changeable lifestyle. However, while the Sagittarian simply prefers to be unfettered, the Aquarian leans more toward a way of life that is totally wacky. It has been said that each sign represents a converse reaction to the extremes of the previous sign, and perhaps no sign illustrates this more clearly than Aquarius. Capricorn tends toward conservatism and tradition; Aquarius is usually ahead of its time, flying in the face of tradition. The sign Aquarius is associated with radical politics, labor unions, humanitarianism and universal brotherhood, modern technology, and unconventional relationships.

Thus, your Aquarian lover may not give you exactly the type of relationship you expected. He or she may tend toward "open marriage," or life in a commune. Like the water-bearer (Aquarius' symbol) pouring knowledge on the world, the Aquarian individual often feels the need to spread love everywhere. Therefore, it may be difficult to expect fidelity of the Aquarian lover, unless, of course, other factors in the chart offset this tendency.

Altruism, or love of humanity in general, is often preferable to the Aquarian than committed love with a single individual. If you are involved with someone whose chart has a strong Aquarian influence, particularly if that person is inclined toward politics, you might find yourself playing "second fiddle" to causes. Sometimes you may wonder if the nameless faces in the crowd mean more to your lover than you do.

The Aquarian probably has taken this incarnation for the purpose of spreading knowledge and freedom to all of humankind, rather than for developing a romantic union with one other person. If you share his or her interest in causes, the relationship can be quite rewarding, but if you are more interested in an exclusive partnership, the relationship may never be satisfying for you.

If your Aquarian partner's interest is spreading scientific or technological knowledge rather than politics and causes, you may find the relationship slightly more rewarding—if you also are interested in your partner's work and can allow him or her to expound upon it at length. Intellectual exchanges with you may spur your lover on to greater knowledge, and therefore, his or her interest in you is intensified. Sharing knowledge and insights is so important to Aquarians that often they are happiest with other air-sign people, or partners who have Mercury prominent in their charts. Because most Aquarians are seeking intellectual stimulation in their partners, they usually are attracted only to those whose intelligence is close to their own.

If you are an emotional and/or sensual type, you may find the Aquarian's intellectualizing frustrating and your Aquarian partner might seem cold and detached. However, if there is some influence from earth or water signs in your partner's chart, the combination of intelligence and feeling can produce an exciting romance.

If your Aquarian partner is a student of psychology, you must be prepared to have every aspect of your life constantly psycho-analyzed! This tendency may be frustrating, but it is not a sign of lack of caring.

Remember, the key phrase for Aquarius is "I know." The Aquarian wishes to use his or her knowledge to enrich every aspect of life. The "coldness" and intellectualizing traditionally associated with this sign can be a defense mechanism. Aquarians are as idealistic as Sagittarians or Pisceans. They believe in the basic goodness of human nature and in the brotherhood of all beings. When their ideals are threatened, they tend to retreat into their intellect and the safety of their belief systems.

Because of their innate faith in human nature, I find that Aquarians can love as passionately as any Cancer or Scorpio, though they might think of their partners more as members of the human race than individuals or love objects. As with the other air signs, the Aquarian's sexual nature often depends on other influences in the chart. Since Aquarius is a fixed sign, unless a relationship becomes intolerable they usually stay with a partner once a commitment is made, even though they may stray from time to time. Their tendency to love everyone may be confused with sexual love.

For an intelligent, unconventional person, an Aquarian can be an exciting lover. Aquarians thrive on the unusual and are often inclined toward trying new things and taking chances that people of more conservative signs fear. Life with an Aquarian can indeed be an adventure, and if you are looking for a relationship that will never be dull, you'll probably be happy with the Aquarian.

The Pisces Lover

Without a doubt, Pisces is the most romantic sign of the zodiac. Sensitive, highly emotional, and mystically inclined, Pisceans are eternally seeking an exalted spiritual union. Like Sagittarians, their expectations for relationships are high, but these high expectations are often pure fantasy. Pisceans are impressionable, and many have been brain-washed by images from movies and romantic novels.

Perfectionists, they seek mates who are perfect. Unlike Sagittarians, however, who may leave a relationship when their partners turn out to be less than perfect, Pisceans project their images of perfection onto their partners and, when those persons prove to be less than ideal, they make excuses for them and continue to live in a fantasy world. Pisceans wish for partners that are beautiful in every way, from whom they may absorb beauty themselves. Unfortunately, all too often they see perfect beauty in people who actually possess very little, and therefore leave themselves open to disillusionment and disappointment.

Strangely enough, Pisceans frequently attain the mystical union with their lovers that they seek, at least at times. They may be able to communicate with their partners on a subconscious level, and therefore be aware of what is going on in the partner's inner being. Often Pisceans sense their partners' thoughts, even though there may be miles between them. This can be inspiring to some signs, but others, particularly fire-type people, find this disconcerting. Both fire and air-types tend to find such closeness stifling.

Though insightful and intuitive, at times the Piscean lover appears to be lost in a fog, totally unaware of what is going on with the partner. At these times, Pisceans can be so completely oblivious to others that they seem cruel and insensitive. This is not the case; they simply are so preoccupied that they see nothing but their own inner visions.

Escape is a word frequently used in connection with Pisces, meaning that the Piscean goes through life trying to escape from the harsh realities of life on Earth. Sometimes these people escape into art, music, drama, metaphysics, and spirituality, other times they escape through alcohol and drugs. When Pisceans are bruised by reality they retreat, withdrawing into their private dream worlds, leaving their partners feeling hurt and excluded. If you are involved with a Piscean, be aware that this will happen from time to time and give your Piscean lover space to retreat and regather strength.

Pisceans often are attracted to practical signs like Taurus and Capricorn, and the pragmatism associated with these signs is an excellent balance for the Piscean dreamy idealism. However, unless there are some practical indicators—such as a strong Saturn or earth-sign planets—in the Piscean's chart, more practical types may be too cynical for the person with Pisces dominating. It is difficult for those who have little faith in God or humankind to empathize with the otherworldliness of Pisceans. Often, these skeptics do not see much value in metaphysical or spiritual beliefs, beliefs most Pisceans embrace wholeheartedly. Some Pisces individuals make their religious beliefs the focus of their entire lives.

Pisces is the "I believe" sign of the zodiac. It also is associated with self-undoing; however, this side of Pisces only comes out when these individuals feel that their God has abandoned them and their faith has come to nothing. Even Jesus, whom some researchers believe had the Moon, Jupiter, Saturn, and Uranus in Pisces, cried out in despair "My God, my God, why hast thou forsaken me?" as He hung on the cross. If you are involved with a Piscean, you should be aware of this vulnerability to despair and disillusionment, and accept that you may be called upon to reinforce your partner's beliefs. When black moods descend upon your lover, you may have to do your best to restore his or her faith. A Piscean cannot be truly happy without faith to draw upon. For this reason, it is best for the partner of a Piscean to have some faith as well.

If two people who both have Piscean factors prominently figuring in their charts and little balance from earth signs or Saturn become involved with each other, the relationship can be a disaster! It may succeed on a metaphysical or artistic level—but such people's practical affairs probably will be a mess for the whole of their lives.

Another unhappy condition that may plague Pisceans in their darker hours is paranoia. They may lose faith in everyone around them, even their partners. If you love a Piscean, this is something you may have to live with from time to time. Romantic Pisceans may experience paranoia when they first realize that their partners are not Divine, or not what they had fantasized. However, as they grow to love you and your human failings, they will have more faith in you as a person instead of an ideal, and probably will be just as romantic after the illusions have passed.

Pisceans are sensitive, kindhearted, compassionate, and self-sacrificing, and can be devoted partners. If you are not dependent on a partner for practical guidance or financial support you may find a Piscean a sweet and loving partner. And if you are looking for old-fashioned, medieval-style romance, there is no one better than the Piscean.

Notes

1. Clemens E. Benda, M.D., *The Image of Love,* (New York: Glencoe, 1961), p. 13. Quoted from Plato, *Symposium,* trans. Clemens E. Benda, M.D., (New York: Glencoe, 1959).

2. Nathaniel Branden, *The Psychology of Romantic Love,* (New York: Tarcher, 1980), p. 3.

3. Robert A. Johnson, *We: The Psychology of Romantic Love,* (San Francisco: Harper & Row, Publishers, 1983), p. xi.

4. This statement is one of many expounded upon by Werner Erhard and other est trainers in the est training.

5. "Update," *TV Guide,* October, 1986, (Radnor, PA: Triangle, 1986).

6. Johnson, p. 47.

7. M. Scott Peck, M. D., *The Road Less Travelled,* (New York: Simon & Schuster, 1978), pp. 103-104.

8. Johnson, p. 92ff.

9. Ram Dass, *Grist for the Mill,* (New York: Unity Press, 1976), p. 96.

8

Animus and Anima: The God and Goddess Within

The concept of the animus and the anima was outlined in Chapter 2. However, to recapitulate briefly: Swiss psychiatrist and metaphysician Carl Jung postulated that every person is a composite of both masculine and feminine attributes. In men, the outer personality is primarily masculine and the feminine side is subconscious, or internalized. In women, of course, the opposite holds true: the outer personality is primarily feminine and the masculine side is subconscious. As we travel through life, we have to come to terms, to unite, so to speak, with the masculine or feminine side within.

This need is often reflected in our search for a lifetime partner; we seek a husband or wife who best reflects the subconscious partner within us. Too often, however, we lose touch with the true inner partner, and we find ourselves catapulted into a relationship with a man or woman who only appears to reflect the inner partner, or who may possess some qualities shared by our inner partner, but not others.

Jung maintained that only through intense self-analysis could we unite with our inner partners and express freely the animus or anima—and only after achieving this union with the male or female within could we actually find happiness with another person. Men need to feel free to express their feminine side—their need to nurture, be sensitive and emotional—and when they have learned to do this, they are less dependent on women to satisfy those needs for them. Conversely, women need to be able to express their masculine side—to be able to assert themselves and go after what they want so that they will be less likely to expect their partners to provide for and protect them. When each individual is less dependent on a partner to provide the feeling of inner unity, he or she is more free to develop a relationship that is satisfying to both.

The nature of the animus or anima within each individual is difficult to nail down, but current schools of thought tend to fall back on the traditional concepts of masculine and feminine types, as personified by the ancient gods and goddesses. These archetypes are very old—perhaps going back to the beginning of human history—and, therefore, they are deeply ingrained within our psyches. The inner partner within each person, therefore, may assume the traits and attitudes associated with one of the ancient gods or goddesses. Current astrological research seems to confirm this idea; the gods and goddesses—and their parallels as found within each sign of the zodiac—are now popular subjects for astrological books and lectures.

Most authors and lecturers tend to concentrate on the Greek and Roman pantheon for their archetypes, perhaps because the Olympian gods and goddesses are the best-known to most Westerners. However, in my research, I find that too often patriarchal prejudice, inherent in Greek and Roman thought, precludes finding a god to suit each sign. For example, the sensitive and yielding sign Cancer has no real male archetype among the members of the Greek pantheon. To the patriarchal mind, feminine qualities such as those associated with Cancer were incompatible with the nature of a male god. However, if we look to other times and cultures, we find deities like the kind-hearted Indra, king of the gods in ancient Hindu Vedic thought, who seems to personify the Cancerian animus nearly perfectly. I also could find no Greek god to personify the male side of Libra; the Greeks, for the most part, thought of women as inferior creatures and of marriage as a necessary institution existing mainly for the purpose of creating male babies. But in ancient India, women, as personifications of the goddess Kundalini Shakti, were revered. The Hindu tradition boasts of the devoted and uxorious Rama, who overcame powerful obstacles and fought many wars simply to ensure the rescue of his beautiful kidnapped wife Sita.

Although the Greek goddesses were undoubtedly regarded as powerful, few expressed power such as that bestowed upon the Hindu goddess Durga—and, therefore, it appears that of all the gods in Aryan tradition, Durga seems most representative of Scorpio. If, in the following paragraphs, I seem to jump indiscriminately between the Greek and Hindu pantheons, and also include divinities such as Mithras or Mary (Pisces) who are part of neither culture per se, please bear in mind that all these gods and goddesses are descended from archetypes who were once a part of the primal Indo-European tradition. Therefore, they are all a part of the collective unconscious of Westerners.

It is tempting to digress here and relate how a small tribe of fine-featured, well-formed, chestnut-haired nomadic people living in the Ukraine in preliterate times (roughly 5000 B.C.), called by philologists and anthropologists the Indo-Europeans, eventually branched out and gave birth to nearly all the languages and cultural traditions from Ireland to India — but we shall not do so. For the purposes of this chapter we are interested mainly in only four segments of that tribe: the Aryans who migrated east and settled in India, the Achaeans, who sought the lush seacoasts of Greece, the Keltoi, who became the ancestors of the Gauls and Britons, and the proto-Persians who settled in what is now Iran[1]. We shall simply accept that most Westerners are genetically and culturally descended from that particular people, and, therefore, the gods and goddesses they worshipped are part of each one of us.

The origins of these gods and goddesses are shrouded in mystery. Sources differ; old myths and legends often contradict each other. Because of the antiquity of these characters, most ideas about their origin are, by necessity, speculative. Some figures, like Bacchus, Rama, and Mary, are based on historical or semi-historical figures who actually may have lived. Others, like Indra, Apollo, and Ceres, seem to personify various forces of nature. Still others—Mars, Athena, Hermes—appear to represent various aspects of the human personality.

It is tempting to associate each sign with the god or goddess whose name is the same as that sign's planetary ruler. In some cases, this association holds true. In others, however, the nature of the god or goddess and the astrological function of the planet of the same name seem to be markedly different in many ways. For instance, although the planet Jupiter, ruler of Sagittarius, does have much in common with the god that bears its name, the god Jupiter (Zeus in Greek, Dyaus in Indo-European) is, like most gods associated with patriarchal thought, too stern and vengeful to constitute an exact parallel with the good-hearted, jovial nature of Sagittarius. Therefore, I have chosen the centaur Chiron for the animus associated with that sign, even though his name has been given to a newly-discovered planetoid. (Many astrologers are inclined to award co-rulership of Sagittarius to Chiron.)

Although the Moon rules Cancer, the moon-goddess Diana is hardly typical of this sign. Rather, I find her cold, unapproachable, and sometimes cruel nature much more compatible with the opposite sign, Capricorn. This correlation seems logical when we also consider that Capricorn is an earth sign—and Diana, as goddess of the hunt, was associated with the Earth and the life forms sharing it.

We must recall that the gods and goddesses, although recognized as having traits that are all too human, were considered incomprehensible to human beings, and were therefore worshipped and adored. The god or goddess within each of us, therefore, is a part of ourselves which we do not understand very well, so we constantly search for that god or goddess, hoping to find him or her reflected in a lover. By studying the sign positions of certain planets in the natal chart—the Sun and Mars in the chart of a woman, the Moon and Venus in the chart of a man—we can find clues as to the nature of our own animus or anima. Although the characteristics represented by these archetypes will undoubtedly prove to be oversimplifications (the innermost depths of the human psyche are virtually impenetrable) they can enable us to at least scratch the surface of our inner partners.

To do this most effectively, it is best to consider the archetypes represented by the sign positions of the applicable planets. For instance, if a woman has the Sun in Aries and Mars in Taurus, her animus probably blends characteristics of the gods Mars and Bacchus. I know a woman with these planetary placements, and in her relationships she alternates between men who can be identified roughly with either Mars or Bacchus—but rarely with a combination of the two. Therefore she has never been totally happy with any of her relationships.

Since lovers are not made to order for us, finding an exact composite of our two preferred archetypes can prove difficult, if not impossible. However, by recognizing that this sort of composite is what we are seeking subconsciously, we can come to terms with the fact that we can only find that particular being within ourselves. In this way, we can work on acknowledging this inner archetype, on expressing this hidden side of ourselves, and on learning to love it. By doing so, we will be less likely to look for an ideal reflection of our animus or anima in a romantic partner.

The woman referred to above, for example, was reared in a traditionally-oriented family, where a woman was expected to defer to and be totally dependent on a man. These values were deeply inculcated into her attitudes, therefore she does not seem to be able to express the Martian qualities of assertiveness or leadership, or the Bacchian ones of perseverance and practicality. She depends on the men in her life to express those qualities for her, and so far, all have fallen short. If she would learn to develop her own assertiveness and leadership, as well as perseverance and practicality, she would probably find herself less dependent on her men to live out those qualities. Quite likely, she also would be more appreciative of the sterling qualities which her lovers do possess.

Uniting with your anima or animus may seem like a pretty tall order—and it is. Doing so takes a great deal of self-analysis and the determination to make your inner ideals a reality. But isn't having a strong, rewarding relationship that can result in a lifetime commitment worth it?

When you look at two charts in terms of synastry, you may find that the Moon or Venus in a man's chart (the Sun or Mars in a woman's chart) corresponds to the Sun, Moon, Ascendant, or prominent planets in the chart of a prospective partner. This often occurs because the archetypes seem to express themselves through their corresponding zodiacal signs.

However, this is not always the case, because the reflection of the inner partner is not always discerned from what a flesh-and-blood partner actually is, but from what the lover believes him or her to be.

Here, then, are our god and goddess archetypes—as represented by the twelve signs of the zodiac.

Aries

The God: Mars

The god Mars was traditionally associated with war and its cruelties. Tall, strong, and muscular, Mars was traditionally an amoral figure, who gave no thought to right or wrong and was concerned only with the desolation he could wreak upon the enemy. These traits may sound exceedingly repulsive to our twentieth-century Aquarian Age minds, but remember that to the Greeks and Romans, who were constantly fighting wars to defend and to expand the borders of their homelands, such traits were not only acceptable but desirable in a leader. Many were the sacrifices performed in the temples of Mars prior to a major battle, by soldiers praying for his leadership and for victory.

Mars was adventurous, challenging, and impulsive in love as well as in war. One of the most famous stories about him tells of how he cuckolded the lame god Vulcan by carrying on a passionate love affair with Vulcan's wife, love-goddess Aphrodite. The story showed that Mars was regarded as having a passionate love nature and was driven by desire for his beloved—and that he was willing to chance the wrath of his father, Zeus, the vengeful king of the gods, for her sake.

Therefore, a woman who has her Sun or Mars in Aries hides within her an inner partner who is both passionate and cruel by nature, who takes what he wants without considering right or wrong, and who is capable of inspiring others to do the same. Such women seem to attract men whose treatment of them alternates between passionate adoration and abusiveness.

The Goddess: Athena

Athena also is associated with war, but she is less concerned with the actual fighting and killing than with the planning. She is interested in the battle maneuvers, and the skills and strategies necessary. For this reason, Athena is also considered the goddess of wisdom. Athena's prominent role in Homer's *Iliad* reveals that she was regarded as the divine protectress of all warriors. Because of her efforts and her leadership, the Greeks were rescued from many potentially disastrous situations throughout the course of the Trojan War.

Romantically, Athena was one of the three virgin goddesses and, therefore, considered unattainable by man and god alike. She was certainly beautiful and vain of her beauty—it was partly her vanity that led to the Trojan War—but she bestowed her romantic favors upon no man. If the man was a skilled and important soldier, she would grant him her protection and, to some degree, her attentions, but for the average mortal she had no regard.

A man whose Moon or Venus in Aries, therefore, probably carries within him a woman who is beautiful, clever, capable, wise, and protective, but at the same time proud, self-important, and unattainable, who only bestows her attentions upon men who have proven themselves worthy of her regard. As a result, these men are generally attracted to women of this type, and they seem to thrive on the challenge of winning the favor of the woman they love. Sometimes they succeed; sometimes they seem to set themselves up for rejection by women whose standards appear to be impossibly high. Yet rejection, insults, even abuse, seem to make these men more determined to win the love and respect of the proud and unattainable Athena.

Taurus

The God: Bacchus

Bacchus is remembered mainly as the god of wine, a god who delighted in sensual pleasures, and who loved to seek out the company of his fellow gods and get them drunk. However, there was much more to the nature of Bacchus. He was also the god of husbandry, who watched over farmers and peasants who tilled the soil, and he participated in growing the grapevines as well as enjoying their fruits. Bacchus was the prime force in the development of all forms of agriculture, and the care and breeding of domestic beasts. Like other gods who grew to prominence in the Age of Taurus, Bacchus's symbol was the bull.

Bacchus was also the god of commerce, associated with formulating laws and building cities. According to Greek and Roman tradition, it was Bacchus who developed trade and merchandising, and establishing the business practices associated with commerce. Bacchus has been credited with taking an army to India and thereby opening up trade between that nation and Greece. (Some anthropologists believe this to have been an actual event.) Ancient representations of Bacchus show him as being a very handsome man, though somewhat plump (from indulging in the fruits of his labors). He was quite attractive to women and surrounded himself with throngs of female worshipers; in their company, Bacchus constantly celebrated life in every possible way.

Women who have the Sun or Mars in Taurus, therefore, possesses an animus who is clever, inventive, and business-oriented, and yet still sensual and attractive, capable of enjoying physical life to its fullest. Once these woman find such a man, they devote themselves to him whole-heart-edly, as Bacchus's female worshipers devoted themselves to him, and they won't give him up easily. Too often, however, one side of Bacchus is more prevalent than the other in his human counterpart; the man either is too interested in making money, or overly devoted to having a good time.

The Goddess: Aphrodite

Aphrodite, or Venus as the Romans called her, is perhaps the most famous of all the Greek goddesses. The goddess of love, Aphrodite is always repre-sented as a voluptuous woman with a sweet and lovely face. As the pro-totype of the ideal lover, stories of Aphrodite and her many love affairs reveal that she was sensual and promiscuous, though not in an exploitive manner. Every man she slept with, she loved, even though the relationship never lasted. She was warm, generous, and giving, especially to those who sacrificed to her for love, but she was also somewhat self-centered, and, like Bacchus, enjoyed indulging in sensory pleasures such as the consump-tion of fine food and wines. She is also supposed to have been a charming companion; the Homeric hymns to Aphrodite refer to her as "the Golden One" and as "Lover of laughter."

Men whose charts contain Moon or Venus in Taurus, have an inner partner whose primary interest in life is giving love on all levels, especially to her man. These men are generally attracted to women who are outward-ly pretty and curvaceous, and who radiate an aura of sensuality. The at-traction is usually highly sexual in nature, though these men appreciate kindness and generosity in women as well. Problems often result when this type of man is attracted to a woman who, on the surface appears to be an Aphrodite-type, but who is also intelligent and, therefore, wants to be appreciated for more than her love-nature.

Gemini

The God: Hermes

Hermes is one of the oldest of the Olympian gods; anthropologists trace his history back to before the pre-Hellenic era. He is known as the messenger of the gods, swift, youthful, and skilled in the arts of communication. Traditionally, Hermes is regarded as the mediator between gods and humans, being the most diplomatic among all the Olympians. He also was the friendliest of the gods, to mortals and immortals alike. Hermes' charm lay not only in his friendliness, but in his need for freedom as well. Hermes never committed himself to any permanent home, but was "always on the road between here and yonder,"[2] exploring different territories and different peoples, and bringing what he'd learned back to his companions on Mount Olympus. Another appealing aspect of Hermes is his penchant for mischief. In the Homeric hymns to Hermes, the story is told of how on the day he was born, Hermes sang with joy to his parents (Zeus and Maia) and at the same time was already planning to play tricks on them.

Sometimes Hermes is viewed as asexual, but this is erroneous. As a lover, Hermes was rather active, according to the stories about him that tell of his numerous *amours* with both goddesses and mortals. He had many children, including the famous *hermaphrodite,* the child of Hermes and Aphrodite, which bore the organs of both sexes.

Women who have the Sun or Mars in Gemini often are attracted to younger men, or men whose personalities are youthful in spite of their age. The inner man, corresponding to the god Hermes, is intelligent, talkative, diplomatic, and somewhat mischievous. He also is friendly, charming, and a lover of freedom. The sort of man who reflects this image, however, may demonstrate a darker side of Hermes as well, one that includes lying, deception, infidelity, and, in extreme cases, criminal tendencies. Women with this type of animus need to approach romantic relationships with some caution so as to avoid these potential problems.

The Goddess: Saraswati

To the ancient Indo-Europeans, land-locked as they were in what is now the Ukraine, the rivers were of prime importance. Therefore, the people presupposed the existence of a series of river-goddesses, one for each waterway. When the Aryans migrated to India, one of the swiftest and most serviceable rivers was the one to which they gave the name Saraswati. As water spirits were generally regarded as the prime givers of inspiration and wisdom, the chief river-goddess, Saraswati, eventually came to be known as the goddess of speech and learning. Early hymns to Saraswati praise her as the mother who purifies and scintillates the intellect, the bestower of intellectual, moral, and spiritual advancement, and beg her to allow the hymn-singer "to nurse at the breast of Mother Saraswati, so that I may drink in all your knowledge and eloquence."[3]

Saraswati was regarded as handmaiden to the Great Earth Mother Goddess, and is often represented as a twin to Lakshmi, goddess of prosperity. Images of Saraswati depict her as being narrow-waisted and wide-hipped, with generous breasts, and often standing near books or scrolls with complex inscriptions. Saraswati's wisdom was regarded as being so lofty that she attracted the eye of the god Brahma, the Creator, and became his wife. Her intellect did not preclude her having human failings, however; she was quite capable of turning from a wise and eloquent queen into a quarrelsome child. When Brahma took a second wife, it is said, Saraswati became so angry and jealous that she cursed Brahma, proclaiming that he could only be worshipped once a year. Saraswati is also presented as having been constantly at loggerheads with her twin sister Lakshmi; on one occasion, she is said to have been quarreling with another goddess when Lakshmi intervened and tried to make peace. Saraswati became so angry with Lakshmi that she cursed her, causing her to be reborn as a tree and then later as a river.

Men who have the Moon or Venus in Gemini, therefore, seek a partner who is brilliant and willing to share her knowledge, but who tempers her intellectual superiority with a retreat into childish behavior from time to time. Such men may view occasional quarrelsomeness and unpredictability as indicative of a versatile nature, a guarantee of excitement within the relationship.

Cancer

The God: Indra

Indra is perhaps the oldest known god in Indo-European culture. The king of the gods in the most ancient Hindu tradition, Indra appears to have been related to thunder, and therefore, may have been the prototype for the many European and Arabic hammer-gods, such as Thor in Norse mythology, Ptah in Egypt, and Finn MacCoul in Irish tradition. When claps of thunder sounded in the heavens, Indra was said to be swinging his hammer.

Indra was also the god of fertility and of the harvest—in earliest times the spirit of the corn—and through his influence the Earth gave forth a wealth of food, both animal and vegetable. Indra was regarded as the Great Father, he who breathed the air of life into the bodies of all human beings. And he protected his children; he was the dragon-slayer, the giant-killer, and the nemesis of all who threatened those whom he had created. He was kind-hearted, impulsive, and a heavy drinker. Images of Indra depict him as a large, burly man, with strong arms, a handsome face and a "beer belly."

Women with the Sun or Mars in Cancer, are attracted to men like Indra: strong, kind-hearted, generous and gentle, yet capable of being ferocious when their loved ones are threatened. Physically, these men often appear to be big, handsome Teddy bears, rather like Merlin Olsen or Luciano Pavarotti. It is as if these women want to be cherished and protected, and look for Indra-types who are both nurturing and physically impressive. Too often, however, this type of man possesses all the necessary characteristics except the capacity for fury. Few men or women whose nature is to be kind and nurturing are equally capable of swinging a terrible hammer.

The Goddess: Ceres

Ceres, goddess of the harvest and of fertility, seems to be a later descendant of the Great Earth Mother Goddess worshiped during the Age of Taurus. In Greek and Roman mythology, Ceres (known to the Greeks as Demeter, from *da mater,* "Earth mother," and identified with the Hindu *Sri* and the Irish *Da Nu*) was regarded as the perfect mother. Images of her generally depict a beautiful, voluptuous, mature woman, often draped with wreaths made of vines and flowers. Ceres, as mother, was considered to personify the principle of unconditional love, such as that which a mother gives to her children. As nurturer, the mother is responsible for taking care of her children's material needs (with food and shelter), emotional needs (with love and support), and spiritual needs (through guidance and wisdom); Ceres represents the ideal bestower of all these needs. And yet, Ceres also can be the angry mother, she who disciplines her children when they transgress.

The most famous story about Ceres is the tale of her search for her daughter Persephone. Persephone, a lovely young maiden, was ravished by Pluto, god of the underworld, and abducted to Hades to live as his wife. Upon hearing of the rape of her daughter, Ceres immediately set out to rescue Persephone, and appealed to Zeus and the other Olympians for help. But the marriage of Pluto and Persephone had already been consummated, and so Zeus and the others saw no way for Persephone to return to her mother.

Ceres went into mourning, and the Earth mourned with her. A terrible winter settled upon the world; no trees bloomed, no flowers grew, and, most important of all, no food was produced. Humankind began to die of starvation. Zeus and the other Olympians grew concerned; without humanity, who would worship them? Zeus, therefore, worked out a compromise with Pluto: for half the year Persephone would live with her mother, the other half she would remain in the underworld. And ever since, during the months in which Persephone is with Ceres, the Earth flourishes; when she is with Pluto, the barrenness of winter prevails.

Men who have the Moon or Venus in Cancer have the ideal mother as the goddess within, and, therefore, they look for the maternal nature in their romantic partners. These men need the eternal nurturing and guidance of an ever-present mother, even though they (hopefully) have broken childish ties with their own natural parents. Such men need to remember that having a motherly partner does not relieve them of their responsibility to develop self-sufficiency in themselves.

Leo

The God: Apollo

Worship of the Sun god is among the oldest religions on planet Earth, and many anthropologists and philologists trace the worship of the Indo-European Sun god to the earliest known pre-Aryan civilizations. The tradition of the handsome Sun god driving his chariot across the skies each day appears to be almost universal in Aryan cultures, and therefore Apollo has several parallels, including the Norse god Wotan and the Hindu Surya.

Apollo is one of the most attractive of the gods. Statues of him show a slender, but well-muscled physique, a beautiful visage, and curly hair. Apollo was a born lover; many were the nymphs, demigoddesses, and even mortal women who were forced to go to ridiculous extremes to avoid the amorous advances of the Sun god. Legend presents Apollo as being incredulous that any woman would reject him. He always saw himself as being worthy of all mortals' worship. Apollo could be kind and generous indeed, but when facing rejection he was, like so many handsome, self-centered men, inclined to be childish and somewhat petty. The later stories portray Apollo as capable of cruelty and vengefulness, but these stories seem to be a product of the patriarchal ideas typical of classical thought rather than of the god's true character.

Apollo is associated with music, poetry, healing, and the arts, as well as with prophecy—gifts bestowed by the generous (though somewhat condescending) deity whose light makes life on Earth possible. Apollo in his chariot rises to the heights of creation; hence his association with ambition.

Women who have the Sun or Mars in Leo in their charts are drawn to Apollonian men, gorgeous, gifted individuals who shine like the Sun, who feel they are doing a woman a favor by showing interest in her. Too many women fall prey to their charms and become virtual handmaidens to their Apollos, giving these men the worship and ego-gratification they crave. This can be nice for awhile, but, like Apollo, these men tend to grow restless and move on to other lovers. The women feel betrayed, as if all their devotion was for naught. Such women need to learn to worship the Apollo within themselves, for this is the only Apollo who will return her favors in kind.

The Goddess: Hera

Another cultural descendant of the Great Earth Mother is Hera (*he era* = "great mother"). Hera, the eternally patient wife of Zeus, is portrayed as the ideal married woman, and therefore some astrologers associate her with Libra. However, some aspects of Hera's personality are inconsistent with Libra. For example, her continuous cruel and vindictive battles with Zeus are hardly typical of Libra, which is associated with justice, harmony, and "doing the proper thing." Also, although Hera is totally committed to her marriage, the bonds of the marriage never really contain Hera; for the most part, she does what she wants, without deferring to Zeus. The constant quarrels between Zeus and Hera seem more typical of the antics of insecure lovers than the actions of committed married people, and therefore, in actuality, it appears that Hera's character is more attuned to love-oriented Leo than to justice-oriented Libra.

Above all, Hera is the queen of the gods, and even when shamefully humiliated by Zeus' infidelities and his insensitive treatment of her, she never loses her queenly dignity. Envisioned as a tall, regal, beautiful woman, she is very much aware of her beauty and its effect upon men and gods alike. She is ultimately desirable; even the incorrigible Zeus, who was constantly flaunting his betrayals of her, maintained, "Never has such desire, for goddess or woman, flooded and overwhelmed my heart . . . never have I felt such love, such sweet desire, as fills me now for you."[4] Man and god alike pursued Hera, and this proud queen had many chances to betray her husband as he had betrayed her; yet she sent her suitors away, never once giving in to the temptation. She was extremely desirous of children, but not for their own sake; she wanted children as symbols, the fruit of her love for her husband. In short, it was through love of her partner, and this love only, that Hera found purpose in her life.

Men who have the Moon or Venus in Leo, therefore, seek a proud, beautiful, woman, queenly in her bearing, desired by all men, and yet totally committed in her love for him and willing to sacrifice all else for the sake of this love. This ideal may seem unattainable, but surprisingly enough I have often seen it apparently fulfilled. However, I have noticed that men with this planetary placement who find this woman of their dreams too often become like Zeus and take their mates for granted. And Hera, who stuck by Zeus in spite of all his cruelties, is only an ideal. Flesh-and-blood women, especially those as lovely as Hera, are more inclined than she would have been to move on.

Virgo

The God: Vulcan

The lame god Vulcan has long been associated with Virgo; in fact, some astrologers in the past maintained that the mythical intramercurial planet Vulcan is the true ruler of Virgo. However, modern astronomy, with its increasing use of space probes, seems to indicate beyond a shadow of a doubt that this planet does not exist physically. Nevertheless, the god Vulcan appears to be the male archetype which most closely parallels the astrological function of this work-oriented sign.

The parthenogenically-born son of Hera, Vulcan is said to have been conceived in anger, and thus he was born lame. His strength and skill, however, had no equal among the Olympian gods. He grew up to be god of the forge, the Divine Smith, the Master Artisan, a dedicated worker who did most of his work in private, then modestly presented the wonders he had fashioned to gods and humans alike. It was said that he, in collaboration with Athena, fashioned the form of the beautiful maiden Pandora.

Despite his lameness, Vulcan's skills were enough of an attraction to enable him to capture Aphrodite's heart. She married him, although she certainly didn't remain faithful to him. The most famous tale of Aphrodite's infidelity is the story of her affair with Vulcan's more dynamic brother Mars. However, Vulcan ingeniously devised an invisible golden net which trapped the two lovers *in flagrante delicto,* which testifies not only to Vulcan's skills as an artisan, but to his resourcefulness and somewhat resilient sense of humor.

Greek mythology also includes a rather pathetic tale telling of how Vulcan, ignored and betrayed by Aphrodite, transferred his blighted affections to his partner in creativity, Athena. However, as we have seen, Athena was an unattainable virgin goddess, and in spite of their artistic involvement together, Athena rejected him as she had every other suitor.

In fact, Vulcan's shyness and self-effaciveness seem to have invited rejection. Yet his drive and dedication to his creative endeavors was unquenched.

Women who have the Sun or Mars in Virgo, therefore, would seem to carry within an animus that is shy, self-effacive, and yet, in his own way, devoted both to her and to his work. The flesh-and-blood counterpart of this animus can be very attractive, especially if he is also resourceful and has a sense of humor. If such women are not careful, however, the basic protectiveness of Virgo, (which is part of their own nature), might cause her to attract men whose lack of self-confidence can prove crippling—remember, Vulcan was the lame god.

The Goddess: Vesta

It seems strange that even though Virgo is an earth sign, both the male and female deities associated with Virgo have a strong affinity with fire. Vulcan is the god of the forge, and Vesta is the goddess of the hearth.

The pictorial symbol for Virgo, the maiden holding the sprig of wheat, represents Vesta. Known as Hestia to the Greeks, Vesta was the daughter of Saturn and Rhea, and sister to Zeus and Hera. Worship of Vesta, as the keeper of the sacred flame, goes back to the earliest Indo-European traditions, and parallels to the fire ceremonies performed by the Vestal Virgins are found in the yajna fire celebrations of Hindu yogic practice. In Celtic communities, the hearth fire was never permitted to go out, for it symbolized the solidity not only of the home, but of the tribe as well.

Vesta, then, symbolized the perfect housewife. She was guardian of both home and community, and hence she represented continuous unity of the state, which obviously helped to ensure a united front against all enemies. Vesta embodied the very essence of honesty and fair dealings, and she was also the primary advocate of the sacred law of hospitality: sharing the hearth, food, and shelter with strangers. Like Vulcan, she also embodied the principle of dedication to one's work, and to attaining specific goals and missions in life.

Vesta was the second of the three virgin goddesses. Unlike Athena, whose virginity was due to her unattainability, Vesta was virgin because she had no need of a male; she was whole in herself, a symbol of self-confidence and autonomy. In the few stories we have of her, Vesta is presented as being deeply suspicious of close personal attachments, preferring impersonal relationships, and she is often referred to as the Divine Sister.

Men who have the Moon or Venus in Virgo, therefore, seek a partner who is dedicated to the idea of unity within the family. Their ideal partner is loyal and dependable, and devotes herself to creating a warm and comfortable home, a safe refuge for family, friend, and stranger alike. And yet, these men seem to want a woman who is autonomous and undemanding, who makes few emotional claims upon them. In my work I find that the basic self-effaciveness of Virgoans causes these men to become threatened by women who project the self-confidence associated with Vesta. These men need to realize that this inner confidence rarely interferes with the devotion of Vesta-types; rather, it enhances it.

Libra

The God: Rama

Rama is one of the few gods in our Indo-European pantheon that appears to have been based on a real person. Some anthropologist/historians believe that Rama was the leader of the first group of Aryan invaders who left the original Indo-European homeland in the Ukraine for the rich and verdant country in the north of India. Rama also is said to have been instrumental in the composition of the earliest Hindu scriptures, the Vedas.

In mythological terms, Rama was an earthly incarnation of the god Vishnu, who was born a prince of a small but prosperous kingdom in ancient India. By the time he was sixteen, Rama was popular and well-loved throughout the kingdom, known for his skills in leadership and martial arts as well as his love of peace and justice. A well-known saint rewarded the prince for slaying a demon that plagued him by instructing Rama in all the principles of knowledge and wisdom.

The daughter of a neighboring monarch, a lovely young girl named Sita, fell in love with Rama and they were married. When a dispute arose over succession to the throne, Rama, Sita and Rama's brother Lakshman were exiled from the country and spent many years wandering in the wilderness. During that period of time, a demon kidnaped Sita and brought her as a prize to the king of a rival nation. Many years of war followed, during which time Rama proved his devotion to Sita again and again. In the early part of the *Ramayana,* Rama is presented as the ultimate leader, fair, just and yet stern. He also is shown as the ideal married man, so devoted to Sita that he puts his own life on the line many times for her sake.

Strangely enough, however, at the end of the epic poem Rama seems to turn on Sita violently. Because she has lived in the same building with another man—even though the gods attest that the man never touched her—Rama, pressured by his counsellors, exiles the wife who had been totally loyal to him for so long. Some mythologists, in order to find justification for this act of seemingly extreme cruelty on the part of the hero-god who had been so just and fair until then, maintain that Rama, as a king, had to keep his own reputation intact, and in spite of Sita's fidelity there would always be people who wondered about her. In short, Rama gave in to the typically Libran obsession with "doing the proper thing."

Women who have the Sun or Mars in Libra and the corresponding animus appear to look for a partner who is wise, just, and fair—and totally committed to his marriage. However, along with the well-balanced and uxorious side of Libra comes the preoccupation with society's mores. Though a situation so drastic as Rama's exile of Sita may not occur, from time to time problems may arise if his deep concern for doing the right thing is not shared by the woman.

The Goddess: Themis

Those who regard Hera as the ideal married woman seem to forget that Zeus had another wife who was just as devoted to her marriage and caused Zeus much less aggravation. This was the Titan, Themis, goddess of wisdom and justice, the guardian of the law.

The daughter of Gaea and Ouranos (and supposedly, by association, Zeus's aunt as well as his wife), Themis was connected with the preservation of natural order and harmony in the cosmos. After the formation of order out of Chaos in creation, Ouranos gave the assignment of keeping the delicate balance of creation intact to the strong and capable Themis. Later, after the emergence of humankind, Themis (whose name means "law") was revered as the goddess of justice and righteousness. Worship of Themis as guardian of universal order seems at times to have superseded even the regard for the Great Earth Mother. Themis has her parallels in Irish mythology as the Danaan goddess Ana, and in Hindu lore as the goddess Kundalini Shakti, both of whom represent the feminine principle of unity in all creation.

As the goddess of law and justice, Themis is usually depicted as tall, straight, and handsome, often blindfolded, holding a sword in one hand and the scales of justice in the other. Her marriage with Zeus represents the ideal partnership, and in the early days of his reign, the guidance Themis gave Zeus was invaluable. Not only was she the guardian of order and the patron of fairness, she had been blessed by Ouranos with foreknowledge of the future. It was Themis who convened assemblies of the Olympian gods, and it was from her that Zeus derived his judicial authority. Themis was also hailed as the goddess of Peace and the mother of the Fates: Eunomia (good government) and Dice (judgment). As Zeus's power on Olympus grew, however, Themis began to wane in her importance. According to some mythologists, this symbolizes the increasing power of the patriarchy and the denigration of the feminine principle.

Themis is such an extraordinary figure it is difficult to believe that there are many human women who even give the impression of being cut from the same cloth as she. There undoubtedly are men, however, who carry within them an anima who exemplifies the feminine principle of justice and order. The closest human type we can imagine reflect this type of anima is the classic Libran type, a woman who is devoted to her marriage and treats it as a partnership, and who respects and upholds all principles of law and order, exemplified by her adherence to society's mores and etiquette. Perhaps of all the ideals mentioned in this section, the image of Themis is the most difficult to maintain. And, I have observed that men with Moon or Venus in Libra are often the most quickly disillusioned, although their Libran devotion to harmony and order usually causes them to deny this disillusionment, even to themselves.

Scorpio

The God: Shiva

Worship of the Horned God is among the oldest known on Earth. It was widespread throughout India, the Near East and the Mediterranean area long before the days of the Indo-European migrations. The Horned God seems to date from the earliest years of the Age of Taurus, as one of his symbols was the bull, and it appears that he shared the worship of his subjects with the Great Earth Mother. The Horned God was primarily a fertility symbol; he was the god of vegetation, of trees, and the vine, and also was regarded as Lord of the Animals.

In the course of the development of Western culture, in the midst of the Taurean Age, before the Aryan migrations, the Horned God was raised to the prominence of personification of the ultimate male (yang) force of the universe, ruling beside the Great Mother, or ultimate feminine principle (yin). When the Aryan invaders reached India and discovered that the aboriginals in that land (Dravidians) also worshiped the Horned God, they became further convinced of his power, and he was endowed with the name Shiva ("auspicious"). Somewhere along the line, Shiva became confused with the Aryan sky-god Rudra, the Destroyer, and thus was associated both with death and rebirth. Shiva was also considered a sexual symbol, the god of potency—and this is still part of Shiva-worship today. The phallic symbol "Shiva lingam" is found in Shaivite temples throughout India, even though now the Shiva worshiped in India is more of an impersonal godhead rather than the Horned God of mythology.

The Shiva of tradition is a rather pragmatic figure; stories tell of how he destroyed villages populated by his devotees in order to accomplish a higher good. As the Destroyer, Shiva constantly demolished the old and outmoded to make way for the newer and better. He taught his followers to disregard human laws so that they might rediscover the truth of Divine law. His potency, sexual and otherwise, unleashed the powers of soul and of body. Shiva is associated with that which is chaotic, dangerous, and unexpected. Some anthropologists see Shiva as a parallel of Bacchus, because orgies were known to have been held in his name. The madness induced by sex and wine was meant either to raise the reveler to the heights of awareness, or to destroy him/her.

The personality of the Shiva of myth is rather perplexing. The story of his love for the goddess Parvati, daughter of the King of the Mountains, and his constant trials to win her hand even though her father disapproved, indicate his indomitability. Shiva was insanely jealous of any of Parvati's other suitors and he fought courageously to overcome them. Perversely, however, as soon as they were married Shiva taunted his newly-won bride for being black! Parvati, so the story goes, then retreated and performed austerities until her skin turned a lovely golden brown.

Women who have the Sun or Mars in Scorpio and the corresponding animus, are attracted to men who can induce in them the madness of love and sensual pleasure. Those who are more aware also seek partners who can cause them to see the transcendent side of themselves. Such women must also bear in mind, however, that the Horned God within such men causes them to seek continual transformation themselves and, as Shiva was known to destroy the villages of his followers for a higher good, these men will leave their loves behind if they feel that doing so will aid them in their own growth. These men may even turn on their partners, as Shiva once turned on Parvati. The only way to avoid this type of abandonment is for the woman who holds this animus within her to work steadily towards her own growth—as Parvati did to transform the color of her skin—and thus, continually prove herself worthy of the Horned God whom she cannot help but worship.

The Goddess: Durga

At one time, the Hindu goddess Durga was at associated with the rugged, awe-inspiring mountains, and for this reason she eventually became regarded as one of the most powerful of all goddesses. Some etymologists trace her name to an old Sanskrit word meaning "difficulty," and indeed one of Durga's main functions was to free her devotees from any difficulty. She was the prime benefactress in the Hindu pantheon, having the power to give prosperity and to destroy enemies, to eliminate sins and to purify the soul, to ward off troubles and to satisfy desires. Even the gods acknowledged the supremacy of Durga; of all the goddesses she alone was entitled to bear the conch and the discus, which were the principle weapons used by the god Vishnu. Images of her in Hindu temples portray her as a war-goddess of great beauty, wearing the lion clasp—a badge which no other female deity was allowed to wear.

The war-goddess Durga was supportive and beneficent toward her followers, but to her enemies she became the hideous and bloodthirsty Kali (who has a Celtic parallel in the ogress Cailleach of Scottish legend). As Kali, this goddess destroys without mercy, taking delight in dancing on the skulls of her foes, and in one story she even laughed cruelly as she danced on the living body of her husband, Shiva. Kali is represented as the mysterious betrayer, able to conceal herself in her long, abundant hair, ready to show herself to her enemies in all her evil grotesqueness at the first sign of trouble. Just as Scorpionic people are often seen as either the greatest of saints or the vilest of sinners, so the goddess associated with that sign has two vastly different sides: as Durga, the just and loving benefactress, or as Kali, the dealer in death.

Men with Moon or Venus in Scorpio, and the corresponding anima, are drawn to women who project unusual power, women who can play the role of beneficent high priestess, and who bestow their favors on those men who shower them with devotion. Yet these women also have the power to destroy those who turn on them, to inflict pain such as was never felt before. The goddess within these men seems to warn, "Adore me or else." The secret of a successful relationship with a Durga-type seems to be having the resiliency to deal with the Kali within the lover—or the power to keep her from ever showing her face.

Sagittarius

The God: Chiron

Before the rise of the Olympians, the god Saturn fell in love with a lovely sea nymph named Philyra, and set about to seduce her. However, in order to avoid the watchful eye of his wife Rhea, Saturn mated with Philyra in the form of a horse. The fruit of this union was the centaur, Chiron.

It is said that Philyra was so repulsed by the sight of her half-horse son that she cast him away from her to fend for himself. However, because he was an immortal like his father, he could not die. The god Apollo took pity on him and instructed him in the arts of healing, divination, music, and the higher wisdom, which the Sun god felt would help the young centaur to rise above his bestial nature. Apollo discovered that the boy had a brilliant, expansive mind, and was an eager student.

As a result of Apollo's guidance and patronage, Chiron grew to be a famous teacher, physician, prophet, and sage. Kings sent their sons to Chiron to be educated in all the arts that would be useful to them in their future roles as leaders: hunting, riding, archery, combat, medicine, and the beginnings of natural science and philosophy. Among Chiron's more famous students were Jason, Achilles, and Asklepios.

Chiron is credited with the invention of the spear. It is said that he drew up the design and presented it for approval to the gods on Olympus. Athena polished the shaft and Vulcan forged the blade. Chiron then presented the finished product to Achilles.

The centaur's fame as a healer spread far and wide. He was said to have surpassed even Apollo in his skills as an herbalist, physician, and surgeon. During the Trojan War, Chiron was reported to have performed many near-miraculous cures.

Even though Chiron was involved with such serious matters as teaching and healing, he also had a lighter side. He was known to all as "the kindly, gentle Chiron," and certainly enjoyed a good time. He spent many hours roving through the woods, playing his pipes as he went. He was often seen cavorting and romping in the hills and forests with his fellow centaurs, and is reported to have become entangled in some rather touchy scrapes. On one occasion, Chiron and his fellow centaurs were driven from their mountain home because they had gone to a wedding and become embroiled in a drunken brawl when one of the centaurs tried to rape the bride.

A woman who has the Sun or Mars in Sagittarius possesses an animus that is brilliant and gifted, with expansive inner vision, who is also a free spirit who enjoys a good time. Perhaps she is attracted to men who have had a disadvantaged start in life, but who have used their talents to overcome setbacks. The problem with Chiron-type mortals is that they have so many diverse interests that they find it difficult to settle on one path. The charm and versatility of this type can be irresistible; however, the very multi-talented nature which at first is so appealing can prove frustrating for a partner who wants a conventional domestic life. If you are involved with a man who embodies your inner Chiron, you might have to accept that adventure will be a way of life for both of you.

The Goddess: Epona

In the early days of the Indo-European migrations, the pre-Hellenic branches of the original tribe migrated to the southwest, into Greece, and the Keltoi migrated to the northwest, into what is now France. In Greece, a peninsula where the primary mode of transportation was by water, the Great Earth Mother Goddess of the primal Aryans remained pretty much the same as she had been to the original people. But the Keltoi, living much farther inland, began to see the Earth Mother in a different light. For as their contact with other peoples became increasingly important, the Keltoi found themselves more and more dependent upon the horse for transportation. So, for the Keltoi, Demeter, the Great Earth Mother, eventually assumed the guise of Epona, the Horse Goddess.

Epona was envisioned as a tall, slender young woman with blue eyes and an abundant mane of long fair hair, who possessed the power to turn into a horse. In that guise, she travelled among the various villages of the Keltoi, seeking the ideal home and winning over even those who were hostile. She was known for her laughter, her good nature, and her sweet complaisance, and she attracted the attentions of man and god alike.

Yet Epona cherished her freedom above all else; Celtic legend tells of how the god Pwyll fell in love with Epona (called Rhiannon by the Welsh) and pursued her on his fastest horse, but could not overtake her, for she had assumed her usual guise of a white mare and left both him and his horse far behind. There are many old stories of love-chases which owe their origin to tales of Epona; among them is the story of Lady Godiva.

Like Chiron, Epona is also associated with healing. Old fables tell of how at first she concentrated on treating horses, and then, somewhat unwillingly, later began using her gifts to heal her people as well.

Religious rites performed in Britain and Ireland to honor Epona and the sacred horses who were her charges celebrate the symbolic union between the king and the Horse Goddess. Perhaps this is the reason why later Welsh and Irish legend portrays the Horse Goddess as a married woman with children, the queen of a Celtic kingdom. Yet the main charm of Epona seems to be her dedication to the ideal of unfettered freedom, an ideal that even today is symbolized, particularly in America, by the image of the wild horse.

A man who has his Moon or Venus in Sagittarius, therefore, seeks a partner who is a free spirit, unbound by convention, who desires no permanent home, but instead dedicates herself to her ideals and aspirations. Indeed, such women can be appealing, but it is hard to hold on to them, just as it was impossible for Pwyll to capture Epona. The commitment of Epona-types is not to a conventional life, but to freedom, and men who also are dedicated to liberty would be happiest with them.

Capricorn

The God: Saturn

The god Saturn is always presented as a very old man, with a long beard, bearing a scythe in his hand, quite similar to Father Time. In fact, many anthropologists maintain that Saturn and Father Time are one and the same. The second king of the gods, Saturn is often presented as a rather terrifying figure; he is said to have been so coldly determined to hang onto his position as king of the cosmos that, upon the forced abdication of his father Ouranos, he ordered that all his male children be brought to him as soon as they were born so that he might devour them, one by one. At first, this was easily accomplished; his orders were carried out and his throne was safe. In spite of this cruel practice, however, he proved to be a wise and capable ruler. The reign of Saturn is said to have been a Golden Age, when the Earth produced all that was needed for the survival of its inhabitants in peace and comfort, without labor or hardship.

Nonetheless, Saturn's false security could not last. His wife, Cybele, soon grew tired of seeing her male children murdered by their father, and so when Zeus, Poseidon, and Hades were born, she hid them away and instead gave Saturn stones to eat. When the three sons had grown to young manhood, she surprised her husband with them, and he was so taken by their young manly beauty that he forgave his wife. When Saturn's brothers, the Titans, declared war on him, it was Zeus who led the forces against the Titans and stopped the rebellion. Saturn was again secure in the continuation of his rule.

Yet the skill and cunning of Zeus in overcoming the Titans frightened Saturn. He therefore plotted against Zeus and had him thrown into the depths of the underworld. Saturn's own blind ambition proved his downfall. Zeus was angered because his father had betrayed him after Zeus had saved his throne. The powerful young god escaped from the underworld and finally overthrew his father.

Saturn's determination to remain a king was too strong to keep him down for very long, however. He retreated to an obscure corner of Italy, where he took charge of the rather barbaric inhabitants and reclaimed them from the wildness of their ways. He introduced him to civilization, the arts, and happiness, and thereby created again a Golden Age.

The woman with Sun or Mars in Capricorn, therefore, carries within her an animus that is reminiscent of a father-figure. This man is determined to lord it over others and can be somewhat ruthless in pursuing this end. Once he achieves his goal, though, he is capable of being a fair and just leader. If this type of woman is not well-integrated with the inner partner, she appears to be less independent than most and seeks to re-create the relationship she had with her father (or her subconscious ideal of a father-daughter relationship). If well-integrated, the Saturn-type woman may be independent and ambitious, but still seek a man who is a leader.

The Goddess: Diana

It may seem strange at first to see the name of the Moon Goddess ascribed as the figure for the sign opposite the one ruled by the Moon. Sources indicate that Diana's legendary dominion over the Moon is a fairly recent addition to the Diana persona; according to anthropologists, Diana was not associated with the Moon until the post-Homeric period. It appears that Diana was originally a nature spirit, the Indo-European goddess of the wood; both the Hindu tree-goddess Aranyani (also called Danavi) and the Celtic tree-goddess Nematona are considered parallels to the Greek Diana. In fact, the latter is sometimes referred to as Diana Nematona.

Diana is the third of the traditional virgin goddesses: Athena, Vesta, and Diana. Diana's virginity was due to her role as "the other."[5] She is dedicated to solitude, to being alone with the wild creatures of the wood, and she is hostile to any god or human she meets. She is not at home on Mount Olympus, nor does she share any affinity with her fellow immortals, except possibly with her twin brother Apollo. Diana is associated with the birds and beasts, and yet there is nothing spiritual or sentimental in her involvement with them; to her the animals are simply there, and they are hers.

Feelings have no place in Diana's world. Emotions do not lead either to sexual fulfillment or creative passion; they simply exist to be observed, dispassionately and discriminately. In mythology Diana is presented as tall, slim, attractive but forbidding, mysterious, remote, uncompromising, and essentially alone. She "compels delight but cannot love."

Although it appears clear that the goddess's original name was Dione or Diana, Homer and other Greek poets called her "Artemis"; some etymologists have traced this name to a pre-Hellenic phrase meaning "she who slays." Apollo, it is said, was a healer; Diana was a poisoner. Diana is so dedicated to being alone in her forest that she must kill anyone who comes too close. One of the most popular myths concerning Diana involves the hunter Actaeon, who became separated from his companions after a day's chase in the woods and, exhausted, fell asleep. He awoke to find Diana bathing with her handmaidens in a nearby stream, and presumed to observe the goddess in all her naked glory. Diana retaliated by turning him into a stag and then setting her hounds upon him; for Actaeon's impudence, the dogs tore the stag to pieces.

The man with Moon or Venus in Capricorn, therefore, bears within himself a goddess as remote, unfeeling, and unapproachable as Diana. He often may wonder why he constantly is attracted to women who project pride and desirability, yet are cold and remote, giving no thought to his feelings, and who, at times, seem to punish him merely for loving them. This is a difficult anima to come to terms with, for the goddess within keeps even her outer half at a distance, however, the conflict can possibly be resolved by concentrating on development of the more positive attributes of Capricorn, such as inner strength, stability, and dependability.

Aquarius

The God: Vishnu

In the *Rig-Veda,* which is the earliest written chronicle related to Aryan mythologies, Vishnu, the Solar Logos, is treated as only a minor god. Later chronicles are more explicit as to Vishnu's nature and function. As the spirit of the Sun, Vishnu is concerned with the preservation of our Universe, and constitutes one-third of the Hindu Trinity: Brahma, the Creator, Vishnu, the Preserver, and Shiva, the Destroyer.

Perhaps Vishnu's most salient characteristic is that, unlike Indra, Shiva, and other gods, there are virtually no accounts of his adventures *as a god.* As a god, Vishnu remains in the heavens, and only when he takes human incarnation do his activities come into the spotlight. In short, Vishnu represents the Aquarian ideal: God moving among human beings. He generally is depicted as sitting in the ocean on a lotus-flower, and represents the ultimate in love of humanity: He is the god of grace and of benevolence, and never hesitates to shower his largess upon his many mortal subjects. Although in the beginning, he was regarded mainly as a solar deity, it was later said that his domain was the infinite ocean of the Universe, where he allowed the water of beneficence to pour down upon the Earth and all who dwelt there. Of all the Hindu gods, Vishnu was perhaps the most ingenious. His own personal weapon, which he devised, was the discus, and with it he slew countless demons. He is also said to have been connected with the invention of the spear and the bow and arrow.

The stories of Vishnu's various earthly incarnations also illustrate his cleverness. There are said to have been eight main incarnations of Vishnu: the fish, the turtle, the boar, the man-lion, the dwarf, Rama, Krishna, and Buddha. (Notice the parallel to modern theories of evolution.) The most well-known story of Vishnu (other than the epic tales of

Rama in the *Ramayana* and of Krishna in the *Mahabharata*) is the story of his legendary three steps. According to mythological accounts, in his dwarf incarnation Vishnu took three steps: one which took him through the underworld, the second which encompassed Earth, and the third which took him to the region of the gods. In this way he established his supremacy over all three worlds. This tale has many parallels in other Aryan traditions, particularly the Celtic tale of the dwarf Cuchulain's leap across the bridge.

It would seem, then, that the woman with Sun or Mars in Aquarius carries within her an animus who projects humanitarianism, who expresses a powerful love of humankind, but who does not set himself above them; rather, he is willing to move among the masses, as one of them. This type also expresses ingenuity and cleverness at their best. Few human beings can devote themselves to humanitarian ideals without sacrificing their personal relationships to some degree, however.

The Goddess: Lakshmi

In Hindu myth the wife of Vishnu, Lakshmi, appears to trace her origin to an ancient Indo-European corn goddess. Eventually she became identified with the primal ocean and is often pictured standing on a lotus flower in that vast sea with flowing springs as well as gold coins falling from her fingertips. Lakshmi is the goddess of wealth and prosperity, of grace and benevolence, and therefore, like Vishnu, she illustrates the ultimate in love of humanity.

Like the Greek Aphrodite, Lakshmi is said to have sprung full-grown from the ocean. It is said that as soon as the beautiful Lakshmi appeared in the cosmos, the god Shiva desired her. But he was already wed to Parvati, and so the newly-born Lakshmi was given to Vishnu. Thus began the legend of what perhaps was the most devoted marriage between deities in all of Aryan mythology.

Although there are many stories of Lakshmi's life as a goddess, the main focus of her activities seems to be taking human incarnation and moving among her people, as was true also of Vishnu. Her devotion to Vishnu was such that she could not bear to be parted from him and so when he took incarnation as Rama, she assumed the role of Sita; when he incarnated as Krishna, she became his beloved Radha. In spite of Rama's betrayal of Sita and Radha's eventual separation from Krishna, the commitment between the two exalted beings seems to have remained unscathed.

Lakshmi was and still is perhaps the best-loved goddess in the Hindu pantheon. Even in India today (and in yogic communities the world over) devoted followers of this beneficent deity chant to her the ancient hymn written and dedicated to her, the *Lakshmi puja,* hoping to attract her favor.

Therefore, it would appear that the man with Moon or Venus in Aquarius hopes to attract a woman with strong humanitarian ideals and a great love for humankind—but who nonetheless is totally dedicated to him, as Lakshmi was to Vishnu, and to preserving peace in the world, as Lakshmi tried to preserve peace among the gods.

Pisces

The God: Mithras

Some readers acquainted with mystery religions may be surprised to find Mithras categorized under Pisces, since he was the patron saint of soldiers and his rites involved the ritual slaying of the bull of the Age of Taurus, symbolizing the advent of the Age of Aries. However, the exact nature of the god himself appears to have been quite different from that of the rites practiced by his followers.

Mithras was the Persian Sun god, whose origin may be found in the original Indo-European trinity—Mitra, Varuna (Ouranos in Greece), and In-da-ra (Indra in Hindu lore). Like Shiva and Bacchus, his symbol was the bull, demonstrating his rise to power during the Age of Taurus. As the Sun god, his function was originally to allow the life forces to flow freely onto the Earth and its inhabitants, to promote fertility, wealth and abundance, and to bless his followers with life and happiness.

However, after the Age of Taurus had passed and the Age of Aries grew to full flower, the day of the warrior had truly dawned. No longer did different tribes co-exist in peace; they all coveted the same land, the same riverbanks or seacoasts, and they began fighting each other in order both to maintain their hold on what they considered theirs by right, and to gain new territory which they felt they deserved. Suddenly the gods began to change; the fertility gods and goddesses of the Age of Taurus gave way to a series of powerful warrior-gods. An attitude evolved that there were two sides to the Universe: the good, and the evil. In short: *we* represent good, *they* represent evil. The warriors of each side sought the blessing of their individual gods. And with the development of this dualistic, good versus evil philosophy came the rise of Mithras.

Mithras was the savior-martyr of the Arien Age, a precursor, if you will, of the savior-martyrs of the future Piscean Age. No women were allowed to join the cult of Mithras, yet there were no social barriers; a slave could be initiated side by side with a king's son. The cult of Mithras resembled somewhat the Freemasons of today; it was a metaphysically-oriented group who believed in life after death. Before every major battle or military campaign, the priests of Mithras held their initiation of the soldiers into the cult. They would climb down into a sacred pit, and then a sacred bull, supposedly the god Mithras incarnate, would be slaughtered over them; its blood would pour over their bodies and bathe them in its infinite life force, assuring them of an afterlife should they meet death on the battlefield. In short, Mithras died so that his followers might live. There are those who say that Christianity owes much to Mithraism, and this may be true. But the mythological archetype of the savior-martyr king actually long predates Mithraism, probably having its beginnings in the guilt experienced by the hunter when he deprives the animal which he must eat of its life. In early hunt-oriented societies, it was accepted as fact that someone must pay for this guilt—and often a sacrifice, sometimes even the king himself, was offered to the gods in order to atone for the lives of the animals killed in the hunt.

The woman with Sun or Mars in Pisces, therefore, carries within her a god such as Mithras—the benevolent, life-giving Sun god, so devoted to his people that he is willing to give up his life so that they might live. These women are generally attracted to men who are attractive and charismatic, but at the same time are capable of compassion to the point of self- sacrifice above and beyond the call of duty. These men may also be mostly unaware of their magnetism, and therefore their compassion is less a product of true altruism than a means of insuring the continuing love of those around them by letting themselves be used.

The Goddess: Mary

The mythological archetype which eventually became attached to the persona of the very real historical figure who was the mother of Jesus of Nazareth is as old as civilization itself. This archetype, called by Robert Graves "The White Goddess," goes beyond the concept of the Great Earth Mother and encompasses more what the Hindus called the Goddess Kundalini Shakti. In other words, this archetype represents the transcendental feminine force or yin energy which permeates the entire Universe. The earthly personifications of this force throughout mythological history appear to encompass omniscience, boundless wisdom, never-ending love and compassion, and total awareness of everything in the hearts and minds of men. Among the mythological figures that were representations of this White Goddess were the Egyptian Isis, the Persian Astarte, and the Irish St. Bridget (in pre-Christian days the Goddess Bridget). Strangely enough, many of the lesser-known goddesses from the days before the birth of Christ who symbolized this particular type of figure bore names similar to that of Mary. The Greek Cypriot goddess Mari, the Cretan Mariandyne, the Near-Eastern Mariamne, and possibly the Hebrew prophetess Miriam are only a few. Robert Graves traces this name to an old Aryan name for the White Goddess, "Anna," from an Indo-European root meaning, "heaven." According to Graves, the roots of this name were the Indo-European "Amma," meaning mother, "rim" meaning to bear a child, and "enna," meaning heaven; hence, "fruitful mother of heaven." Other etymologists trace the name to the ancient Indo- European root "mare," meaning "of the sea" or the Hebrew "Maryam" meaning "sea-brine." The latter etymologies parallel the idea that this goddess represented the Divine cauldron which was regarded as a source of inspiration, the mystical receptacle of the Holy Spirit. For this reason, both Astarte and St. Bridget of Ireland were associated with poetry and music, supposedly the products of divine inspiration.

Whether the flesh-and-blood woman who gave birth to Jesus of Nazareth actually possessed all these superhuman personality traits is uncertain, as the New Testament devotes very little time to the character of Mary, except to present her as an individual with limitless faith in God who was pure enough to merit the honor of giving birth to a Divine incarnation. The popular Christian image of Mary, however, represents that she was aware that she was bringing up a child whom she would some day lose—who would be offered as a sacrifice for the purpose of redeeming all who would believe in Him. If only half the stories about Jesus's mother told in the Gospels are true, it would appear that she was aware of her son's destiny at least to some degree—and crucifixion is hardly a fate any mother would want her child to face. It would seem that only Mary's boundless faith could possibly have kept her sane in the years between the Nativity and the Crucifixion. It is no wonder, then, that those pagans who later became Christians saw in Mary still another representation of the greatest of all female deities, the White Goddess, the Kundalini Shakti of the Universe.

It seems, then, that the man with Moon or Venus in Pisces carries within him an anima representative of Mary, she who was worthy to be a receptacle for the Holy Spirit, a source of divine inspiration, a woman possessing enough transcendental knowledge to maintain unquestioned faith in the wisdom and justice of the Powers that Be, willing to make the ultimate sacrifice. These men are generally attracted to women who project a transcendental image, who possess a high level of love and compassion, who are willing to sacrifice their interests for the sake of others, and who are gifted in the fields of music or poetry. Few human beings can uphold the image of the White Goddess for very long, however. These men have to bear in mind that the women they love are human beings who will probably need to receive compassion as often as they give it.

Notes

1. Rafael Lopez-Pedraza, *Hermes and His Children,* (Zurich: Spring Publications, 1977), p. 37.

2. Demetra George, *Asteroid Goddesses,* (San Diego, CA: ACS Publications, 1986), p. 152.

3. Christine Downing, *The Goddesses: Mythological Images of the Feminine,* (New York: Crossroads, 1981), p. 157ff.

9

Astrology and Sex

Chart comparisons usually give much attention to sexual compatibility between prospective partners. The prime factors considered are the man's Mars and the woman's Venus; however, new evidence indicates that there is a strong, magnetic attraction between partners with Venus-Uranus aspects, and that lovers with Venus-Pluto connections often experience a healthy and active sex life.

These aspects also are important in an individual natal chart. A person who has major aspects (harmonious or stressful) between Venus and Mars, Venus and Uranus, and/or Venus and Pluto usually has a strong sex drive. Harmonious aspects between these planets usually make the person sensual, spontaneous, and uninhibited. In general, stressful aspects between Venus and Mars can produce tendencies toward violence; hard aspects between Venus and Uranus can encourage preferences for unusual sexual practices; and squares or oppositions involving Venus and Pluto can indicate manipulation and power plays in sexual matters.

The Moon is also an important factor to consider when analyzing a person's sexual nature. However, the Moon is less concerned with an individual's actual physical drive than his or her emotional need for sex, and therefore, the Moon will not be emphasized in this section.

The zodiacal signs that are prominent in a person's chart also are significant factors in his or her sexual nature. For the most part, Taurus, Leo, and Scorpio are highly-sexed signs, and Gemini, Capricorn, and Aquarius are not; the others lie somewhere in between, varying by degrees. (See chapter 7, "The Aries Lover," etc., for more on this.) The eighth house and planets either positioned in or ruling that house also provide information about the individual's sexual nature.

In order to analyze the sexual compatibility between you and a partner, you need to understand your partner's sexual potential and your own, as well as the degree of attraction between the two charts. Potential is shown in an individual's birth chart; the degree of attraction is discerned by comparing two charts. It is essential to consider both, for, as mentioned earlier, two people might have many indicators of attraction but have essentially different natures, so that despite their "chemistry" the relationship won't last.

The Eighth House

Traditionally, the eighth house is connected with all that is mysterious, hidden, and powerful. We can certainly see why this house is associated with sex!

A person with an accented eighth house—occupied by two or more planets, or by the Sun, Mars, or Pluto—generally is preoccupied with sex for one reason or another. I have counseled individuals whose charts indicated indifference toward sex, except for the emphasis on the eighth house. For some of these people, sex was seen as a way of conveying power rather than expressing love or pleasure. At other times, this type of individual possesses an intellectual interest in sex as a creative force of nature, but has little interest in actual sexual activity.

However, if a person has an unoccupied eighth house, and the planetary ruler of the sign on the eighth house cusp is not oriented particularly toward sex, other factors in the chart must be considered. An unemphasized eighth house does not necessarily mean that the individual lacks a strong sex drive. However, if the overall chart reveals a person with powerful sexual desires, but the eighth house is badly afflicted, the sex life will be frustrated or inhibited in some way, and the individual probably will need to find another outlet for his or her desires.

For example, the chart of one of my close friends has a strong Taurus-Leo-Scorpio influence, revealing a highly charged sexual nature. Yet his eighth house contains a Moon-Saturn conjunction which opposes Mars. This combination of influences has manifested in his marriage to a woman who does not satisfy him sexually. He has been married to her for nearly twenty years, loves her deeply and would not even consider leaving her, yet the lack of passion in their relationship is frustrating to him. At times, he has attempted to satisfy his needs through affairs with other women, yet as he grows spiritually he has become more and more uncomfortable with this practice. Now, as transiting Pluto conjuncts his natal Sun in Scorpio, he is coming to realize that his sexual nature probably will have to be transformed and sublimated through creativity and spiritual practices. Yet the romantic ideas surrounding sex are hard to abandon, and he is having difficulty facing the path ahead of him.

The Sun in or ruling the eighth house suggests that the person identifies the will with sex. If the Sun is in one of the more sensually-inclined signs, especially if it also is well-aspected, this individual can be a skillful lover. If the Sun is in one of the less sensual signs or badly aspected, the person may use sex to manipulate and control, and is not above using another's romantic attachment to him or her for selfish ends. If you are involved with someone whose chart contains this Sun-eighth house combination, you will need to use your head to control your heart (and your passions), though this may not be easy. Remember, allowing someone to dominate and manipulate you is not beneficial for either of you.

The Moon in or ruling the eighth house indicates that sex is seen as an expression of deep feelings. If the Moon is well-placed by sign and well-aspected, the person can be a loving and satisfying partner. If the Moon is afflicted, however, the person may try to bind a lover to him or her through sex, and if Neptune is involved, this person's emotional dependency can be suffocating. If Uranus is involved, the person may be emotionally and sexually erratic, insatiable one minute, withdrawn the next. If you are involved with such a partner, do not be confused; a person with an eighth house Moon usually has a strong sex drive. If he or she withdraws from lovemaking it does not indicate a lack of desire, but rather an emotional cry for help, a signal that your partner's emotional needs are not being met. Try to help your partner open up and tell you why he or she feels this way.

Mercury in or ruling the eighth house implies an intellectual approach to sex, or a tendency to talk excessively about it, or both. This person may enjoy "talking dirty" during lovemaking. Mercury is an intellectual and communicative planet and, therefore, is not an indicator of sensuality in itself. However, if other planets, particularly the Sun, Moon, Venus, and/or Pluto, are also posited in the eighth house, the person's sensuality may be verbally frank—which sometimes can prove embarrassing to more inhibited partners. If Mercury is afflicted, particularly by Saturn, the person will be reticent about expressing his or her needs to a partner. If you are involved with this sort of individual, you will need to discern your partner's desires through means other than verbal communication, for it is difficult for him or her to talk about things as private as sex.

Venus in or ruling the eighth house denotes a strong connection between sex and love. Depending on other factors in the individual's chart, this could manifest as a desire to have sex only with people he or she loves. Or, it could suggest a tendency to "fall in love" even with casual or temporary sexual partners. Venus in this position almost always indicates a sensual lover who is uninhibited in sexual matters. However, if Venus is afflicted by Saturn, the individual rarely finds a partner he or she considers worthy of love, and therefore has a rather limited sex life. Marriage may occur late in life, or this person might wed an older partner, or possibly someone whose sex drive is low. If Venus is afflicted by Uranus, strange or unusual liaisons are likely, and such a person is capable of bringing these attractions to fruition. If Venus is afflicted by Neptune, the individual has unrealistic expectations of sex and often feels let down if an encounter does not produce ecstasy. In any aspect to Pluto, an eighth house Venus produces a sex drive that is practically insatiable, but if the aspect is a difficult one, there is a tendency to use sex to control partners.

Mars in or ruling the eighth house indicates that the person has much enthusiasm for sex and channels a great deal of energy into sexual activity. He or she enjoys impulsive, spur-of-the-moment encounters, and might be the type who likes sex in situations where the possibility of being caught in the act adds to the fun. Risk only makes such a person more determined. A woman with Mars in this position is generally more aggressive than others. If Mars is badly afflicted, there can be a tendency toward roughness or violence. Or, the individual might satisfy his or her own needs with little consideration for the partner's. Traditionally, Mars has been associated with sex because of its identification with the archetypal male or yang principle, but it is my experience that Mars represents the *energy* a person channels into sex, not sex itself. Sex per se appears to me to be associated more with Pluto.

Jupiter in or ruling the eighth house indicates a healthy and enthusiastic attitude towards sex, and, in most cases, an abundance of sexual partners throughout life. The person is generally free and easy in his or her practices and has few inhibitions. This individual is tolerant of the sexual attitudes and practices of others, even if they conflict with his or her own. In some cases, an eighth house Jupiter may indicate large or especially sensitive genital organs. An afflicted Jupiter in this position does not seem to inhibit the individual's sex drive, but instead limits or exaggerates his or her sexual expression, as is suggested by the aspecting planet. For example, a person with an eighth house Jupiter in hard aspect to Venus has a tendency towards promiscuity and is inclined to "fall in love" with each object of desire. Jupiter in hard aspect to Uranus implies many sexual encounters of an unusual nature, or a succession of sexual affairs that begin and end suddenly. In any aspect to Saturn, an eighth house Jupiter implies sexual fidelity; however, if the aspect is a difficult one, the person's expression of sexual love is often inhibited, even with a partner to whom he or she is committed.

Saturn in or ruling the eighth house suggests an inhibited sex drive, or, if the remainder of the chart is overwhelmingly sensual, makes it seem as though some force beyond the individual's control is inhibiting his or her sexual expression. Unless Leo, Taurus, or Scorpio is prominent in the chart, the person may give the impression of sexual coldness. This aloofness either will dampen the interests of prospective partners or challenge them to be more aggressive. Such people may be sexually faithful, but unless Venus is involved this fidelity is due less to love and commitment than to lack of interest in sex. Unless there are contradictory influences in the rest of the chart, Saturn in or ruling the eighth house is not a harbinger of an active sex life, and if you are involved with such a person, your instances of lovemaking together may be rather infrequent.

Uranus in or ruling the eighth house implies an erratic sex drive, marked by unconventional appetites or practices, brief affairs, and sporadic encounters. If the chart is dominated by air signs or by Capricorn, the person is not interested much in sex; such people either are too intellectual or too ambitious to be concerned with matters of the flesh. While someone who has Saturn in this position can appear to be blocked sexually, Uranus can imply that he or she has no sexual desires at all. If the chart is otherwise a sensual one, the individual may experience periods of being intensely passionate, interspersed with long stretches when desire is nonexistent. This person has an uncanny knack for sublimating sexual desire through self-expression. There is little inclination towards sexual fidelity: Uranus in this position seems to separate the idea of sex from that of love and commitment. Unless other factors in the chart counteract the tendency, these people can be totally amoral where sex is concerned, and unless water signs are prominent, they usually don't bother to hide their peccadillos from their partners. If you have this aspect in your chart, you may need to come to terms with the fact that most people do expect fidelity from a marital or romantic partner, and, if you can't curtail your practices, at least learn to be discreet.

Neptune in or ruling the eighth house indicates that the person has romantic ideas about sex and unrealistic expectations of the sexual experience. Neptune in any house represents a desire for an altered state of consciousness, or for escape from or through matters ruled by that house; the eighth house is no exception. It is possible, of course, to reach the heights of ecstasy and transcendental experience through sex, but it is not likely to happen at every encounter, or with every partner. If Neptune is afflicted by Mars, Mercury, or Saturn, there can be lies and deception with regard to sexual matters. Perhaps this individual, even after committing to a lifetime partner, still continues to seek the ideal sexual experience. However, unless Neptune is posited on the cusp of the seventh and eighth houses, he or she does not necessarily identify the perfect sexual experience with the perfect relationship. If you have Neptune in the eighth house, you need to reassess your expectations of sex and become more realistic, in order to increase your chances of having a rewarding relationship.

Pluto in or ruling the eighth house, particularly if in aspect to the Moon or Venus, produces a sex drive that can be quite compelling, even insatiable. The person is a passionate lover, has few inhibitions, and enjoys giving a partner pleasure. The sex drive, however, can be sublimated and transmuted into exalted artistic or magical experiences, and while involved in such activity this person may lack interest in sex. I have a female client with this planetary placement whose lovers have accused her of "wearing them out." Yet this same woman, who is a talented painter, has gone for years without sex and hardly missed it. If Pluto is badly afflicted, there can be tendencies toward manipulation, power struggles, and even violence.

Venus Aspects

Venus, the planet of love, is the principle indicator of a person's potential for a rewarding sexual relationship. Though Pluto rules the sex drive per se, Venus shows the person's need to relate, and therefore, Venus' aspects need to be considered. This holds true for individual chart analysis or chart comparison. The aspects in this section, therefore, can be applied to either situation.

Venus in aspect to Mars produces a blend of the love and affection of Venus with the enthusiasm and energy of Mars. In a chart comparison, aspects between one partner's Venus and the other partner's Mars represent a connection between the yin of the one and the yang of the other. When considering the sexual potential—either of an individual or of a relationship—any aspect between Venus and Mars is better than none. Harmonious aspects produce a warm, easy, and compatible sexual nature. Squares add a touch of stress, risk, and excitement. The opposition intensifies the effect of the square, but in extreme cases it can produce a sexual nature that is somewhat brutal. In a chart comparison, if there is a Venus-Mars opposition between the two partners, the Venus-person may bring out whatever latent violence exists in the Mars-person.

Venus in aspect to Uranus indicates strong powers of attraction. The person is magnetic and unexplainably attractive sexually. Relationships are unusual and unorthodox in some way. In a chart comparison, a Venus-Uranus combination can indicate a compelling attraction between two individuals, sometimes what is called "love at first sight." In an individual chart, if the Venus-Uranus connection is a stressful one, there can be an inclination towards alternate sexual behavior such as homosexuality, sado-masochism, or other unconventional practices. Sexual relationships can be intense, but are often brief and erratic, ending as quickly as they begin. In a chart comparison, it is generally the Venus-person who is first drawn to the Uranus-person. As the relationship progresses, it is the Uranus-person who seems most strongly attached, though the Uranus-person may give the impression of wanting "a long leash." If the aspect between Venus and Uranus is a difficult one, the partners may break off and then reunite several times before they either separate completely or make a commitment. If the aspect is an opposition, chances are they won't stay together—though with Uranus one must always expect the unexpected!

Venus in aspect to Pluto endows the individual with a powerful sex drive, which can be either loving and giving (harmonious aspects) or manipulative and somewhat brutal (stressful aspects). The person is passionate and demanding. In a chart comparison, the Venus-person is powerfully drawn to the innate sensuality of the Pluto-person, and the Pluto-person responds to the love of the Venus-person. If the aspect between Venus and Pluto is a hard one, the relationship can be fraught with power plays, and each individual might try to control the other through sex. Any aspect between Venus and Pluto—in a natal chart or a chart comparison—represents a need for the individual (or for the couple) to seek transformation of the inner self through love and sex. The keyword for Pluto is, after all, regeneration.

10

The Neptune Connection

Earlier in this book, I discussed the tradition of "courtly love" and how it has affected our current attitudes toward love relationships. Though the practice of courtly love is more than a thousand years old, its legacy is still with us. Many contemporary people still believe that the perfect lover is out there waiting for them, a partner who will love them forever and devote his or her life to making them happy.

In the initial stages of a relationship, when excitement masks a lover's deficiencies, it is easy for us to project our own desires onto our partners and imagine that they are everything we seek. As the relationship progresses, these projections have a nasty way of fading and we are forced to view our partners more realistically. Sometimes we find that our lovers are pretty exciting as they are, faults and all. Too many times, however, we discover that we were mistaken, and that our partners aren't what we wanted after all.

To some degree, romantic illusion affects us all when we first meet a person to whom we are physically and emotionally attracted. Some people are more pragmatic than others, though, and view everyone with a discriminating and critical eye—even during the first rush of romantic love. Other people accept the initial fantasy and enjoy it, but take time to get to know their partners before making a firm commitment. Then there are those who are so attached to their illusions that they hang onto them desperately, even after it should have been blatantly obvious that their partners are nothing like what was initially desired and imagined.

To find out how susceptible someone is to romantic illusion, look at the planet Neptune in his or her chart. Neptune is associated with other worlds, other dimensions and states of consciousness, fantasy, and escape. At its highest, this planet can produce an exalted awareness of that which exists beyond the physical plane, a mystical feeling of union with God or the forces of nature—the highest form of spiritual love. When Neptune is placed in an angular house in a person's birth chart and harmoniously aspected, that person has the potential for all these experiences. However, an afflicted Neptune clouds perception and leads to possible dishonesty, confusion, misconstrued perceptions, and deception. In love relationships, it is often *self-deception* that proves disastrous.

Neptune Aspects

Sun/Neptune

The will and all matters ruled by Neptune—fantasy, idealism, illusion, confusion—are linked. If the aspect between these two bodies is harmonious in an individual's birth chart, he or she will be romantic and idealistic, but able to keep some perspective in relationships. This person enjoys romance and "falling in love," but is not likely to let the illusions get out of hand. If the aspect between the Sun and Neptune is a stressful one, however, the individual's perception of reality is clouded. Often this person has a difficult time letting go of romantic illusions. If the Sun is otherwise well-aspected and/or well-placed by sign or house, however, the person is not as susceptible to the devastation of broken dreams as might otherwise be the case. The inner strength and self-confidence provided by a strong Sun enables the individual to face difficulties with greater clarity than someone whose Sun is in hard aspect to Neptune.

When Sun-Neptune aspects show up in a chart comparison, the relationship seems mystical and ideal. The Sun-person sees the Neptune-person as a channel through which to express his or her divine nature. If the aspect is a harmonious one, the relationship eventually may reach the state of mystical union we all crave. If the aspect is stressful, the Sun-person's perceptions of the Neptune-partner fluctuate between fantasy and reality. The Neptune-person is aware of the partner's idealistic view of him or her and often plays on these fantasies when it is advantageous.

Moon/Neptune

Any aspect between the Moon and Neptune, be it stressful or harmonious, indicates an emotional attachment to romance and illusions. If this combination shows up in an individual's birth chart, the person's perception of reality in general and emotional involvements in particular is clouded by his or her emotions. This individual has high expectations of any kind of relationship. He or she is able to feel and give the highest form of spiritual love, and will shower partners with the unconditional love all of us so desperately desire. However, if the aspect between the Moon and Neptune is a stressful one, it can cause problems. If you are involved with someone who has a Moon-Neptune aspect, try not to take unfair advantage of your partner's devotion, nor take this devotion for granted. Stressful aspects between the Moon and Neptune also can cause the individual to fasten affections on the wrong person. However, this person will be so attached emotionally to romantic illusions that he or she will cling to the relationship even if it proves destructive.

The effect of a Moon-Neptune aspect between two charts is similar to that of a Sun-Neptune aspect, except that the Moon-person perceives the Neptune-person to be an expression of his or her emotions. If the aspect is a trine or sextile, the Moon-person's emotional need for romance and illusion is satisfied easily by the Neptune-person, and each partner gives the other the closest possible thing to unconditional love. If the aspect is a square, opposition, or inconjunct, the Neptune-person might use emotional blackmail to control the Moon-person by playing on the latter's need for romance. How susceptible the Moon-person is to such manipulation depends on aspects in his or her natal chart.

Mercury/Neptune

Aspects between Mercury and Neptune imply an intellectual fascination with romantic love and an ability to express romantic feelings verbally. These individuals often are gifted poets, novelists, or songwriters. If the aspect between Mercury and Neptune is a stressful one, however, the person is reluctant to communicate romantic feelings and may be rather cynical about such verbal expression; he or she isn't likely to use endearments when speaking to a lover and doesn't want lovers to use them either. If you have Mercury in a stressful aspect to Neptune and are involved with a partner who wants you to verbalize your love, you will probably need to make an effort to overcome your innate cynicism. If you are involved with someone who has this type of aspect, remember that just because your partner may not say it very often doesn't mean he or she doesn't love you.

When Mercury/Neptune aspects appear in a chart comparison, the Mercury-person is usually more communicative than the Neptune-person, although the two of them generally relate well about artistic, spiritual, and romantic matters, especially if the aspect between the planets is harmonious. If the aspect is a difficult one, however, the Mercury-person at times may feel that his or her communications are not understood by the Neptune-person, especially if the latter is a daydreamer.

Venus/Neptune

Venus in aspect to Neptune causes the person to idealize all relationships—between parent and child, friends, lovers—and he or she has high expectations from any kind of involvement. If the aspect is harmonious, the person also realizes that there will be many times when these idealistic desires are not fulfilled, and he or she will not feel too let down on those occasions. If the aspect is stressful, however, the person is probably incapable of maintaining any kind of distance. All relationships—especially romantic ones—are clouded in a haze of fantasy and rarely perceived as they actually are. The individual cannot give up his or her illusions, and when fantasy dissolves into reality and reveals something other than what this person desired, he or she either writes the relationship off totally or clings to it desperately, making attempt after unsuccessful attempt to recreate the initial romantic image.

When a Venus/Neptune aspect shows up in a chart comparison, this aspect can produce a beautiful, harmonious, and spiritually-attuned relationship—if the aspect is a conjunction, trine, or sextile. If the aspect is a square, opposition, or quincunx, however, the partners may *perceive* that the relationship expresses these positive qualities, but in reality it is based almost totally on fantasy. The Venus-person may feel that in expressing love to the Neptune-person, he or she constantly is hitting a wall.

Mars/Neptune

Mars in aspect to Neptune signifies that the individual channels a great deal of energy into romance, and sees romantic partners as a source of inspiration. This person generally has a sporadic interest in romance and may either drift from one involvement to another, or, if married, may alternate long periods of seeming disinterest with periods of intense concentration on the partner. If the aspect between Mars and Neptune is harmonious, the person's romantic relationships represent a channel for spiritual or artistic aspirations, as well as a source of motivation to live a better life. If the aspect is stressful, however, the person craves romance and never seems to get enough, even if he or she appears to be "lucky in love." For this reason, such an individual may allow him- or herself to be exploited and deceived by lovers.

When Mars and Neptune are in aspect in a chart comparison, this connection suggests an aura of deception in the relationship, even if the aspect is harmonious. The Mars-person's energy and activity sometimes are too much for the Neptune-person, so the Mars-person goes ahead and does what he or she wants to do without telling the Neptune-person. If the Mars/Neptune aspect is harmonious, a great deal of energy is channeled into the romantic mystique that exists between the two partners, and deceptions don't always appear to hurt the relationship—especially if the Neptune person is too deeply involved with his or her own dreams to pay much attention to the Mars-person's activities. If the aspect is stressful, however, the deception is often vindictive, and the Neptune-person may feel used and exploited.

Jupiter/Neptune

Jupiter in aspect to Neptune conveys happiness through romance, and perhaps is the aspect most likely to offer potential for a highly-evolved and spiritually-based relationship. The individual is capable of depth and richness in love and emotional expression. Compassion, devotion, and excessive generosity are also likely. If the aspect between the planets is harmonious, the person will probably be lucky in love and experience great spiritual growth through romantic experiences. If the aspect is stressful, however, happiness may be elusive and frustratingly unattainable; just when it seems to be within reach, it vanishes into nothingness. The person may try to spread the *agape* he or she wishes to express to too many partners. This individual is easily influenced by romantic pronouncements, whether true or false, and there is a tendency to idolize everyone he or she loves.

Harmonious Jupiter/Neptune aspects in a chart comparison usually convey a lasting feeling of happiness in the relationship, even through tough times. Romance will last throughout the partners' lives, and to spiritually-inclined persons, the relationship will seem blessed by God. Even stressful aspects cannot produce too much strain on the happiness in the relationship (though they can create confusion), unless hard aspects from other planets make the attachment a difficult one. In these cases, the partners may cling to the relationship because of the potential for *agape,* but may find the potential heart-rending because of the other problems between them.

Saturn/Neptune

Saturn in aspect to Neptune can block the expression of romantic feeling. The person's capacity for fantasy, and how important romantic mystique is in his or her relationships, can be judged best through other factors in the chart, but Saturn's aspects to Neptune can reveal what the person does about that capacity. If the aspect between these planets is harmonious, the individual possesses self-restraint and a discriminating attitude in romantic matters. This person exercises caution, foresight, and practicality in relationships, and is less likely to see potential lovers through an illusory haze. The individual also possesses an above-average capability and willingness for self-sacrifice.

In a chart comparison, easy Saturn/Neptune aspects suggest that the romantic feeling in the relationship is a lasting one. Even when the initial rush of passion has past, its memory can help to sustain the romantic mystique for many years. Each partner is willing to make sacrifices for the other, and there is a loyalty and devotion between the two that is unrivaled. However, hard aspects between Saturn and Neptune often block romantic feeling and expression. If a love relationship is entered into between two people with such an aspect, there are often other considerations involved besides romance, since it is unlikely that there are any overwhelming romantic passions between them.

Uranus/Neptune

If the Uranus/Neptune aspect is harmonious, it indicates an exalted capacity for inner vision, insight, and illumination, and a keen combination of intellect and emotion. The person may feel exhilarated by romantic emotions, yet he or she is capable of keeping them in proper perspective and doesn't allow them to cloud perceptions of a potential lover. Generally magnetic and attractive, this individual has no problems drawing partners to him or her. However, if the aspect is a stressful one, the person lacks control of romantic feelings, and will often plunge into a passionate love affair without any forethought. There is extreme susceptibility to illusion, nervousness, insecurity, and emotional instability. Romantic relationships are often short-lived, unless other aspects in the chart counteract this effect.

Aspects between Uranus and Neptune are often de-emphasized in synastry because the outer planets move so slowly that all people born within a given time period will have the same Uranus-Neptune aspect in their charts. However, if either planet is angular, or conjunct the Sun, Moon, or Venus, the effects of that planet in chart comparisons is intensified. Positive aspects produce a relationship based on sound spiritual insights; negative aspects will probably mark the relationship with instability and insecurities, and only strong Saturn aspects between the two charts can render this involvement a lasting one.

Pluto/Neptune

For the greater part of this century, Pluto and Neptune have been in sextile aspect. The principle underlying a positive connection between these two planets involves an identification of romance with sex, a high degree of susceptibility to fantasy, and transformation through relationships. The generations born under this aspect generally have embraced these attitudes, as shown by the sexual revolution, the popularity of romantic novels and movies, and increasing expectations from marital commitments.

If either planet—in an individual natal chart or a chart comparison—is conjunct the Sun, Moon, Venus, Ascendant, or MC, the effects listed above will assume greater importance for that individual or the relationship. A close friend of mine has Pluto conjunct the Moon and Ascendant, and Neptune conjunct the Sun; he is known in musical circles for his intensely powerful love songs. Although he has never married, he has had several romantic relationships which have been sources of inspiration and transformation for him.

11

The Fifth and Seventh Houses

Traditionally, romantic involvements in which no commitment is involved are ruled by the fifth house; marriage or relationships with a strong degree of commitment are ruled by the seventh. Sometimes these distinctions are clear to the astrologer, other times they are not. For instance, it is often difficult to discern whether a "living together" arrangement involves a commitment or is merely a convenient domestic extension of a casual affair. There are also occasions when two people choose not to live together, but are just as committed to each other as some who have been married for years.

Although the fifth house is associated with "love given," it is primarily the house of self-expression. It is also one of the first six houses, which traditionally denote the individual. Therefore, even though this house does rule love and love affairs, it is still concerned mainly with the person as an individual. Relationships ruled by the fifth house, while they may be warm and filled with love, are still those entered into for the sake of personal gratification. The individual seeks an involvement with another human being for purposes of personal fulfillment and ego-gratification, to enhance his or her own needs for happiness. While fifth house relationships may grow into the kind of committed partnership represented by the seventh, they do not always. A person who has a concentration of planets in the fifth house and few (or none) in the seventh house probably will not embrace the idea of marriage too eagerly. This type of individual has taken incarnation for the purpose of experiencing less serious romantic relationships, and while he or she may love you devotedly, it is doubtful that your partner loves the idea of being committed.

The seventh house type of relationship, on the other hand, represents a commitment on the part of the two individuals involved, not only to each other, but to society as a whole. The two persons involved in the relationship see themselves as being a unit in a larger whole of society. There is a sense of facing the world together, with a common destiny and a specific socio-cultural goal or "job" to do together for the betterment of the whole to which they belong. In past eras, marriage was often viewed as a business arrangement, for the purpose of uniting two lineages or land-holdings, or for the social or financial advancement of one or more parties to the relationship. Hence, the seventh house is associated both with marital relationships and business partnerships.

At what point in the course of a relationship does the involvement cease to be a fifth house affair and become a seventh house partnership? This issue is debated by astrologers and often is difficult to discern. Does it happen when the two people pledge their troth, or when they move in together, or when the romantic haze fades, or simply when they begin functioning as a couple?

In *The Astrological Houses,* Dane Rudhyar states that one of the keywords for the seventh house is *function,* and that relationships falling into the sphere of the seventh house are those with a particular function—that is, the aforementioned common goals and destiny. He maintains that the values surrounding marriage have changed so much in recent decades that too often, there is no committed socio-cultural purpose for a relationship, that most marriages now are entered solely for the purpose of personal happiness.[1] If this supposition is correct, it would appear that some marital relationships, in spite of wedding ceremonies, children, and years of living together, never actually progress beyond the fifth house stage. Perhaps this lack of function is the reason for the high divorce rate in modern society; it could be that a marriage needs a function above and beyond personal satisfaction in order to weather the ups and downs of life. Rudhyar goes on to say that a marriage for love between two people does not cease to be ruled by the fifth house and progress to the seventh at the marriage ceremony, but rather after the honeymoon is over.[2] However, judging when in the course of a relationship "the honeymoon ends" still poses something of a problem. Suffice it to say that the fifth versus seventh house issue is not a question with a cut-and-dried answer. It varies with the relationship and the individuals involved—and their values and expectations regarding romance and marriage.

The planets in the fifth or seventh house give a good picture of the person's attitudes about the type of relationship ruled by that house, and the life circumstances he or she will face with regard to those relationships. When no planets are posited in the house, look at the ruler of the signs on the house cusps.

As indicated above, if a person has a strong fifth house but a weak seventh, that person is probably romantic and will be more inclined to seek love affairs that are primarily pleasure-oriented, rather than committed partnerships. If, on the other hand, the seventh house is strong but the fifth house is weak, the person's relationships throughout life might be rocky simply because in modern Western society, we expect a lifetime commitment to be preceded by a period of mystical courtship. In my chart, for example, I have Saturn, Mars, and Pluto in the fifth house, and Jupiter and Neptune in the seventh. Therefore, for me, romantic relationships have always been difficult, to say the least. All my "successful" involvements with the opposite sex by-passed the initial romantic phase and proceeded directly into some sort of partnership, disguised, generally, as a religiously-oriented (Jupiter-Neptune) or businessoriented (Jupiter) relationship. However, my potential partners eventually grew restless because of the lack of romantic mystique in our involvement and went looking for it elsewhere—but they still were unwilling to give me up! (Saturn in the fifth).

Planets in the Fifth and Seventh Houses

The Sun

The Sun in the fifth house generally indicates a generous, loving, and charismatic person who has no trouble attracting lovers. These individuals may or may not marry, but if they do, even after marriage they remain attractive (and attracted!) to members of the opposite sex and can be flirtatious. Whether such persons actually follow up on these flirtations depends on other factors in their charts.

If Taurus, Cancer, or Capricorn is prominent in the chart, you can probably depend on your partner's fidelity in spite of his or her attraction to other members of the opposite sex; to these people lasting love (or the illusion of it) is vital. If Leo or Scorpio is prominent in the chart, your partner may be inclined toward sexual infidelity but won't end the involvement with you unless it is inadequate. If Gemini or Sagittarius is prominent, however, your partner is probably fickle by nature, and therefore, unless other factors in your partner's chart overwhelmingly offset this, don't count on a lasting commitment from this person. Simply treat such a friendship as a good time, and Gemini-Sagittarius types with a fifth house Sun can certainly show you a good time.

People with the Sun in the seventh house generally do not function well without a partnership of some kind. Almost all their business arrangements are partnerships; in friendship they usually attach themselves to one person and make that person a part of all facets of their lives. This individual is not happy single, and though he or she may divorce (sometimes frequently), such a person never stays single for very long. In my experience, most seventh-house-Sun people are married or otherwise committed again within a few months of a break-up. Sometimes this type will cling to a destructive relationship out of dependency, while keeping an eye out for a better partner. This person is easy to catch on the rebound; if you are involved with such an individual, you should take care not to exploit his or her vulnerability.

The Moon

The Moon in the fifth house produces a similar overall effect as the Sun, except that in the case of the Moon, an emotional attachment is more evident. The person is less confident in romantic matters than the fifth-house-Sun-type, and, especially if the Moon is afflicted, it sometimes appears that this individual is almost desperate to prove his or her attractiveness—and thus enhance self-esteem—through constant flirtations or other romantic involvements. The individual is not comfortable without a romantic relationship, and may have a tendency to settle for whomever is around during a "lean period," and then move on when someone better appears. If you are involved with such a person, look to see if there are strong Saturn aspects between your charts before expecting a commitment. Without a powerful Saturn connection between you, there is no guarantee that a relationship with this type of person will last.

The person with a seventh-house Moon is the type that pushes for marriage because of an intense emotional need for the security of a partnership. If the Moon is afflicted, this person may seek marriage with anyone who appears romantically interested, often before the other person is ready to consider it. Therefore, this type may be frustrated constantly in romantic situations because he or she scares off potential partners by committing too soon. If you have this aspect in your chart, I would advise learning some self-control; your efforts to obtain emotional security by pushing for a premature commitment will probably prove counterproductive—unless your partner also has a seventh-house Moon! If you are involved with such a person, unless the relationship is inadequate in other ways, do not write this partner off for talking commitment before you are ready. Simply communicate your feelings and ask that he or she be patient with you. This type usually is more patient than it appears.

Mercury

The individual with Mercury in the fifth house generally attracts and is attracted by charm, wit, and intelligence. This person is probably a writer or speaker, and has a way with words. Depending on other aspects in the chart, this person probably is drawn to younger lovers—sometimes much younger. Even if married, he or she still tends to notice attractive young people, but unless other factors in the chart overwhelmingly imply fickleness, the attraction probably will not extend any farther than simple admiration.

If Mercury is in the seventh house, the person either marries young or takes a partner who is much younger. This individual is attracted to partners who are intelligent and articulate, and involvements are primarily intellectual in nature. This type of person generally gets along well with the public and may spread his or her friendship among many. However, this is not something a lover should regard as a threat. If you are involved with such a person, you should realize that your partner simply enjoys exchanging ideas with many different people.

Venus

The person with a fifth-house Venus can outcharm them all. More loving and generous even than the individual with a fifth-house Sun, this individual places a great deal of emphasis on love. He or she has few casual affairs; even if promiscuous by nature, this person usually feels a strong and moving affection for sexual partners, and remembers all of them fondly even long after the involvement is over. This person is probably an artist and sees love affairs as a source of inspiration. Venus in the fifth generally renders a person faithful and loyal to lovers; if you are involved with such a person, unless other factors in the chart suggest otherwise, you can probably count on fidelity. However, if Venus is afflicted, this person can be self-centered where love is concerned. This does not mean that he or she is selfish, rather that this individual often cannot comprehend a partner's point of view.

A person with Venus in the seventh house cannot separate the two ideas of love and marriage. When Venus is afflicted, wealth or social prestige might motivate this person to enter into a commitment; even then, he or she probably still will love the partner devotedly and remain loyal for the most part. As with the seventh-house-Sun-type, this person generally feels insecure without a committed partnership, and almost never remains single or unattached for very long. Such people are generous with partners and more than willing to share all resources. However, if Venus is afflicted, there can be a tendency to give the partner too much. If you are involved with such a person, you should try not to take advantage of your partner's generosity.

Mars

Mars in the fifth house generally indicates an ardent lover, sometimes one who appears to be sexually insatiable. The person directs a great deal of energy into love affairs. Particularly if Mars is afflicted, there can be a great deal of tension in relationships and sometimes such involvements can be quite stormy. This quarrelsomeness does not suggest a lack of love, but rather an abundance of it; the relationship is very important to the fifth-house-Mars individual. Men with this placement claim to like a woman with "spirit," and may like to amuse themselves by getting their partners angry. Women with Mars in the fifth like men who stand out in a crowd; usually part of their drive toward self-aggrandizement is channeled through men whom they believe everyone else finds exciting.

Mars in the seventh house implies marriages that are tempestuous, which is fine if both parties enjoy a good fight once in a while. If Mars is badly afflicted, however, especially by Saturn, the person's happiness in marriage is greatly limited. Yet he or she places much importance on marriage and continues to try to wrest marital happiness even from a destructive relationship. Usually this type of individual is reluctant to take responsibility for an unhappy marriage and prefers to blame the partner. If Mars is afflicted by Uranus, the person will probably be divorced more than once. If Mars is afflicted by Pluto, violence might be involved in the person's marital relationships.

Jupiter

Many of the benefits of a fifth-house Sun or Venus are also apparent when Jupiter is positioned here. However, unless other factors in the chart denote otherwise, the person with Jupiter in the fifth does not have the same attitude toward fidelity as someone with a fifth-house Sun or Venus. This individual probably will have many love affairs and may be capable of juggling several at once. Jovial and good-natured, his or her romantic involvements appear to be superficial, but this person tends to overly-idealize lovers and, if Jupiter is afflicted, can be terribly disillusioned when partners fall off their pedestals. Still, these people enjoy their love affairs immensely, and will probably gain much emotional and psychological benefit from them.

Jupiter in the seventh house obviously suggests several marriages.

People with this planetary placement enjoy the feeling of unity and common purpose that comes with marriage, and whenever one ends, through death, divorce, or separation, they are anxious to renew the marital state simply because they like it so much. Unlike Jupiter-fifth house individuals, these people take their marital vows very seriously and are more likely to embrace fidelity. If Jupiter is afflicted by Saturn, the person will experience blocks in forming marriage relationships, but once established, they generally last. If Jupiter is in stressful aspect to Uranus, the individual will experience many separations and broken relationships. Jupiter afflicted by Neptune indicates very high ideals regarding marriage, a danger of attracting the wrong sort of person, and an unfortunate tendency to sacrifice all for partners, even those who are unworthy.

Saturn

Saturn in the fifth house renders love affairs difficult. Often these people cut themselves off from romance entirely, either through work or family obligations. Or, they tend to be attracted to people who don't reciprocate their feelings, and attract others whom they cannot stand. These individuals are reticent—perhaps too reticent—about expressing romantic feelings; sometimes prospective lovers will approach them, but will be turned off by what appears to be a lack of enthusiasm. If Saturn is afflicted by Neptune, the person may fall desperately in love with someone who does care, but plays "hard to get" until the opportunity for romance has been lost. Often such individuals fear close involvement, probably because their parents didn't show them much love.

If you have this combination in your chart, you need to overcome your fears about expressing your feelings and learn to accept your vulnerability; otherwise you may never experience love and the happiness it can bring. Saturn, however, does not necessarily deny anything. A fifth-house Saturn does not have to block you from romance for your entire life, though it may delay satisfaction through love affairs until you reach maturity.

Likewise, Saturn in the seventh house does not preclude marriage, but may postpone it until late in life. As with Saturn in the fifth, this individual may be attracted to partners who are much older or more mature. If Saturn is well-aspected, he or she can look forward to a firm, strong marriage that will probably last a lifetime. If Saturn is afflicted, the person has much to learn karmically about relationships and marriage, and probably will experience many problems in relating to other people. If you are involved with a person who has an afflicted seventh-house Saturn, you are likely to experience difficulties in your relationship together, especially if Saturn ties in synastrically with your birth chart.

Uranus

Uranus in the fifth house signifies many love affairs which begin suddenly and end suddenly. People with this planetary placement have a tendency to fall in love at first sight, particularly if Venus is involved in any way. There may be a tendency toward unusual relationships, and this individual often is attracted to people of vastly different social or ethnic backgrounds, age, etc. There is also a possibility of homosexual attachments. These individuals are generally quite magnetic, but, unlike the charisma bestowed by the Sun, Venus, or Jupiter in this position, the magnetism of Uranus is not necessarily a positive one. If Uranus is afflicted, these people can project a strange hypnotic power over potential lovers and use that power for their own selfish purposes.

Uranus in the seventh almost always signifies a separation or divorce from a marriage partner at some time in the individual's life. Still, these people often remain attached in a strange way to their former partners, sometimes maintaining a friendship, sometimes reflecting nostalgically on their past loves. If you have Uranus in the seventh house, or if you are involved with someone with this placement, the best possible manifestation of the Uranian energy is to stay open to an unconventional relationship that allows both partners to have plenty of freedom. Dependency, clinginess, and jealousy have no place in this person's relationships, and partners generally are happier if each has a life separate from the partnership as well. In this way, the separating energy imposed by Uranus can serve to enhance rather than destroy the relationship.

Neptune

An individual with Neptune in the fifth is, needless to say, a hopeless romantic. Deep within their psyches, people with this placement carry powerful attachments to the archetypal ideals of perfect romances, like those of legendary lovers Romeo and Juliet, Lancelot and Guinevere, Tristan and Iseult. The problem with these legends is that almost all the relationships portrayed in them ended in tragedy. Especially if Neptune is afflicted, it seems that individuals with a fifth-house Neptune attract relationships where there is a rush of idealized romance and an overwhelming feeling of perfect mystical union at the onset of the affair, but as the relationship escalates, so do the problems. Sometimes these individuals seem to go out of their way to create problems in a relationship that may actually be progressing well; they hold on to a deeply-ingrained idea that perfect love has to be painful.

If you have this placement in your chart, or if you are involved with someone who does (or if there are Neptune afflictions between planets in your chart comparison), one positive way to use this Neptunian energy is to embrace spiritual studies together and channel your need for the perfect attachment into a common relationship between yourselves and God.

Neptune in the seventh house does not have quite the same effect on marriage as a fifth-house Neptune does upon love affairs. In fact, this placement of Neptune may endow the individual with high ideals regarding not only marriage but the function, or socio-cultural purpose, of marital partnerships. Thus, this individual may possess a more powerful commitment to marriage than most people ever consider. If Neptune is well-aspected, the person probably will be rewarded for these ideals through his or her relationships. If Neptune is afflicted, however, the commitment this person seeks will probably prove elusive, or he or she will tend to focus that commitment on the wrong person. Traditionally, Neptune in the seventh is associated with marriage to people who are dependent on the Neptune-person, or who desperately need this individual and whatever he or she has to offer. Sympathy also can play a large part in the relationship.

Pluto

Pluto in the fifth house traditionally is associated with a lover who dies, and in my work too often I find this actually does occur. It does not always happen in the course of the romance; more often than not, a person with a fifth-house Pluto hears about the death of a former lover after the affair has ended. Pluto in the fifth is also associated with self-transformation through love affairs, and, while this certainly does occur when a partner dies, the death of the relationship itself can cause the transformation, too. People with Pluto in the fifth often are forced to confront not only the shortcomings of a lover, but their own shortcomings which are mirrored in the partner. I have had friends and clients with this placement who have emerged from seemingly disastrous love involvements as stronger, surer, and more confident individuals.

Pluto in the fifth generally renders the person a skilled and ardent sexual partner. If Pluto is badly afflicted, however, this planetary placement can incline the person towards violence—which may be directed at loved ones.

Pluto in the seventh house indicates transformation through marital relationships, and it can have the same effect upon marriages as love affairs. This placement also can suggest marriage to a partner who dies. Power struggles are likely in the course of the relationship, and the partnership probably has a strong emphasis on sexual attraction.

Notes

1. Dane Rudhyar, *The Astrological Houses,* (New York: Doubleday, 1972), p. 95ff.
2. Ibid., p. 98.

12

Case Studies:

Romance and Marriage

No two relationships are alike, for each one involves two separate and unique individuals with their own particular needs, desires, and karmic lessons to learn. Undoubtedly, we would all like to read case studies with which we can readily identify, and hopefully each of us can see traces of our own conditions in the three cases I have chosen. The three stories I have selected personify what, in my experience, are the three most common reasons for entering into a romantic relationship: a need for companionship, a passionate attraction, and mutual goals and ambitions. We will examine each of these relationships in light of what has been discussed in earlier chapters.

George and Martha Washington:
A Marriage Based on Friendship

Few Americans think of the Father of Our Country as having had any kind of love life. We think of him as the rather grim-looking face on the dollar bill, or as he is portrayed in famous paintings of him crossing the Delaware, heading the Constitutional Convention, and others. All these representations of our first President are taken from a portrait of him that was painted when he was an old man by artist Gilbert Stuart. This is a shame: Most people who knew George Washington personally, particularly Martha, did not like the Stuart portrait, believing it to be unflattering and not a good likeness.

Actually, George Washington was a handsome and rather dashing country gentleman, witty, intelligent, a gifted conversationalist. He was tall—over six feet, which was unusual for his time—and something of a dandy, enjoying fashionable clothes and the salient appearance they conferred. His early portraits, though not as technically correct artistically as the later Stuart portrait, project Washington's charm much more adequately and give us a better understanding of why he was constantly surrounded by female friends (some who would have loved to have been his mistresses) well into late middle age.

In colonial days, however, there were few women. Although as a young man Washington seems to have had some flings, no woman captured his fancy until, at the age of nineteen, he became acquainted with a new neighbor, George William Fairfax, heir to an old English family and to a peerage. Will, as Washington called him, had married the daughter of an old Virginia family, a woman named Sally. A bright and witty charmer, she immediately ensnared the heart of the young George Washington. He grew to love her as deeply and as passionately as was possible under the circumstances—perhaps more because of the hopelessness of the relationship.

Some historians have speculated that Sally regretted her marriage and was bored with Will Fairfax at the time she met George Washington. Others believe that she was flattered by the young planter's attentions and was simply indulging her flirtatious nature. However, there is no doubt that she did to some degree return young Washington's feelings and encouraged the development of a romantic relationship between them. Her letters to him are coquettish, teasing; there are times when she reveals that she has felt neglected and asks where she has gone wrong. She does not express passionate love or desire, but since she was married, putting such feelings on paper, sincere or not, would have posed a danger. There is also the possibility that Washington saw the danger in such communications and, if there were any, destroyed them.

But George had considerations other than romance. His plantation was growing fast and needed more attention than he himself, with his military career blossoming, could give it. Most of Augustine Washington's fortune had gone to his eldest son by his first marriage and George's mother, Mary, Augustine's second wife, was dependent on her son for support. Understandably, in spite of his feelings for Sally Fairfax, George began to look for a wealthy bride. There are also biographers who maintain that George was desperate for relief from the traumatic entanglement with Sally and saw no way out except marriage to another.

Another neighbor, twenty-seven-year-old Martha Dandridge Custis, whom George had recently met and liked immensely, was recently widowed. Her late husband, Daniel Parke Custis, had left her a fortune. Several portraits of the young Martha Dandridge Custis survive, and, fortunately, the artists who painted them were much more adept at capturing personality than Gilbert Stuart. Martha was blonde and pretty, petite and elegant, with large eyes and wide brows. The lure of both her beauty and money insured that she certainly didn't lack for suitors. But Martha had loved her husband deeply, and had not yet recovered from the shock of his death. Though polite and friendly with the men who came to call, she wasn't interested in rushing into a second marriage, and didn't encourage anyone—that is, until she fell prey to the charms of George Washington.

It is not known how much, if anything, Martha knew about George's feelings for Sally Fairfax. Some biographers believe that she did know; others portray her as having lived her life with George in blissful ignorance. Since George and Martha, in the early years of their marriage, were thrown together constantly with Will and Sally Fairfax, it seems that she would have at least had suspicions of their involvement, though she might have chosen to ignore it. There are also historians who believe that Martha was as haunted by Daniel as George was by Sally, and therefore, she was more understanding than another woman in a similar position might have been. Nonetheless, from the start of their marriage, it appeared that George and Martha were going to have a good relationship. They had a great deal in common and liked and respected each other immensely.

Schoolchildren learn about George Washington's military skills and the fact that he was our first President, but few people learn anything in school about George Washington the man. He was actually quite gifted in many ways; he was a surveyor in his youth, and was admired for his skill in that field. He thought of himself primarily as a planter; he loved that life and constantly sought and invented methods to make the land more productive, while at the same time treating the soil well and making certain it remained fertile for the next planting season.

What is also largely unknown is that George Washington may have been the first active feminist in the Americas. One of his most cherished causes was curbing and doing away with the exploitation of wives and their property by avaricious husbands.

In spite of the fact that the marriage did not begin with romance, passion, and desire, there is no doubt that George did love Martha deeply, and never regretted his marriage to her. He told friends that his marriage was the event that had contributed the most to his happiness. In 1775, when there was talk of his going to Europe, he wrote to Martha from his position on the battle front: "I shall enjoy more real happiness at home with you in one month than I have the most distant promise of finding abroad, if my stay were to be seven times seven years."[1] One wonders about the significance of this line and what it meant to Martha, inasmuch as Will and Sally Fairfax had by this time returned to England so that Will could claim the family estates and the peerage.

In another letter, George wrote to Martha: "I return an unalterable affection for you which neither time nor distance can change."[2] In one of his most famous letters testifying to the success of his marriage, Washington wrote to his step-granddaughter that she should not allow passion to gauge her choice of a marriage partner, inasmuch as the extreme happiness he had enjoyed with Martha had not begun with such an emotion, and yet he would not have traded it for any passion in the world.[3] We also wonder about Martha's feelings for George, since her letters to him are more indicative of an intense friendship than romantic desire.

So what kind of person was Martha, this woman whom our first President so deeply loved? First of all, we should note that most men who knew her saw her as the type of woman a man wanted to protect. Not only was she small and delicate in stature, Martha was a bit nervous and apprehensive, and somewhat mistrustful where her affections were concerned. She was also extremely fearful for those she loved—and this fear was not without foundation, considering the untimely demise of her first husband, the losses of two babies during her marriage to Daniel Custis, and the later premature deaths of her other son and daughter by Daniel.

We have already observed that after Daniel's death she was surrounded by suitors. We know of George Washington's commitment to shielding women and their property from exploitative husbands. Though she possessed strength of character, was economically clever and superbly capable of carrying out the plans of others, Martha was known to be without initiative and was totally ineffectual when it came to practical considerations of any sort. Is it too far-fetched to believe that George saw Martha's many callers as vultures waiting to pounce on an unsuspecting widow, and therefore sought to make certain no one did—even though he himself was much better off financially after he married her?

Although today, Martha Washington's lack of initiative might make her appear less than admirable, in her time this particular characteristic, along with her dedication, her talent for bringing the projects of others to fruition, and willingness to work hard made her a perfect wife. Also, even though we know that Martha, always fearful for those she loved, must have been petrified every time George went off to war, there is no indication of it in any of their letters; such reticence on Martha's part must have taken a great deal of inner strength. Martha was not brilliant, nor was she particularly ambitious, either for herself or for her husband. Her intelligence and imagination were focused on building relationships with others, and whatever ambitions she had were mainly social. However, her social skills were impeccable. She was chatty, friendly, loyal, and possessed beautiful manners; no one is known to have ever regarded her with enmity.

Both Martha and George were hopelessly sociable and loved a house filled with guests. They were always entertaining and regarded the departure of their friends with regret; they considered an unfilled dining room "lonesome" and an empty house "dull."[4] They were both generous and philanthropic, and few whom they knew to be in need remained so.

Their life together, therefore, was quite happy, and it was clear that George appreciated it more than most men. Even though, as we have observed, he was surrounded by female friends throughout his life and could have had his pick of mistresses, there is no indication that he was ever unfaithful to Martha. Their one disappointment was that they had no children; historians have drawn the ironic conclusion that George Washington, the "Father of His Country," was probably sterile. There is no record of his ever having fathered a child, and Martha had borne Daniel Custis four children. Washington was a good stepfather to Martha's surviving son and daughter. All indications are that the relationship between Washington and the Custis children was quite good, but Washington was never to know the joys of having a child of his own.

Unfortunately, there appears to be no recorded birth date for Sally Fairfax; it would have been interesting to study her chart, too, and to try to ascertain what kind of woman had so intrigued the young George Washington. However, when studying the natal charts of George and Martha Washington, one can see why these two individuals would have had an excellent relationship.

The heavy air concentration in both charts demonstrates that both of them valued communication highly, probably above all else. In George's chart, Mercury and the Sun in Aquarius, and Venus in Pisces indicate an idealistic nature. Martha's ninth-house concentration, which includes a Sun-Neptune conjunction, implies that she shared his idealism and was willing to sacrifice to make her ideals a reality.

George Washington's Aquarian concentration demonstrates his potential for being one of the Founding Fathers for a new nation that was based on democracy and human equality. Aries rising and Mars in Scorpio suggest military skills. The Moon in Leo in the fifth house testifies to the charisma and magnetism that enabled him to capture the imagination of the colonists.

It is evident from looking at George's chart that relationships were very important to him and would be a dominant part of his life. The Moon's fifth-house position and the Libran emphasis, which includes the seventh house cusp, are significant. So is the grand air trine between Neptune in brother-oriented Gemini, Pluto in marriage-oriented Libra, and the Sun in friendship-oriented Aquarius. The Moon in Leo and Venus in Pisces indicate that his ideal woman, his anima, was probably a combination of Hera and Mary—a charming, queenly woman, willing to sacrifice her own interests to those of others, particularly her husband's. From

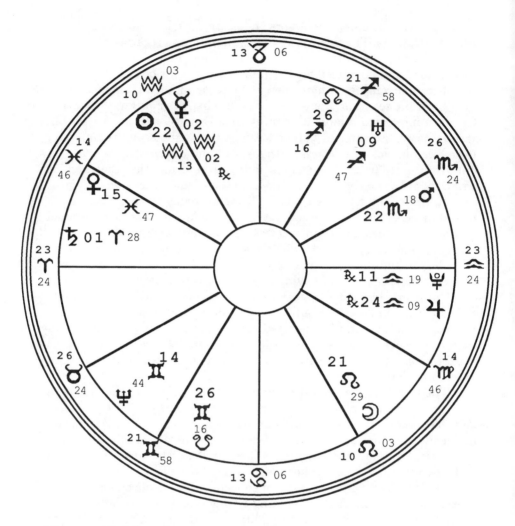

Figure 12.1
George Washington
February 11, 1732 9:42 am
Alexandria, Virginia
Placidus house cusps

our study of Martha's personality, we can see how she, with her charm, prettiness, idealism, and lack of initiative matched this inner woman almost perfectly.

In Martha's chart, the Gemini Sun testifies to her chatty friendliness;

the Libran Moon and Ascendant show her sociability and her need for relationships, particularly marriage. Venus in Taurus indicates a kind and loving disposition that caused her to make many friends and no enemies. The placement of both Sun and Mars in Gemini, conjoining Neptune, implies that her animus, or her ideal man, was Hermes personified, and that she idealized this type of man. Washington, who was exceptionally intelligent (experts have calculated that his I.Q. was at least in the high 120s)[5] as well as mischievous (he enjoyed engaging in land deals that were somewhat shady) was certainly a close match to Martha's ideal.

If we do a synastry comparison of the Washingtons' charts, we can observe that there probably was a very effective energy exchange between them. The two Suns are in an exact trine—the most harmonious blend of two wills and ego drives. Her Moon and Ascendant are in a wide trine to his Sun, and his Moon sextiles her Sun, representing a mutually beneficial exchange between their wills and emotions. Her Moon trines his Mercury and his Moon sextiles her Mercury, symbolizing good communication on both a mental and emotional level. The exact sextile between their two Venuses suggests a deep and powerful love between them. The mutual trines between the two Neptunes and the other air planets implies a certain degree of romance between them, even if it did not manifest early in the relationship. Their sex life must have been intense; her Venus opposes his Mars, her Mars squares his Venus, and his Jupiter conjoins her Pluto. There are also mutual trines between their many air planets and both of their Plutos. The close, out-of-sign conjunction between his Moon and her Jupiter implies an abundance of emotional energy between the two of them. From looking at their individual charts and the synastric connections between them, we can judge that any relationship between these two people would have been a good one.

This is not to say they had no problems. A relationship without stress of some sort becomes boring, and certainly this marriage was anything but boring. When we look at the connections in these two charts, however, we find that the stressful aspects between them were not destructive ones. The square between Martha's Venus and George's Sun indicates that she did not always find it easy to express the love she felt for him. The square between her Mercury and his Saturn shows that there probably were times when he clammed up; perhaps her chattiness got to him, particularly when he was in a dark mood or wanted to be left alone (Saturn in the twelfth). The square between Jupiter in her chart and Uranus in his hints at separations through travel—and, of course, George was constantly going off to war. Even after the war was over, his need to travel frequently between Mount Vernon and Philadelphia separated him from Martha. All things considered, however, if an astrologer studies a relationship and finds stressful aspects no more difficult than these, there will undoubtedly be good news to pass on to the client!

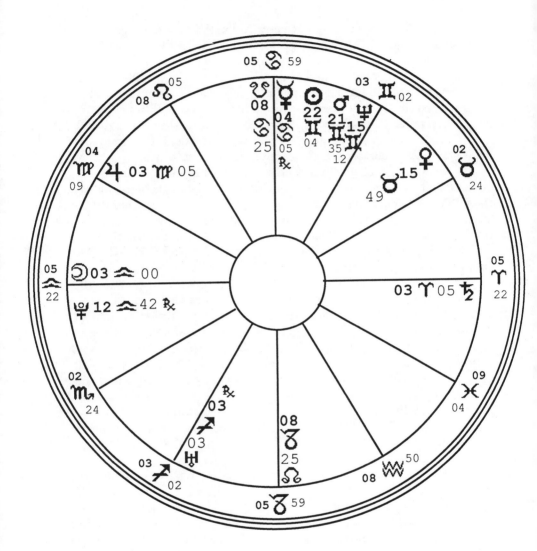

Figure 12.2
Martha Washington
June 13, 1731 1:00 pm
Chestnut Grove, Virginia
Placidus house cusps

These two were friends first. What happens in a relationship based primarily on romantic passion? The following case study is a good example.

Chopin and Sand:
Passion Personified

Composer Frederic Francois Chopin met author George Sand, *née* Aurore Dupin, at a musical review in Paris in the summer of 1837. Chopin, a native of Warsaw, Poland, had been traveling throughout Europe as a pianist, and his genius was acknowledged by many. Though thin and unhealthy-looking, he was nonetheless an attractive young man, with soulful dark eyes and a graceful demeanor, and many beautiful young women followed him from concert to concert, hoping to attract his attention.

However, the young Chopin was a romantic, known all his life for purity of character; his childhood and youth had been marked by a series of highly romantic friendships, some with young girls, some with young men. The musician's idealism barred him from casual dalliance with eager women; though friendly, he kept his distance from all the nineteenth-century groupies who pursued him avidly.

George Sand was as different in character from Chopin as one can imagine. Earthy and outspoken, she had already had several affairs by the time she met the pianist. The kindest description of her appearance is that she was "not a beautiful woman."[6] A more apt description might have been "plain" or even "homely." Swarthy and square-jawed, with a broad, thick nose, George Sand was somewhat heavy-set, and took few pains with her appearance, preferring mannish outfits and unremarkable colors. She also smoked cigars, which Chopin believed to be a disgusting habit and often deplored in his friends and associates.

Nonetheless, Sand possessed a charisma and magnetism that few beautiful women can boast; her energy, intelligence, and brilliant conversational gifts attracted many friends and associates. She was thirty-three when she met Chopin—six years older than he—and far more worldly and down-to-earth than he, with an innate strength of character that the neurotic young artist lacked. She was not musically inclined herself, yet she enjoyed music and liked to attend concerts, both for their cultural and social value.

On that fateful day in July of 1837, when she first met Chopin, she was not only impressed by the young man's talent, but by his waif-like sex appeal as well. She noticed how he politely but firmly rejected the advances of all the young women who flocked to his concerts, and his resistance to them posed a challenge to her. Like the other women at the concert, she wanted him—and she was determined to have him.

Sand had a rather wicked reputation, and was known to "trample on all the social and ethical conventions."[7] Though Chopin was repulsed at first, both by her reputation and her somewhat vulgar habits, he eventually succumbed to Sand's magnetism. Perhaps in spite of her coarseness, perhaps on some level because of it, he developed a passion for her that remained unmatched throughout his life.

Paris has long been a center of cultural superiority, an inspiration to both artists and lovers. But this was the Paris of the Romantic era—an era when medievalism, including its courtly love, was revived and idolized, and summer in Paris, with its myriads of gardens and blossoming trees, was undoubtedly a fertile ground for romance and passion. Chopin and George Sand were as susceptible as any, perhaps more so, because of their high-strung artistic temperaments. They began a relationship that alternated between intense mutual desire and rank incompatibility.

In 1838, during a bout of the illness that had plagued Chopin all his life, the two of them, along with Sand's two children and other members of her household, traveled to Majorca. Chopin's constant bad health plagued not only him, but his lover as well; it was not easy for a woman of her energy and vitality to pander to the moodiness of a neurotic and unhealthy musician. Yet Sand was quite maternal, and her impatience with Chopin's sickliness was often replaced by smothering love and care. Chopin seemed to thrive in the presence of his lady. She was apparently his intellectual superior, and she proved an inspiration for his composing again and again.

They traveled to Nohant, to Genoa, and finally back to Marseilles, and he was constantly writing, writing, writing. Much to Sand's frustration, he was often impatient with his work and destroyed it before she could stop him. She, in turn, wrote about him—her work of the time is marked by thinly-disguised autobiographical inferences to the alternating passion and frustrations in their relationship.

Eventually they returned to Paris, where Chopin was again plagued by ill health. Sand, however, refused to pay homage to her lover's sickly reclusiveness; she was anxious to rejoin her many friends and admirers. Chopin was often jealous. Sand, in her previous relationships, had been known for her infidelity, and there were many men in Paris who admired her and who were stronger and more robust than he. It cannot have been easy for a man of such refinement and delicate sensitivities as Chopin to move in the circles of coarse and outspoken reprobates that Sand enjoyed. Nonetheless, Chopin was ecstatically happy with Sand; he enjoyed the company of her children, and was wildly jealous when she insisted on leaving him to a sickbed while she moved in the social whirl of Paris.

Their relationship at this point became stormier than ever; servants, as well as Sand's two children, bore witness to their violent quarrels and passionate reconciliations. Chopin and Sand loved each other, it seemed, but there was an abysmal gulf between them. He abominated her coarseness; she had no patience with his hypochondria. But there was no doubt about it; they needed each other.

Chopin recovered to some degree; he began giving concerts again, and suddenly he found himself performing for the social elite of Paris. He was much in demand both for concerts and for upper-class *soirées,* and found himself surrounded by admiring countesses and other women of the Paris upper crust. The tide of jealousy turned; Sand suddenly felt threatened, and she again became the loving, maternal figure she had been in Majorca and Nohant.

However, there are indications, in her letters and other works, that she was becoming bored with Chopin and his manic-depressive nature. She grew more and more impatient with his jealousies and insecurities and his dependency on her. Chopin's intense desire for Sand had not waned, though, and he tried to be what he thought she wanted. He joined in her literary evenings and swallowed his revulsion over many of her acquaintances.

It is no surprise that her periods of coolness toward him coincided with a return of his illness. She then became overwhelmed with guilt and returned to being a mother to him. Sand was known to have had other love affairs during her relationship with Chopin; she treated the composer as a child, a toy, a pet, and she was not above dominating or manipulating him through emotional blackmail. He complained, he cried—and she returned to him, contrite and loving, filling his being with her motherly presence. But it could not last; a woman of her intense physicality could never totally respect a man who was constantly taking refuge in an illness.

In 1847, they parted for good. In early 1848, Chopin died, and there were those among their circle of acquaintances and in the musical world who, in mourning the death of their revered genius, blamed Sand for Chopin's death. It is true that after she finally left him, his health deteriorated even more; he seemed to have lost all hope. Is it overly romantic to suggest that this brilliant and gifted musician died of a broken heart?

It is not known whether George Sand felt any responsibility for her former lover's death. After hearing the news, however, she shut herself in her room for days, and servants reported that her eyes were reddened with tears whenever they saw her during that time.

What powers of attraction, what needs within each of them, drew two basically incompatible people into such a powerful attachment? George Sand's chart is highly indicative of the magnetic, strong-willed person which we know her to have been. Uranus squaring her Sun shows her unconventionality; the presence of Pluto in the first house bestows power and magnetism. Venus in Leo attests to her creativity and charisma, and the presence of Mars in Taurus implies the physical strength, stamina, and boundless energy which Chopin lacked. The Cancerian Sun bestows the sensitivity and the maternal nature which more or less bound her to Chopin, and the presence of the Moon in Aries in the first house denotes the self-centered ego which rendered her incapable of understanding the weaknesses of another.

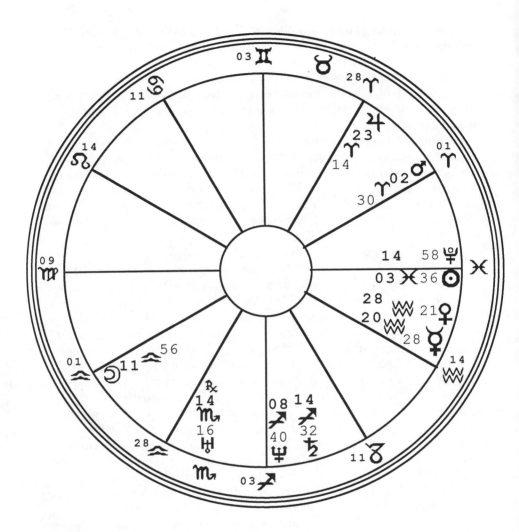

Figure 12.3
Frederic Chopin
February 22, 1810 6:00 pm
Warsaw, Poland
Placidus house cusps

Chopin's chart, on the other hand, with a Virgoan Ascendant and a sixth-house Piscean Sun squared by a Saturn-Neptune conjunction demonstrates that he would probably suffer from ill health much of his life. The Piscean Sun, along with the Libran Moon and Moon-Neptune sextile hints at Chopin's musical talent, and the Virgoan Ascendant testifies to his perfectionism. The presence of Venus in Aquarius suggests that, in spite of the conventionality, high ideals, and dislike for vulgarity imposed by the Virgo-Libra-Pisces concentration, he would tend to be drawn to an unconventional woman like George Sand.

Sand's attraction to Chopin is something of an enigma, however. The presence of Mars in Taurus and the Sun in Cancer imply that she would have been more inclined to seek out Bacchus-Indra types: more specifically, men who were more muscular, sensual, and robust physically than the thin, delicate, neurotic Chopin—and indeed, the other men with whom she allied herself in the course of her life seem to have fit these particular archetypes. However, the Cancerian Sun indicates that the urge towards mothering was an innate need within her—and certainly Chopin needed a mother. Her Arien Moon suggests that she found a challenge in Chopin, who resisted the attentions of all his beautiful young admirers.

Both of them have strong seventh houses, implying that relationships were quite important in their lives; perhaps this is why they stayed together in spite of the conflicts between them. That sex was also an important part of their lives is demonstrated by both charts. George Sand, with Venus in Leo, Mars in Taurus, and a first-house Pluto in Pisces, in mutual reception with Neptune in Scorpio in the eighth house probably had a sex drive unmatched by the refined young ladies of the time. Chopin, though his ill-health and dislike for coarseness probably precluded his being too active sexually, was most likely quite passionate and idealistic where sex was concerned. His eighth house contains sexual Mars and idealistic, enthusiastic Jupiter. In terms of synastry, they probably were quite compatible sexually. Her Venus squares his Uranus and is in a wide trine to his Mars and Neptune; his Venus trines her Uranus and his Pluto trines her Sun.

Both charts indicate an intense need for a partner with whom they can communicate easily. Sand has Mercury in Gemini and Chopin has Mercury in Aquarius. The two Mercurys trine each other, supporting the idea that there was a strong intellectual bond between them and that each found the other a source of intellectual and artistic inspiration. The presence of Chopin's Venus in this configuration suggests that the intellectual bond was more love-inspiring for him than for her—though Sand's Venus in Leo, sextiling her Mercury, and balancing Chopin's Aquarian concentration (which conjoins her Ascendant) is only slightly less indicative of this need for love through intellect. The conjunctions between her Moon and his Jupiter, and his Moon and her Uranus demonstrate not only an attraction, but also good feelings in the relationship.

The differences between them, however, are easily discerned. Her Mars in Taurus opposes his Uranus in Scorpio, suggesting not only an explosiveness between them, but also that her impatience (Mars) with his lack of vitality (Taurus) often gave rise to rebellion (Uranus) against her manipulativeness (Scorpio). The opposition between his Neptune-Saturn conjunction and her Mercury indicates that he tended to over-idealize (Neptune) her intellect (Mercury), and this limited (Saturn) their relationship.

The square between her Sun and his Moon implies an attraction, but at the same time a basic conflict between her will and his emotions. The effect of this square is intensified by the fact that it is her Sun and his Moon; the energies are easier to live with, particularly in a chauvinistic society such as theirs, if the man's Sun and the woman's Moon are involved. The manifestation of this was probably that he saw her masculine traits (supported by the Aries Moon)—adopting a masculine name, wearing mannish clothes, smoking cigars—as emasculating to him. The very rebelliousness which had caused her to make a success of herself in spite of the prevailing prejudices against women may have caused her to use this attitude of his to needle him. His Piscean Sun and Virgoan Ascendant undoubtedly undermined his self-esteem to begin with, so this tendency on the part of his lover did not help the situation.

The exact opposition between her Pluto and his Ascendant demonstrates that the power plays which she enjoyed so much affected his self-image in a negative way. The opposition between their two Venuses, though attesting to a strong love between them, also indicates a lack of security in expressing that love and a separation between the two love-energies as well.

Although ideally, the synastric energies could have been channeled positively, realistically it seems that in the beginning there was little hope for this relationship. The Mars-Uranus opposition, for example, could have been channeled into seeking excitement outside their relationship, thus avoiding the need to create excitement by quarreling. However, considering their basic character differences, this would have been quite difficult. The Pluto-Ascendant opposition indicates that Chopin could have drawn upon her power and made it a part of his being, but again, his self-effacement, as suggested by the Virgo-Pisces concentration, probably would have made it hard, especially since he had to deal with her Moon-in-Aries ego. The Sun-Moon square probably would have been easier to handle than the previously-discussed oppositions; however, in view of their basic natures, it seems unlikely that they could have done so.

Though Sand and Chopin obviously felt a powerful mutual love and passion for each other, these feelings often fade in the presence of intense conflict. That this relationship lasted as long as it did is probably owing to the strength of the two Mercurys; communication and mutual interests, particularly among intelligent people, are vital to the strength of the relationship.

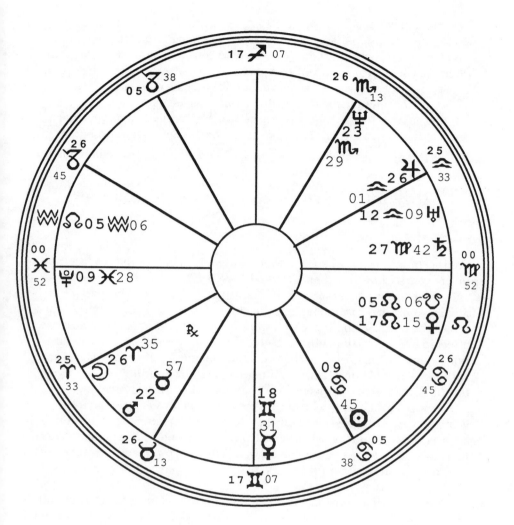

Figure 12.4
George Sand
July 1, 1804 10:20 pm
Paris, France
Placidus house cusps

Strangely enough, abrasive Saturnian aspects are conspicuously absent from the comparison between the two charts—and this is unusual when you consider a chart comparison between two people who are as different as these two. However, it is also Saturn aspects that bind a couple together. Uranus, however, separates, and this chart comparison is loaded with both harmonious and stressful Uranian aspects.

Perhaps in future lifetimes, these two entities will come together to resolve their karma when they have natal charts that do not present them with so many differences.

Roy and Kathy's Repeat Performance

Southern California, where I practice, has an exorbitant divorce rate, and in the years I have lived and worked here, I have found it interesting—and frustrating—to observe how Neptunian ideals for the perfect romance so strongly influence relationships. Hollywood continually reinforces the fantasy, and those who work in the entertainment business are affected even more than others. I have seen people reject potentially satisfying relationships because there was no "magic," and others who stuck with unbelievably destructive entanglements because they couldn't give up the fantasies and expectations they had of their relationships.

Few couples I knew when I first moved to the Los Angeles area eleven years ago are still together, and therefore it is refreshing to know a pair such as Kathy and Roy, whose charts are studied here. Throughout their marriage, they have been involved with the entertainment industry, yet they have been together for twenty-five years and are as much in love now as they when they first met.

Roy is a former rock musician, now an up-and-coming film writer and director; one of his films even won an Oscar. As a small boy, Roy knew that he was different from the other children around him. He was singing, making up detailed stories, and composing little tunes before he was even in kindergarten, but he also was aware that he had a certain power over the material world. He could break up cloud formations by concentrating on them; he could raise the wind and communicate with animals telepathically. When he discovered that other children could not do these things, he felt strange, and began keeping his powers a secret, though he often exercised them in private.

As a high school student he began playing the guitar with a rock-and-roll band, and after graduation he worked as a full-time entertainer. When he met Kathy, she was a college student, a country girl from Virginia. Intelligent and somewhat shy, Kathy had an affinity with nature—perhaps a legacy of many great-grandmothers who were knowledgeable in the herbal arts of the ancients.

Because of a mutual interest in the tenets of the Old Religion, Roy and Kathy found a common bond which few of their contemporaries shared. Roy had visions of making the knowledge of the ancients available to modern Westerners through the media of film and music; Kathy shared his desire, and they formed a partnership with that goal in mind.

After two years of being a rock musician, Roy was becoming restless; nightclubs and concerts no longer seemed an adequate channel for what he regarded as his true profession. He and Kathy, newly married, decided to move to Los Angeles where greater opportunities seemed likely.

Los Angeles was something of a shock to them. In a town made up of hopeless dreamers and hardened skeptics, it sometimes seems impossible to survive working as an entertainer and/or writer. Sacrifices had to be made if Roy and Kathy's dream was to be realized, and together they decided it was worth it.

Roy, a naturally assertive person with an unquestioned belief in his own talent, found "making it" a bit easier than most. He worked as an actor, musician, and writer, and then began directing television commercials and music videos. His goal still was to make feature films with metaphysical themes, and Roy wrote several highly-evolved movie scripts with carefully clothed occult messages, but although they were praised they never were produced.

While Roy struggled to gain respect in the film industry and get backing for his metaphysical films, Kathy worked at a local college and offered her continual support to their mutual goal. In part, Kathy's dedication to their initial vision and her unflagging patience have made their marriage a success. For twenty-five years, Kathy has believed in Roy and his talents; Roy has not forgotten that Kathy provided financial grounding as well as emotional support. Together they have created a framework of mutual respect, support, and dedication—and they present a united front to all who know them. Because of their metaphysical orientation, they believe that their relationship has its origins in previous incarnations, and that this one is only a repeat performance, perhaps the culmination of all the involvements that have come before.

Studying their two charts, it is easy to see why they were initially attracted to each other. One of the most powerful attractions in synastry is a Sun-Ascendant connection, because the Sun-person sees his or her will and ego drive (Sun) reflected in the physical body and personality (Ascendant) of the other. In Roy and Kathy's case, Roy's Sun and Kathy's Ascendant are both in Leo; Kathy's Sun and Roy's Ascendant are in Cancer.

Roy's Leo Sun in the second house, conjoining Pluto and Venus, indicates a person with high self-esteem and a great deal of personal magne-

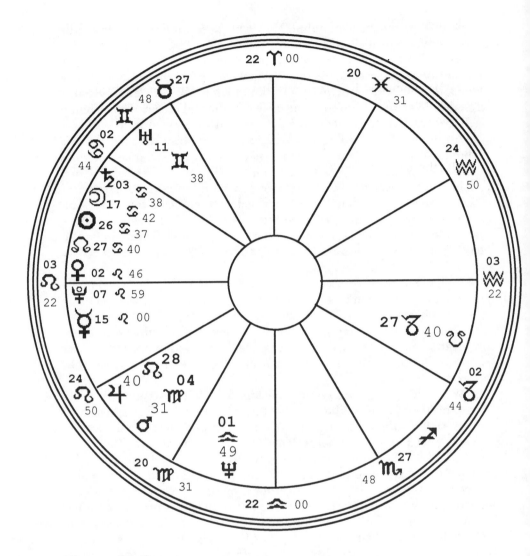

Figure 12.5
Kathy
July 19, 1944 7:00 am
Saltville, Virginia
Placidus house cusps

tism, who enjoys being in the forefront of activity. His Capricorn Moon contributes ambition and a desire for achievement. The trine between the Moon and the Jupiter-Mercury-Mars conjunction in Virgo bestows the tremendous amount of energy—physical and mental—needed to attain goals such as Roy's. The opposition between the Moon and the Saturn-Ascendant conjunction possibly postpones attainment of his goals until maturity.

The Moon in the seventh house implies that a great deal of emotional energy is channeled into relationships, and the trine to Jupiter hints at satisfaction through them. The Cancerian Ascendant denotes a strong attraction to the mother and a desire to seek a motherly, nurturing partner. Venus in Leo and the Moon in Capricorn suggest a Hera-Diana-type anima.

Kathy, with her combination of Cancer and Leo, appears to personify Roy's anima. As a double Cancer, Kathy certainly possesses the maternal warmth that Roy subconsciously sought in a marriage partner. The Cancer factors, including Saturn, in the twelfth house indicate that the shyness of Cancer is intensified by Saturnian reserve and the retiring, introspective nature of the twelfth house.

While Kathy certainly lacks the coldness associated with pure Diana-types, she does possess the reserve. At times, however, Kathy's Leo side, that part of her that is Hera, comes to the forefront. Her eyes sparkle, her dimples flash, her intelligence and sense of humor suddenly make themselves known—and here is the queen of the gods, charming everyone in her presence. Two other sides of these goddesses also manifest themselves in Kathy. In many ways, Kathy, like Hera, lives her life for love—working so Roy can pursue his career and using the power of her imagination to give him what support he needs. However, part of her is like Diana, who needed no man. Kathy is independent enough to have tripled her salary in the twelve years she has held her job and is invaluable to her supervisors and coworkers.

With the Sun, Moon, and Saturn in Cancer in the twelfth house, it is no surprise that Kathy has not been involved in a highly romantic marriage that quickly led to divorce, as is true of so many in Hollywood. This usually is the result of envy and ego-clashes between the partners; each is afraid the other will shine brighter. Kathy obviously prefers to remain behind the scenes, and is comfortable using her intelligence and imagination to aid Roy, rather than trying to outdo him. Roy, on the other hand, with such a strong Leo influence in his chart, obviously prefers to be in the limelight.

Kathy's animus, as illustrated by the presence of the Sun in Cancer and Mars in Virgo, appears to be an Indra-Vulcan combination. The presence of Saturn in Cancer indicates a desire for a father figure who is basically a homey type, perhaps warmer and more nurturing than fathers generally tend to be. If we can recall Indra, the warm-hearted, good-natured, home-oriented god of the land, we can see how Roy to some degree fits that picture.

Unless he is out indulging his Leonine creative urge, Roy prefers to

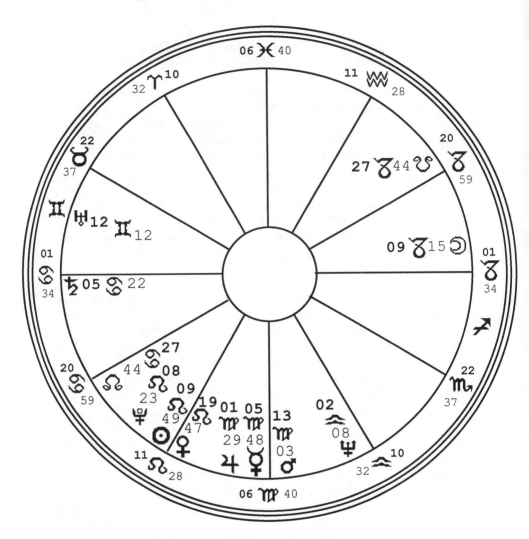

Figure 12.6
Roy
August 2, 1944 2:35 am
Boston, Massachusetts
Placidus house cusps

remain at home, and has a complete office and studio set up in his house.
His favorite hobby is gardening. We can certainly see traces of Vulcan
in Roy: He is indeed a master craftsman, fine-tuning his work—his music,
movie scripts, and garden—until it is perfect. Roy also demonstrates the

family-oriented tendencies inherent in Cancer; he is loyal to his family and rarely makes a decision without first considering how it will affect Kathy and their daughter.

In terms of synastry, we do not see in the charts of Roy and Kathy the combination which so many astrologers consider vital to a successful marital relationship: the Sun-Moon combination. Roy's Moon is in a wide opposition to Kathy's Sun, but, perhaps because of the wide orb, this seems to have little effect on their marriage. Their wills and emotions, represented by the Sun and Moon, most of the time seem to be in harmony. In my experience, the Sun-Ascendant combination can be as powerful and binding as Sun-Moon aspects, and in this relationship it is a double connection, therefore twice as strong.

The Mercury-Mercury link, often considered to be so important, is lacking as well. However, the conjunction between Mercury in Kathy's chart and the Sun and Venus in Roy's, as well as the conjunction between Mercury in Roy's chart and Mars in Kathy's, would appear to compensate for the lack of a tangible link between their Mercurys. Indeed, there is an abundance of communication between these two individuals. The Venus-Mars link, usually regarded as most important for sexual compatibility, is also conspicuously absent here. However, the fact that both of them have Venus-Pluto conjunctions in Leo, with this conjunction right on Kathy's Ascendant and Roy's Sun, suggests that both have strong sex drives and that there is a great deal of passion between them. The Cancerian feature in both charts implies strong emotions, although Roy's Capricorn Moon tempers that somewhat. The easy sextiles between the two Neptunes and the Leonine factor in both charts are offset somewhat by the squares between Neptune, and the cardinal influences. There is just enough idealism in the relationship to keep the romance alive, but not so much that there is a danger of disillusionment, as is the case with so many couples with Neptunian connections.

Of course, there are some problems in this relationship. Kathy's twelfth house-Cancer tendency toward non-communication used to cause Roy some anxiety. Roy's Leonine love of the limelight sometimes embarrasses Kathy. The Mars-Uranus squares, natally and synastrically, show a tendency toward violent differences of opinion—though both charts indicate a reluctance to express such disagreements, which could result in suppressed anger and eventual explosions. However, these differences can be worked out.

At the time of this writing, it seems that Roy and Kathy's dreams will soon be realized, and they are looking forward to living the life they always wanted. Their mutual respect for each other and their shared goals have enhanced and enriched their love.

Notes

1. Blair Niles, *Martha's Husband: An Informal Portrait of George Washington*, (New York: McGraw-Hill, 1951), p. 49.

2. Ibid., p. 50.

3. James Thomas Flexner, *Washington: The Indispensible Man*, (New York: Little, Brown, 1971), p. 39.

4. Niles, p. 67.

5. David Wallechinsky, Irving Wallace and Amy Wallace, *The Book of Lists*, (NY: William Morrow, 1977), p. 5. Quoted from Catherine Morris Cox, *Genetic Studies of Geniuses*, Vol. II, (Stanford, CA: Stanford University Press, 1926).

6. James Huneker, *Chopin: The Man and His Music*, (New York: Dover, 1960), p. 33.

7. Ibid., p. 29.

Part Four

Friendship

13

Gotta Have Friends

Most complex of all relationships is friendship, the only relationship that must maintain a precarious balance of intimacy and distance. Parents and lovers, by the very nature of their closeness to us, expect to be able to share in our most private thoughts (making us sometimes feel guilty if we don't always want to open ourselves totally to them). Good friends, however, care about our feelings and are interested enough to listen, but are also willing to back away and allow us our privacy if that is what we desire. A friend, unlike a parent or lover, should not be too demanding or possessive. A friend is willing to help whenever we need it, but is not obligated to do so. Good friends, it seems, are much more precious than we usually acknowledge.

Friends are not part of our lives due to any bond of blood or romantic passion, but because they choose to be. They see us as individuals who contribute in a positive way to their lives. Friends appreciate us for qualities which they value in others, but don't often find.

It is perhaps for this reason that the most successful romantic relationships are those that begin with friendship instead of a powerful sexual attraction. Passion has a way of fading with familiarity, but the qualities which give rise to a successful friendship can last forever. Unfortunately in our society, friendship is taken for granted too often. As we go about our usual tasks, immersed in our daily routine, we tend to grow too accustomed to the familiar faces we see every day. Our friends become associated with our routines, and sometimes we may find them as annoying as the routines themselves. And yet, when our lives are either very joyous or unbearably unhappy, we often discover that being surrounded by people who care for us is invaluable—and then we realize how important our friends are.

To be sure, friendships have not been immortalized in folklore and literature to the same extent as romances. In Western society, the romantic dyad is the basic unit, and there has been little celebration of other relationships, including friendship. However, we do hear of a few famous friendships, such as the inspiring Biblical friendship between David and Jonathan.

Jonathan was a prince of Israel, the son of the famed warrior-king, Saul. Saul was an ambitious, self-serving man who did not always follow the dictates of the Scriptures or of the prophets who enforced those dictates, particularly the stern and fearsome Samuel. When Samuel denounced Saul for serving his own interests above those of the Lord, the prophet decreed that soon Saul and his progeny would not longer occupy the throne of Israel.

Samuel set out, supposedly with the Lord's guidance, to locate a new king. He found his candidate in the humble cottage of a poor shepherd named Jesse: the shepherd's youngest son, an etherically beautiful, red-haired boy named David, who spent most of his time in the fields playing the harp and composing psalms to the Lord of Israel. After joining Saul's entourage, David proved himself a warrior as well as a singer when he slew the giant Goliath, champion of Israel's most bitter enemy, the Philistines. David then went on to become Saul's commander-in-chief.

The bond between David and Jonathan was forged almost upon their first meeting, and they cemented their friendship with exchanges of gifts and vows. Jonathan proved himself David's devoted friend and ally many times in the following years. Saul apparently became mentally unhinged. The people liked David immensely, and at times seemed to revere the young man more than Saul. Therefore, the king imagined that David was his enemy. Many times Saul, in fits of paranoia, either openly tried to kill David himself or plotted to have him assassinated. And every time, Jonathan was there to take the side of his rather bewildered friend over that of his jealousy-crazed father.

Several times Jonathan tried to reason with his father: David had done nothing wrong, David was Saul's most skilled general, David had raised Israel to a heretofore unimagined greatness. Sometimes Jonathan's logic succeeded temporarily, and sometimes it did not. On those occasions, Jonathan warned his friend, helped him to hide, risked his own life to aid David in his escape. In the end, David and his armies were forced to leave Israel and take refuge in Judah, where David's military prowess eventually raised him to the position of king.

David did not forget Jonathan. At their last meeting, the two had sworn undying friendship and loyalty between their two houses forever.

When the Philistines again attacked Israel and Jonathan was killed, David spent days fasting and mourning for his friend, and composed an elegy for Saul and Jonathan, which is preserved in the Bible to this day.[1]

More recently, another inspiring friendship was brought before the eyes of the public in a critically-acclaimed book and an Oscar-winning motion picture. Playwright Lillian Hellman met Julia when they were children. The only daughter of a wealthy family, Julia exhibited radical political viewpoints while still a young girl. She and Lillian once formed a "spy-watching ring" in their New York City neighborhood, supposedly to discover German spies. They suspected everyone who carried a briefcase or violin case, and once, to the embarrassment of their families, they turned an innocent music teacher in to the police.

Over the years, they spent nearly every weekend together at the home of Julia's grandparents and went on vacations together. Never before had Lillian met anyone as brilliant as Julia. Still, Julia's radical inclinations often flabbergasted Lillian. Once when Julia's grandparents took her abroad, she returned, not with glowing accounts of the beauties of Europe, but with pictures of slum areas and blind children begging in the streets.

Although the two young women remained close through letters, Lillian rarely saw Julia after the two of them reached adulthood. Lillian pursued a successful career as a playwright. Julia moved to Vienna to study medicine, eccentrically choosing to live in a slum area and use her considerable wealth to benefit the poor around her. However, Lillian's love for her fascinating friend never diminished, and she made efforts to visit Julia whenever she was in Europe.

In 1934, Lillian travelled to Vienna, only to find that Julia had been gravely wounded in a Nazi attack on the ghetto in which she lived. Lillian visited her friend in the hospital and tried to help restore Julia's shattered life, but to no avail. Months later, Lillian finally heard from Julia, and her relief was boundless.

Several years later, in 1937, when Lillian was visiting friends in Paris, she wrote to Julia again. Julia replied that she needed her friend's help. Discreet inquiries hinted that Julia was involved in an anti-Hitler movement. Julia wanted Lillian to smuggle $50,000 across German lines to help Jews, Catholics, and other Nazi-persecuted people to escape war-torn Europe and seek relative safety in other parts of the world. Somewhat reluctantly, Lillian complied, and at journey's end found her friend waiting for her in the railroad station. They had a somewhat tearful reunion, but it was of necessity brief. After promising to join her friend in New York soon, Julia again disappeared, and Lillian never saw her alive again.

The following year Julia was murdered by the Nazis—and Lillian was the only person close to Julia who cared enough to claim the body. She later determined that the story of her friend's self-sacrifice would be told, although Ms. Hellman stubbornly kept Julia's true identity a secret.[2]

Not all friendships are as involved as these. There are, to be sure, different levels of friendship. We all have our casual acquaintances—people we know from work, church, the neighborhood, friends of the family, and people we may like but with whom we don't have enough in common to develop an individual relationship. We have our "drinking buddies"—people with whom we share certain interests and enjoy seeing socially, but with whom we never seem to become close friends. There are special interest friends, whom we cultivate because of shared interests, such as art, tennis, or astrology; "convenience friends," with whom we form relationships simply because they live next door or because they are already acquainted with someone else we know; business friends, whom we know through work or other business contacts; transient friends, such as those whom we meet while on vacation; and crisis friends, such as those whom we meet through groups like Alcoholics Anonymous or natural childbirth classes, or because both of us were going through divorces or other painful transitions at the same time. All of these types of friendship can lead to more intimate relationships, but most of the time they do not. We enjoy these people and remember them fondly in later years, but these relationships rarely survive if one party moves away and the bond that formed the friendship no longer exists.

As a matter of fact, urban sprawl often interferes with the development of such friendships. We meet friends at work or through clubs or associations and often grow to care a great deal for them. But we may live many miles from them, and if the regular contact is broken, our busy lives and the physical distance separating us often make it hard to continue the friendship, except perhaps for occasional telephone calls. Americans, in particular, seem to form friendships easily and shed them just as easily, perhaps because the country itself is so big, our cities so vast, and our lives so crammed with activity that it is virtually impossible to stay in touch with everyone we grow to like and even love.

However, even busy Americans leading mobile lives full of constant transitions seem to value their intimate friendships. It is rare that we meet someone with whom we always feel totally and completely at ease, whom we can always trust to be there when we need them, and with whom we feel free to share all our thoughts and feelings. These intimate friendships can be so valuable, so supportive, and so absolutely necessary to our lives that a strange symbiosis can grow between us and our intimate friends. The intense emotions involved can sometimes rival sexual passion. Jonathan's feelings for David, for example, must have been quite compelling if Jonathan was willing to defy his father for the sake of his friend, especially in a culture where the father-son relationship was considered sacred. In *Pentimento* Lillian Hellman writes that her love for Julia extended far beyond "the mere passion of one girl for another."[3]

Both sexes value close friendship. No matter how much love there is between us and our romantic partners, we all need the understanding and companionship of members of our own sex. Men and women, however, do seem to embrace different attitudes toward friendship and form markedly dissimilar types of bonds with their same-sex friends. I recall once reading of a survey in which the men interviewed stated that they loved their spouses best, their closest friends of the same sex next, and their parents and siblings third. Women, on the other hand, claimed to love their spouses and their best friends of the same sex equally, with parents and siblings coming next.

Men's attitudes towards friendship appear to be based on the idea of facing the world together and fighting their mutual battles, as would comrades-in-arms. (Indeed, some of the strongest bonds between men have been forged while they were at war.) Men appear to value the externals of a friendship more: the camaraderie, the "nights out with the boys," and mutual interests in sports, politics, etc. To women, being able to trust someone enough to feel free to share their most private thoughts and fears is important, and they may form almost mystic spiritual unions with other women. It is apparently more necessary for women to be able to share confidences than to be constantly involved in mutually-enjoyed activities.

However, for both men and women, the most significant elements of a friendship are respect and trust. It is important for members of both sexes to feel that their intimate friends will always stand by them, through the best and worst of times, and that their friends will take up their causes and look out for their interests. We like to think that while friends may privately disagree with our viewpoints and may even criticize our attitudes or behavior, to the world they will defend us, even though they may admit they don't always agree with our opinions.

When a friendship progresses to the point of intimacy, it is usually a betrayal of respect or trust that brings it to an end. The famous friendship between the poets Lord Byron and Percy Bysshe Shelley virtually ended after eight years, when Byron's heavy drinking brought out his rudeness and arrogance, and he continuously failed to show Shelley the same respect and admiration which he had given for so many years, insulting Shelley in the presence of others and behind his back.

Friendships between women often end when both of them begin to love the same man. No matter what the facts of the situation, the one who is left behind sees the other's behavior as a betrayal of trust, and the friendship always suffers, if it doesn't actually end. (Strangely enough, men don't always see this type of situation as a betrayal. They are undoubtedly hurt by such an occurrence, but they tend to take an attitude of "may the best man win.")

Still another painful situation may arise in a friendship when one of the parties marries or becomes romantically involved with someone whom the other friend doesn't like. The two friends may work hard at trying to remedy the impasse, but too many times the friend and the spouse simply cannot resolve their differences. Since we do have a way of identifying totally with our romantic partners, the friend who has married sees the other's dislike of the partner as a betrayal, a rejection—and the friendship cools or ends.

We can lose friends through moving away, leaving a job, or, at worst, through a betrayal of trust, and in the course of our lives, we will probably encounter many unhappy situations which will lead to the loss of a friend. For this reason, we do not need to lose friends through petty misunderstandings that may arise because of minor personality quirks, or because of different attitudes or reactions to events. Astrology can give us deeper insights into the characters of our friends and help us to come to terms with the differences between us and them. Astrology can reveal the basic needs and desires of our friends, how we can fulfill those needs and desires, and how those friends can and cannot contribute to our lives.

The Aries Friend

If Aries is strong in your chart, your friends undoubtedly find you exciting and dynamic. Your charm appeals to strangers and attracts them to you. You are full of new and progressive ideas, and if other factors in the chart support it, you have a talent for winning others to your way of thinking and selling them on your ideas.

However, you have trouble empathizing with others, and often may feel astounded when your friends disagree with you or have needs and desires that are diametrically opposed to yours. Aries is the "I Am" sign of the zodiac, and people who have a strong Arien influence in their charts—the Sun, Moon, Ascendant, or a concentration of planets—have a tendency to believe that the world revolves around them, for they have not yet progressed beyond the self-focused vision of the young child. They are not meant to do so; one purpose of their current incarnations is to come to terms with their value as individuals. Therefore, it is not only inevitable, but desirable that their main focus of consciousness is the human self (as opposed to the Divine Self).

The negative side of this trait, however, is that Ariens see others primarily as extensions of themselves and have a difficult time understanding others. Also, Ariens have a way of blaming themselves for events and situations which actually have nothing to do with them, and therefore, they may torture themselves with undue guilt. If you are an Arien, you need to make special efforts to understand and acknowledge the feelings and desires of your friends—even if they disagree with you.

If you have an Aries-Libra karmic pattern in your chart, you often swing between extreme selfishness and total immersion in your relationships, sometimes to the point of allowing yourself to be victimized. By recognizing this, you may be able to find a comfortable midpoint between the two behavioral extremes.

If you have an Aries friend, try to be patient and give the Arien enough space to be self-centered; this may not be easy. It involves giving in more often than you would to your other friends, and also taking the time to convince the Arien of the validity of your own feelings. If the comparison between your birth chart and that of your Aries friend reveals compatibility, you'll find his or her enthusiasm, energy, and leadership abilities can be invaluable and inspiring.

The Taurus Friend

It is difficult to imagine a more loyal, steadfast, and devoted friend than the Taurean. If Taurus is prominent in your birth chart, you have a deep reserve of patience, and will often put up with behavior that would cause other people to end a friendship. You keep plodding along, nurturing the relationship, and sharing your seemingly endless supply of affection when others would have been long gone.

You need to ask yourself, however, are you maintaining the relationship because of love and devotion, and because it actively contributes to your life? Because of stubbornness? Or, do you lack the gumption to stand up for yourself? Often Taureans will devote themselves to individuals who aren't worthy of their friendship simply because they feel comfortable with a known quantity and are too lazy to go out and explore new friendships.

If you have a Taurus-Scorpio karmic pattern in your chart, you may have a lesson to learn about attachment and letting go. Taurus has a tendency to become overattached to things and people; Scorpio rules death and regeneration. Therefore, people with Taurus-Scorpio patterns often find themselves in positions where they are forced to let go of relationships to which they have become very attached. This can bring about emotional agony, yet it is an experience the person has to go through in order to learn the true meaning of non-attachment. The devotion inherent in Taurus can be wonderful, but when carried to extremes it can lead to intense pain.

If you have a Taurean friend, you undoubtedly appreciate the love and loyalty offered to you, but you have to watch a tendency to take advantage of the Taurean steadfastness. You assume that your friend will always be there and may show him or her less consideration than you would others whose friendship is less constant. You also might have to grin and bear it when you see others taking advantage of your Taurean friend. Remember, the lesson of attachment and letting go is one which all Taureans are here on Earth to learn.

The Gemini Friend

Geminis often drive their friends nuts with constant, abrupt changes in moods, opinions, and intentions. If you have a Gemini friend, you need to relax and give your friend space, for changeability is inherent in this sign, and unless other factors in the chart provide some balance, your friend probably will be this way forever. The Gemini friend is quick, curious, and clever, an intriguing conversationalist, and quite good at all forms of communication.

Gemini friends can be too intellectually oriented, and unless Taurus, Cancer, Scorpio, or Pisces factors are present in the chart, the Geminian won't experience the deep emotions we usually expect of those with whom we are closely involved. These people are not meant to do so; at least in part, the Geminian is here to explore all aspects of intellect and to learn to use the mind to its maximum potential. The Geminian can be quite generous with knowledge and intellectual gifts, and those of us with Geminian friends often find them valuable sources of insight and information.

If you are a Gemini, and if you have no fixed signs prominent in your chart to balance your flexible nature, you probably don't even realize how changeable you are. You need to acknowledge your mood swings and try to reach a balance between the extremes.

If you have a Gemini-Sagittarius karmic pattern in your chart, you may often find yourself alternating between idealizing your friends (Sagittarius) and intellectualizing your relationships and the problems connected with them. You need to reach a balance between these two tendencies.

It defies all logic, but surprisingly enough, two Geminis often have a remarkable level of compatibility and can develop a rewarding relationship. One of my most famous celebrity quotations comes from Gemini Bob Hope, whose wife is also a Gemini. When asked how he could have possibly remained married to another Gemini for all these years, the comedian quipped, "All four of us get along very well."

The Cancer Friend

If you have Cancer strongly figuring in your chart, and especially if you are a woman, you need to take care to maintain some distance in your friendships. Cancerians have no difficulty developing intimacy, and they can be wonderful friends when times are tough. Their nurturing nature causes them to enjoy doing things for other people and they never seem to grow tired of giving their friends physical and emotional support.

However, since the very nature of friendship implies the proper balance of intimacy and distance, the Cancerian needs to watch a tendency to smother friends with too much nurturing and emotion. If you are a Cancerian, you also need to curb your possessiveness, and not expect your friends to give you as much support as you give them. Others are not always as devoted and giving as you, and you need to realize this before forming a friendship with someone, since you might not get the same in return. This tendency is much stronger in women than in men; however, it exists in both sexes.

If you have a Cancer friend, you need to know that often a Cancerian will seemingly give of himself or herself unconditionally. Suddenly, however, your friend will expect you to return these favors in kind—often under conditions which you are unwilling to accept. The Cancer friend can seem like your mother, and you may wish to take the line of least resistance with him or her. However, before you do this, you need to either accept that the Cancerian will eventually want to be mothered by you, or be brave enough to tell your friend that you may not be able to return the favor.

The loving and nurturing Cancer friend often can seem to be a haven in a hostile world, and he or she will be a friend for life.

The Leo Friend

If Leo is prominent in your chart, you find it easy to attract friends. You bestow your energy and friendliness upon all you meet, and are generous and giving. Unlike the Cancer friend, though, you don't always care if favors are returned or not; you genuinely enjoy giving whatever you can. You exhibit interest in your friends, their projects, and their problems, although your interest in things that don't directly concern you is rather superficial.

Your friends respond to your loving and generous nature, and respect you for your talents. You provide an image they can look up to and admire. And you certainly enjoy their admiration!

Unlike Taurus, Cancer, and Pisces, however, the Leo is not easily used or taken advantage of. Your generosity only can be pushed so far, and after that, it stops. The Leo individual is not easy prey for fourflushers and freeloaders; such people are likely to find themselves out in the cold—unworthy subjects exiled by their king!

Leo is the sign of the king, and the Leo friend often feels comfortable and secure in that position. Your friends look up to you and you enjoy providing the leadership they appear to want. However, a king is not a king without his subjects, and the Leo person does not function well alone. If Leo is pronounced in your chart, you probably need to watch a tendency to behave like a monarch: arrogant and overbearing. Leo people can go to pieces when their circle of admirers suddenly disburses; without followers, the Leo feels lost and betrayed. If you are a Leo, you may need to develop more independence so that you do not feel lost without your friends and associates.

If there is a strong Leo-Aquarius pattern in your chart, you may find that you are often torn between concentrating on the love and attention you give to your immediate circle of friends (Leo) and your love for humankind in general (Aquarius). As a result, you may spread yourself too thin trying to serve everyone. Your friends can provide you with the emotional support and encouragement you so desperately need.

The Virgo Friend

Serving others comes naturally to you and you enjoy doing things for your friends. You enjoy seeing your friends and family feeling better as a result of your efforts. However, you can overdo this, and sometimes do things for people without being asked. Then, if they don't show adequate appreciation, you may build up resentments and feel you are being "used." You need to ask yourself whether you are giving from the heart or because you feel that it is expected of you. Did you perform a service because you were afraid that your friend might think less of you if you didn't? Other people are not always aware that Virgos tend to keep plodding on, performing little tasks and services, until they are actually told to stop.

Contrary to what one might think, Virgos are not often as critical of their friends as they are of their children or partners. For the most part, Virgo people generally keep their criticisms of friends to themselves. However, when asked, they can let go with a barrage of "constructive" criticism that might be hurtful to someone who is sensitive. Never ask for total honesty from your Virgo friends unless you are prepared to hear the complete, unvarnished truth—as the Virgo friend sees it!

Virgo's eye for detail can be invaluable when it comes to giving advice and guidance. The Virgo friend might need to curb a critical tongue and try to be positive and courteous, however, when asked for an opinion or advice. If you have a Virgo friend, remember that he or she won't gloss over an honest opinion with tact, but you can still appreciate and make use of your friend's astuteness.

Your Virgo friends probably have rather shaky self-images, so any positive buildup you can give them will undoubtedly be valuable to them and the relationship.

The Libra Friend

People who have Libra prominently figuring in their charts are so gracious and polite to everyone that it is hard to know who they feel is special. The Libran often finds friends among all social levels, though a strong sense of social status may cause these people to seek the highest possible level in society. If the Libran factor is afflicted in the chart, the person is overly concerned with what people think, and might choose to let down a friend rather than go against society's norm.

If you have a Libran friend, you must remember this and realize that fitting into society is one of the primary purposes of the Libran's current incarnation. Try not to judge the Libran too harshly for avoiding those who don't live by the rules of society.

Librans are able to see both sides of an issue and will bend over backwards to be fair, therefore, these types often end up playing the role of peacemaker between their friends when disagreements arise. This sometimes puts them in a difficult spot, but Librans will try to find ways to make everyone happy.

If the Libran factor in the chart is strong and well-aspected, there is a keen sense of justice. Such individuals will stand by anyone they feel has been wronged and go out of their way to restore peace and harmony, even if it means creating chaos to do so. The Libran warrior, for instance, fights wars in order to work for peace, rather than enjoying war for its own sake as does the Arien warrior.

If you have a Libran friend, remember that peace and harmony are important to him or her, and do not pull your friend unnecessarily into your quarrels. The Libran loves to give and receive love; you can make friends for life with the Libran if you help your friend find the peace and love he or she needs.

The Scorpio Friend

Scorpions are very choosy about whom they call friend. Loners by nature, they are reclusive and unwilling to reveal too much of themselves. However, once you have made a friend of a Scorpion, he or she is generally your friend for life. You must allow the Scorpion to keep personal feelings buried within, for such people are not inclined to share very much, and you may never really learn what makes your friend tick.

It is difficult to earn a Scorpion's trust. If you have Scorpio prominent in your chart, you might suspect ulterior motives in everyone you meet and should try to curb this tendency somewhat so that you are not so quick to condemn someone. However, Scorpions are natural psychologists and extremely perceptive. It is not easy for people to lie to you and you see what others don't even realize about themselves.

Scorpio people are often blessed with an innate power over the material world, and have a way of making things happen, either consciously or subconsciously. They enjoy power, and if the Scorpion factor in the chart is afflicted, these people may manipulate others for their own purposes. This might be accepted in certain business situations, but in friendship such behavior is totally inappropriate.

Scorpios, though, can be extremely loyal, especially if Venus is in this sign. They sometimes idealize a person or cause and will even fight or die for what they believe in or love. This tendency has been glorified in heroic poems and stories, and even in this modern skeptical age we still admire people with this trait. Devotion to a person or cause is fine within limitations; however, when such devotion becomes obsession or fanaticism, the Scorpio can cause pain to him- or herself as well as to loved ones. Scorpios often need to develop reason and objectivity in matters of love and friendship.

The Sagittarius Friend

Sagittarians make wonderful drinking buddies; they are fun-loving, good-natured, outgoing, and friendly. If Sagittarius is prominent in your chart, you are likely to be intelligent and full of lofty ideas, and therefore can be an interesting conversationalist. Well-liked by all, you often have a large group of acquaintances from which to choose your friends.

However, your friends may find you "flaky" at times and you can be changeable and moody. You also need to work on being more depend-able. You have a short attention span and often have trouble focusing on any one train of thought for long. Part of the purpose of an incarnation as a Sagittarian is to learn many different things and to pursue many dif-ferent courses.

If the Sagittarian factor in your chart is afflicted, you often may find yourself knuckling under to pressure rather than standing by a friend. Or, you may turn on a friend who proves to have feet of clay rather than meeting up to your impossibly high ideals. There is nothing wrong with aspiring toward perfection, so long as you remember that perfection is only a star to shoot for—not something you realistically expect to reach. The key to any relationship with a Sagittarian is space: both friends must learn to give it in profusion if they want the friendship to last.

Strangely enough, while Sagittarius is the sign associated with higher education, many Sagittarians appear to be impatient with conventional learning methods and often will spurn traditional educations. Many drop out of school, yet become widely read and well-educated on their own. Part of the reason for this may be that Sagittarians are ear-oriented rather than eye-oriented (unless other factors in the chart balance this trait) and prefer listening—going to movies, lectures, and watching television—to reading. They also enjoy being read to and a friend could soothe the Sagit-tarian's nerves by reading him or her a story.

The Capricorn Friend

Capricorns are less emotional and demonstrative than people of other signs. If the Capricorn factor in a chart is badly afflicted, and if other fac-tors in the chart do not offset the tendency, the person can come across as cold and forbidding, and therefore, may not attract many friends.

Ambitious and business-oriented, Capricorns meet most of their friends through work or career-related activities. Their aura of success and their subtle sense of humor attract admirers. Another appealing Cap-ricorn trait is their down-to-earth practicality and their skill for handling just about any situation that life may throw their way. Their friends find them to be always dependable—and almost always willing to lend a hand when the chips are down. Major Charles Emerson Winchester, one of the characters in the popular TV series M*A*S*H, is a perfect example of the Capricorn friend. Known for his pompousness, his ambition, his near-obsession with tradition, and his sometimes biting humor, he always stuck up for his buddies.

If you have a Capricorn friend, you should bear in mind that although your friend may seem distant and unemotional, he or she still has emotional needs. Your friend's competence does not mean he or she doesn't need nurturing, too. Rather, the Capricorn probably did not receive his or her share of nurturing as a child, and therefore, friends may find themselves making up for this lack. The Capricorn will not express such a need openly, but friends should be aware of it and to be prepared to provide love and care unbidden.

If the Capricorn factor is afflicted, the person may be rather ruthless and even sacrifice friends for social or career advancement. However, it is my experience that such Capricorns are rare. Most of my Capricorn friends are loyal, dependable, and devoted.

The Aquarius Friend

If you have Aquarius prominent in your chart, you are probably somewhat eccentric and can perplex your more conservative friends. Your wacky charm, however, attracts people to you. Your intelligence often causes others to look to you for leadership, but you are usually reluctant to assume such a position. You see yourself more as a cog in a wheel than as its hub.

Since Aquarius is the sign most often associated with friendship, it is natural to assume that Aquarians surround themselves with friends. However, the Aquarian has few real intimates. When the Aquarian does form a close friendship, the relationship is generally based on a solid foundation of mutual interests, often of a universal, radical, or Utopian nature. Because you don't tend to become intimate with people, many of your friends actually should be categorized as acquaintances, whom you meet through activities or special interest groups.

The famous friendship between Lord Byron, an Aquarian, and Percy Bysshe Shelley, a Leo, was based not only on their mutual love of poetry, but on their concerns for the future of humankind, the fate of the world itself, and idealistic visions of the future. Although Lord Byron's reputation as a hopeless rake with little concern for proprieties attracted many hangers-on, he made very few friends whom he respected and loved. Perhaps the most respected and loved of these few was Shelley.

If you have an Aquarian friend, you probably realize that the Aquarian's purpose for taking incarnation was, at least in part, to break free from the restraints of convention. Probably you were attracted to the Aquarian because of this very "oddness." However, one of your challenges could be trying to convince your friend that there are times when more conservative behavior is appropriate!

The Pisces Friend

If you have Pisces strongly figuring in your chart, you may be quite talented in music, art, poetry, or drama, and you possess more intuition than
most other people. You brim over with kindness and compassion, and
those who are close to you probably love you dearly.

However, you are very shy and may prefer being a "wallflower" rather
than risk rejection. You may be confused and impractical in many ways,
and constructive criticism from friends will only make you more self-con-
scious and increase your feelings of unworthiness. Pisceans were probably
ignored or emotionally abused as children, and because of their sensitivity, they take such treatment very personally. As adults, their self-images
might be poor and they can be extremely self-effacing. These individuals
have a sense of sacrifice and humility, but they also want desperately to
avoid rejection and emotional pain.

Yet friends of Pisceans often find, to their dismay, that Pisceans
sometimes seem to go out of their way to attract the very pain they wish
to avoid. For this reason, being a friend to a Piscean often involves a great
deal of patience. If you have a Piscean friend, remember that his or her
ego needs constant boosting, and that Pisceans rarely recover totally from
traumatic childhoods. Therefore, they require much more encouragement
and emotional support than people of other signs.

Some schools of thought trace the development of the soul through
the signs of the zodiac from Aries—the initial stages symbolic of "self"—
through mystical Pisces and back to Aries, this time symbolic of awareness of the Divine Self. A Piscean who also has a strong Aries concentration, while seemingly confused and self-effacing, may be approaching the
awareness to which all evolving souls aspire. For this reason, your Piscean
friends will probably provide a rich source of inspiration for you—even
though they may not be aware of it.

14

The Mercury Factor: Communication

In a natal chart, Mercury shows a person's ability to understand and relate to others on a mental level. Mercury has been called the planet of communication; however, there is much more to Mercury than this simplistic statement conveys.

Mercury rules the mind, and the mind is a storehouse of experience. Mercury represents the capacity to remember facts and events (as opposed to the subconscious memory of emotions, ruled by the Moon), including our own and others' acts, observations, statements, opinions, and emotions. In addition, Mercury signifies the bridge between emotion and action.

A person with a strongly-placed, well-aspected Mercury has keen powers of observation and a good memory, and is likely to remember when, how, and why a friend has been hurt; he or she also knows what will make that friend happy. This is not to say that the person with a strong Mercury will use those powers to benefit others; such is not a function of the mind. (Look at the Sun, Moon, Venus, and Jupiter to judge how this person will use Mercurial abilities in relationships.)

I once analyzed the natal chart of a nine-year-old boy who had a very well-aspected Mercury and who was quite aware of the feelings and hangups of everyone around him. His Moon and Venus were weak, however, and he had Mars, Uranus, and Pluto all conjunct the MC, indicating a pronounced cruel streak. He combined the effects of the strong Mercury and the difficult conjunction to make the lives of his family members miserable. I advised the boy's family to encourage an interest in modern technology as a way of channeling his energies productively, or, if that failed, to enroll him in military school and utilize the Mars-Uranus-Pluto capacity for a military career.

Another person I know, however, has an unaspected Mercury in Pisces, the sign of its detriment. His Moon, Venus, and Jupiter are strongly positioned and well-aspected. Though he would never deliberately hurt someone, he nonetheless causes his friends frequent pain because his Mercury is so weak. His memory is poor, his powers of observation are minimal, his mind is constantly preoccupied, and he rarely notices how others respond to what he says and does. Though his affections are deep, he rarely has a lasting relationship with anyone because he is unable to understand other people.

As these examples show, Mercury's effect upon relationships goes beyond communication. Not that communication is unimportant—far from it! Mercury represents the ability for two separate individuals to bridge the gap between them. It enables a person, to some degree, to occupy the space of another. It allows us to convert feelings and experience into language, and, through language, to convey those feelings and experiences to others. For the most part, the better a person is at communication, the stronger his or her relationships.

Lack of communication often causes problems in all types of relationships. How many times have friends needed things from you, but refrained from telling you—then, when you failed to fulfill their desires, they were upset? Do your friends and loved ones sometimes expect you to read their minds? An inability or unwillingness to communicate is destructive to any relationship, and I find that in relationships where this is a problem it is usually due to a weak or afflicted Mercury in at least one of the two natal charts.

A strong, well-aspected Mercury represents good communicative abilities and a knack for comprehending the feelings and desires of others. Most charts, however, contain a mixture of harmonious and difficult aspects to Mercury. For instance, I knew a woman whose Mercury was strong by sign (Gemini) but afflicted by a square to Neptune and an opposition to Saturn. Though she extolled the value of communication in relationships, she allowed hurts and resentments to build up without discussing them, then let loose with biting, vindictive pronouncements and accusations. She justified her tantrums as "communication."

The value of communication in a relationship cannot be overemphasized. Yet some people manage to get along quite well even though their powers of understanding and relating are minimal, perhaps because the emotional and karmic bonds between them are strong enough to overcome the limitations of poor communication. If your Mercury is strong, you may find you must do most of the communicating in your friendships. On the other hand, if you are the one with the weak Mercury, you may have to try to relate to your friends in other ways, so that they understand your shortcomings and your efforts to overcome them.

Mercury through the Signs

Mercury in Aries

Mercury in Aries indicates a quick mind, sharp wit, and keen powers of observation. If Mercury is also in aspect to Saturn (any aspect), your memory is good. You are outspoken and spontaneous, and have a way of saying what you think without censoring your words, often injuring the feelings of your friends without realizing it. This bluntness needs to be curbed if you are to avoid hurting others' feelings unnecessarily (and unintentionally).

Mercury in Taurus

Your powers of observation and your memory run true and deep, although both may be colored by a certain fixity of ideas. You don't usually speak until you are spoken to, and don't express your feelings or offer opinions until you are asked—or until circumstances render it absolutely necessary. Nonetheless, your communications reflect warmth and love, and you are always tactful and careful not to inflict pain on your friends.

Mercury in Gemini

Your mind is quick, your eye is keen, and you have a way with words. Unless Mercury is strongly supported by harmonious aspects to Saturn, however, your memory is short and your observations superficial, and you don't always make the connections that you should. Geminians are more concerned with gathering facts and observations than in putting them to work, and therefore, it may take some effort for you to put what you observe to work rather than just storing it away. You love to talk and therefore confidences come easily to you; but you must be careful not to betray the confidences of others.

Mercury in Cancer

You are especially sensitive to the feelings of others and have a good memory. Though you communicate well on a verbal level, your best talent for communication is nonverbal. For you, a touch of the hand or a smile can reveal as much as a thousand words. However, though you respond easily to the needs of others, you do not communicate your own needs and desires as well as you should. If Mars is afflicted in your chart, your unwillingness to express what you want could result in gargantuan slights to you—real or imagined—and violent temper tantrums. You need to recognize that others want to do things for you just as you do for them, and that people who are not as perceptive as you are might require verbal pronouncements.

Mercury in Leo

Your mind is focused on your own projects and ideas, and you draw people to you because you have such an interesting way of talking about these projects and ideas. You may believe that other people who are close to you automatically feel the same way you do. While your creativity and gifts for self-expression do win you many followers, you need to make special efforts to understand your friends' interests, too, and become involved in their lives and projects as well. You need to allow for the differences of others and let your friends have their space, even though you enjoy sharing as much of it as you can.

Mercury in Virgo

You have a good retentive memory and ability to communicate, but tend to concentrate on details instead of paying attention to the whole. For instance, you probably observe, store, and remember several different events in the life of a friend, which seemingly make separate statements about his or her feelings; however, when taken as a whole, the events indicate something entirely different. Therefore, you need to make an effort to see the "forest not just the trees."

Mercury in Libra

You are quite good at allowing your friends their space. You find it easy to see the other person's point of view, and even if you disagree, you respect your friends' opinions. You take an interest, though sometimes superficial, in the opinions of others and are more tolerant than people of most of the other signs. However, you enjoy playing devil's advocate, arguing any point of view for the sake of debate, and if your Mercury is afflicted by Mars or Uranus, quarrelsomeness can result. Sometimes you hesitate to communicate your own needs and desires because you feel it's "not nice" to tell someone you want something. This adherence to convention needs to be overcome; your relationships are much more important than knuckling under to social mores.

Mercury in Scorpio

You are inquisitive, sometimes to the point of nosiness. You are good at getting others to open up and talk about their deepest concerns. Also very discreet, you won't talk about or reveal others' secrets under any circumstances. Your memory is good—sometimes too good—and you have a way of remembering old hurts and slights and holding grudges. Although you can easily induce others to confide in you, you aren't willing to talk much about yourself, even to your closest friends, probably because you are afraid of leaving yourself too vulnerable. You need to learn to communicate more and to learn that it's all right to be vulnerable—in this way, you let your friends know you consider them worthy of your trust.

Mercury in Sagittarius

Your mind is in the clouds, often embracing ideals too high for others even to fathom. Verbally prolific, you are more than willing to share your ideas and beliefs with others, and will do so at any opportunity. However, you have so many diverse ideas and feelings and your mind jumps from one to another of them so easily that your thoughts and words may seem scattered. You are a charming conversationalist and others are drawn to your childlike spontaneity. You might be advised to try to concentrate your mental energies more, and not to talk so effusively that you reveal the confidences of others.

Mercury in Capricorn

You have excellent powers of concentration and, as a result, a good memory. You are thorough in your thought processes and possess a certain amount of cunning, and you are able to put these traits to work in your relationships. This can work to your benefit if Mercury is well-aspected, but if it is afflicted, your cunning can border on manipulativeness. When you wish, you can communicate well enough, but as a rule you don't speak easily and openly because you always want to be sure of your facts before offering an opinion. Your friends may take your reticence for rejection, and you should make sure that they do not misunderstand your reserve. You take all aspects of your life very seriously, and this includes your friendships.

Mercury in Aquarius

A progressive thinker, you are attracted to new and radical ideas. You are free and open about expressing your ideas and opinions, which may seem crazy and eccentric, but may not really reflect your true feelings. You are attracted to groups that share your ideas and throw yourself into their activities whole-heartedly, attracting the attention of many. When preoccupied with a project or cause, you prefer to work alone, and might want to remain incommunicado for days at a time. If your friends understand your involvement with your work, they will leave you alone and not be hurt, but if not, they may be confused, and you must use your concern for fair play to make certain you don't offend others unnecessarily.

Mercury in Pisces

Your feelings, thoughts, and opinions are easily influenced by your friends. This trait may cause you to be indecisive and leave you open to manipulation by others. If Mercury is badly aspected in your chart, your thought patterns can be chaotic and your memory poor. As a result, you might not be too observant or aware of what those around you feel or think. Nevertheless, Mercury in Pisces does convey a certain amount of psychic ability, and if the planet is well-aspected you can be quite sensitive to the thoughts and emotions of others. If you manage to crystallize that energy, your intuitive abilities can be put to work, enriching your communications. Mercury in Pisces also suggests aesthetic appreciation, and you attract many friends with whom you can share your thoughts and ideas freely. Your innermost feelings, however, you keep secret—so much so that you may not be overtly aware of them yourself!

15

Venus and Jupiter

Venus is the planet of love. The oldest astrological traditions, going all the way back to Hindu mythology, present this planet as the ruler of all forms of love—maternal, friendly, romantic, brotherly, even spiritual. Astronomically, this tradition parallels the fact that Venus's orbit is the most perfectly circular and balanced of all the planets'. Hence, her association with harmony and, consequently, love, or harmonious feelings between two human beings.

The placement of Venus in a person's chart, therefore, represents that individual's capacity to experience, express, and accept affection in relationships. A well-placed and strongly-aspected Venus renders a person charming and attractive, and capable of both feeling and expressing love.

When Venus is weak by sign or house, and weakly-aspected (or not aspected at all), the person probably has few real friendships. There may be superficial ones, but only by virtue of proximity or necessity, such as with co-workers or family members. In *The American Book of Charts,* for example, Lois M. Rodden includes the chart of an autistic child.[1] (Autism is a personality disorder in which a child appears to live totally within him- or herself, relating little, if at all, to the world outside.) The autistic child mentioned above had Venus in the sixth house, in Gemini, and the only aspects to the planet were wide squares to Pluto and Uranus. Autistic children can be said to have "relationships" with their parents and siblings, by virtue of proximity or necessity, but they are incapable of actually relating in an interpersonal way to anyone, in the sense of either communication or exchanging affection. Autistic children also lack the charm and magnetism to cause people to want to relate to them.

My cousin once knew a girl who had been diagnosed as semi-autistic and who had undergone years of therapy to help her condition. My cousin, a kind-hearted and outgoing person, made a special effort to bring the girl out of her shell and smothered her with warmth. However, the girl did not seem to entertain any genuine affection for my cousin or anyone else. When my cousin married and moved away, this girl retreated into a reclusive lifestyle, without so much as a goldfish for a companion. Her chart showed Venus in Virgo, sign of its fall, in the sixth house, and totally unaspected except for a square to Saturn.

Of course, this does not mean that everyone with a weak or unaspected Venus is autistic or semi-autistic—only that such people have great difficulty relating to others. It is my experience that a badly-aspected Venus is better than an unaspected one in relationships. Squares and oppositions to Venus create challenges and action in relationships that can render a person exciting. These relationships may be short in duration and fraught with conflict and deception, but the person at least will have them, and hopefully will be able to learn from them.

A person with a very well-aspected Venus often finds that friendships come too easily. People court this individual, and he or she feels no need to put any real energy into relationships. This may work for awhile, but eventually friends disappear, feeling that the friendship is a one-way effort. Of course, a Venus with many harmonious aspects is better than one with no aspects at all, for the person reaps the benefits of others' energies even if he or she is too lazy to give much in return.

Obviously, it is best for Venus to have a combination of stressful and harmonious aspects. In this way, the person can both give and receive affection, and put effort into keeping his or her friendships going. And, if Venus is strong by sign or house, the person can count on warm and rewarding relationships throughout life.

Jupiter expands the effects of Venus. Although not a planet of relationships *per se,* Jupiter rules good feelings in general. So, when he is posited in signs or houses that are associated with relationships, or is in aspect to Venus, he can be read as adding to relationships.

People who have Jupiter so positioned express warmth, generosity, and companionship. They attract many friends and enjoy an abundance of good times with them. Jupiter's love and affection go beyond the idea popularly associated with this planet, that of "a good old boy, out to have a good time." Jupiter represents fellowship that runs very deep, affection on an idealistic and spiritual level, selflessness, and the ability to give freely and easily. A person with a well-placed and well-aspected Jupiter possesses an abundance of good feelings and bestows them generously upon all he or she meets.

As is true of Venus, an afflicted Jupiter does not deny good relation-ships. An afflicted Jupiter always leads to excesses. Where relationships are concerned, an afflicted Jupiter causes the individual to scatter his or her affections promiscuously, and to shower affection on people who don't want or don't deserve it, with little return. Still, as with Venus, poor as-pects are better than no aspects at all. A weak and unaspected Jupiter can denote a person who may have good feelings, but has difficulty ex-pressing them. Or, he or she may find it hard to believe that affection and good feelings actually exist.

If Venus and Jupiter are in any aspect to each other, the person's capacity to love and give to others is greatly increased. If the aspect is harmonious, relationships of all kinds come easily throughout life, and the individual will derive a great deal of benefit from them. If the aspect is stressful, the good effect will still manifest, but the person may either be lazy in maintaining relationships, or might take friends for granted. Or, he or she may choose to associate with and give loyalty to people who are unworthy of that loyalty or affection. If Venus and Jupiter are not in aspect to each other, their signs and house positions, as well as the as-pects other planets make to each of them, must be considered carefully.

Readers may react to the above paragraphs with the idea, "But this is saying that everyone has good feelings!" And that is correct. To some degree, everyone—even the autistic or semi-autistic person—has some good feelings for someone, however deeply buried they may be. We are all familiar with the cliché of the hard-nosed hit man who has a soft spot for birds or stray cats. Adolf Hitler undoubtedly felt some affection for his mother and for Eva Braun. The study of Venus and Jupiter in a natal chart reveals the depths of the individual's capacity to feel and give affec-tion, and can show friends and lovers how best to deal with him or her— and whether or not it would be worth the effort!

Venus and Jupiter through the Signs

Venus and Jupiter in Aries

If you have Venus in Aries you feel love and affection spontaneously and ardently, for your friends as well as your lovers. You need constant stimu-lation from those you love, however, and therefore find yourself seeking new companions frequently. This can jeopardize your long-term relation-ships somewhat because you tend to ignore your established friends for the sake of impressing your new ones.

If Venus is well-aspected in your chart, you are able to balance both old and new friendships. If Venus is afflicted, this is more difficult for you; you may find most of your relationships are transitory in nature, because of your tendency to take old friends for granted. You need to realize that your established friends are usually the most dependable, but even their loyalty may be pushed too far.

Jupiter in this sign bestows frankness and a strong sense of honor, which is beneficial in dealing with both old and new friends.

Venus and Jupiter in Taurus

If your Venus is in Taurus, your ability to feel and express love and affection runs very deep, and your loyalty and devotion know no bounds. There is a passionate intensity underlying all your close relationships, even those with members of the same sex. Taurus is a physical sign, and you enjoy kissing, hugging, and other forms of physical affection.

If Venus is well-aspected, you undoubtedly will have productive and loving relationships throughout life. If Venus is afflicted, you may settle your affections on people who subconsciously feel unworthy of such devotion or are threatened by it. Particularly if Uranus is involved, you may find your friendships disintegrate or your friends disappear, and you do not understanding why. You need to be more careful about whom you shower with affection and make certain you don't overwhelm a friend who is not prepared to accept your effusiveness. If you maintain a comfortable distance, you may experience rewarding relationships even with friends who are not as demonstrative, loving, and devoted as you are.

Jupiter in this sign produces generosity and joviality. It also increases the natural loyalty and warmth inherent in Taurus. If Jupiter is afflicted, however, there can be a danger of lavishing your affections on the wrong people.

Venus and Jupiter in Gemini

If your Venus is in Gemini, you extend charm, courtesy, and sympathy to all. You tend to be attracted to friends with whom you have common interests and with whom you can talk for hours. Your affections, while genuine, are inclined to be superficial and fleeting, and unless Venus is in harmonious aspect to Saturn, you tend not to pursue relationships for their own sake. Though you have many acquaintances, your real friends are few, and you feel more comfortable with relationships based on intellectual rapport rather than on deep feeling.

If Venus is well-aspected, these relationships will bring you the intellectual stimulation and broader views that you so avidly desire. If Venus is afflicted, however, the superficial nature of some of your relationships may cause conflict, especially if the friendships mean more to your friends than they do to you.

Jupiter in this sign gives you good manners and versatility, as well as a desire to have many different and varied friendships. If Jupiter is well-aspected, you are likely to find the associations you desire. If Jupiter is afflicted, the relationships you want always seem to be just beyond your reach, and you may have to work harder to develop them.

Venus and Jupiter in Cancer

If your Venus is in Cancer, you feel protective toward the people you love. At times, you need someone to lean on, too. You want to make everyone a part of your family, and people naturally gravitate toward your warmth. Friends seek out your company because they enjoy the sense of belonging that you provide.

If Venus is well-aspected, you always will be surrounded by a large circle of "family-friends" who both give and receive the nurturing kind of love that comes naturally to you. If Venus is afflicted, some of your friends will not respond to your protectiveness; instead they will see you as trying to smother and control them. You need to realize that not everyone finds your parental inclinations acceptable, and sometimes you will have to curb your natural tendencies to "mother" your friends.

Jupiter is exalted in Cancer. In addition to increasing the effects of Venus, Jupiter in this sign adds abundant sensitivity and a strong sense of justice. If your Jupiter is afflicted, you may feel as if there is really no justice in the world. You need to learn to hang onto your ideals in spite of disappointments.

Venus and Jupiter in Leo

If your Venus is in Leo, you give and attract love easily. You have an abundance of charisma and magnetism so that nearly everyone you meet is drawn to you almost at once. You enjoy being around people, especially if you are the center of attention. Sometimes you may seem like a monarch and your friends like your subjects, but your friends rarely resent this. You are generous with your time as well as with your possessions.

If Venus is well-aspected, your affections are given freely and returned in kind. If Venus is afflicted, especially by Pluto, you might use your charisma and magnetism to manipulate others and threaten to withdraw your love and companionship if friends don't do what you want. This may work for awhile, but does not make for pleasant relationships.

Jupiter in Leo gives you an innate desire to be a leader. It also suggests much popularity, and especially if Jupiter conjoins the Sun, Moon, Ascendant, or Venus, you play the role of monarch naturally. You must be careful not to abuse your popularity, however, which is more likely if Jupiter is afflicted.

Venus and Jupiter in Virgo

If your Venus is in Virgo, you are very choosy about whom you call friend, and sometimes practical considerations outweigh affection when it comes to forming friendships. You can be devoted and loyal, though, and if Venus is well-aspected, this tendency is appreciated by your friends and associates. You enjoy doing favors for those you love, and this how you feel most comfortable demonstrating affection.

At times, you can be moralistic and judgmental, especially if Venus is afflicted. This can hurt your friends' feelings, even though you may not mean any harm. An afflicted Venus also can cause you to feel that your friends manipulate and use you, though it is possible that in actuality you are simply pushing yourself too hard or taking on more than you should. If you have a friend whose Venus is in Virgo, try not to take advantage of his or her generosity with time and resources—even if your friend seems to press favors on you—to make sure that he or she does not feel used by you.

Jupiter in this sign indicates a desire to teach your friends things and do favors for them. Your friends may find your practicality and eye for detail invaluable. However, if Jupiter is afflicted, you probably have to watch a tendency to be too critical of others and might need to develop more tact.

Venus and Jupiter in Libra

If your Venus is in Libra, you are friendly and polite, and quite adept in social situations. You enjoy the company of others, and your obliging manner enables you to make friends quickly. Rarely do you say anything that causes people pain, for you weigh each word carefully.

If Venus is well-aspected, you will always enjoy a busy and productive social life, and your friends will appreciate and return your affection. If Venus is afflicted, however, you have a tendency to scatter your affections too widely and diffusely, rather than investing deeply and wisely in a few, cherished friends. Thus, your love energies do not return to you as they should. Giving affection is a pleasure for you and can be greatly rewarding, but you must take care that your relationships involve both give and take.

Jupiter in Libra expands your gifts for conversation and your love of social contact, and you are probably quite popular. If Jupiter is afflicted, however, you may depend or rely too much on your friends—often on the wrong ones.

Venus and Jupiter in Scorpio

If your Venus is in Scorpio, you have a magnetism and charisma that draw people to you. To those you care about, you show a passionate intensity and loyalty that border on obsession. So long as the person you focus your attention on returns such feelings, all goes well. If, however, the relationship goes sour for any reason, you can direct all your energy and intensity into hate and bitterness.

If Venus is well-aspected, your hostility will dissipate when you find another person on whom to focus your affection. If Venus is afflicted, however, these negative emotions can become vengefulness, and you could harbor a strong desire to hurt the former friend. Obviously, such an attitude is damaging, not only to the other person but to you as well. You need to find some other outlet for your feelings—even fantasizing instead of acting on your desires.

Jupiter in Scorpio increases all the effects of Venus, especially the quest for pleasure and passion. A strong sexual undercurrent underlies all your relationships with the opposite sex, even casual ones. If Jupiter is afflicted, this tendency can be exaggerated so that you are only interested in friendships that involve sexuality.

Venus and Jupiter in Sagittarius

If your Venus is in Sagittarius, you have high ideals regarding your friendships, and often your friends don't live up to your expectations. Your disillusionment is rarely the result of the friend's failings, but rather because your expectations are too high. When this happens, instead of working out your differences, you often move on to other relationships. Thus, your friendships lack stability. If Venus is afflicted, you can hold on to bitterness and bad feelings after a friendship ends. You need to learn to be more realistic in your expectations of human beings and to accept the failings of others—and yourself.

Jupiter in Sagittarius increases your idealism. You also are interested in foreign countries and want to make friends with people from other lands. If Jupiter is afflicted, you might experience intense mood swings, and your friends should be prepared for your emotional changes.

Venus and Jupiter in Capricorn

If your Venus is in Capricorn, you are a constant and faithful companion, and have a strong sense of responsibility toward your friends. You are more than willing to help friends and partners get ahead, and sometimes may work too hard toward that end. Many of your friends may be older than you.

If Venus is well-aspected, your friends generally like and appreciate your efforts and reciprocate whenever possible. If Venus is afflicted, you may project coldness and distance even though you might not really feel this way. You have trouble expressing affection and this may lead to disappointments and separations from those you love. You need to make a special effort to express warmth and appreciation, and try not to be so self-controlled.

Jupiter in Capricorn produces ambition and leadership abilities, and leads you to seek friends and associates through your work or business contacts. If Jupiter is afflicted, there can be a tendency to sacrifice friendships for the sake of ambition, which may result in loneliness.

Venus and Jupiter in Aquarius

If your Venus is in Aquarius, you find yourself surrounded by friends of all kinds. You enjoy group activities and tend to form friendships based on these activities. You have many modern and progressive ideas, and are attracted to people who share your beliefs and interests. Some people may be shocked by your unconventional attitudes about love and friendship, but you are still intriguing to them.

If Venus is well-aspected, your friendships are likely to enhance your life and be a source of stimulation to you. If Venus is afflicted, however, especially if Uranus is involved, your unusual attitudes and stubbornness can lead to separations and disillusionment. Sometimes bitter words and arguments can widen the gulf between you and former friends. You need to use your intelligence and objectivity to analyze a situation before breaking off a relationship. Your friends are important to you, perhaps even more important than your lovers, and you need to keep your disagreements in their proper perspective.

Jupiter in Aquarius brings an abundance of comradeship and good fellowship. You also possess keen insights into human nature and have a strong sense of humanitarianism. Friendships are important to you, and your friends and associates often see you as a leader. If Jupiter is afflicted, you might see the group as being more important than the individual, and your friendships may be casual and impersonal.

Venus and Jupiter in Pisces

If your Venus is in Pisces, you see all forms of love in an unrealistic light. You have an extremely kind and sensitive nature that causes others to love you dearly. However, your high expectations of love can bring you pain and disappointment. Even when disappointed, however, you continue to love and serve your friends.

If Venus is well-aspected, you will find your friends very supportive and loyal. If Venus is afflicted, however, your feelings of inadequacy may cause you to believe that your friends don't want or appreciate you when actually they feel nothing of the sort. You need to be careful not to let your insecurities come between you and your friends.

Jupiter in Pisces increases the kindness of Venus in this position and, to some degree, offsets the insecurities. You enjoy solitude, but if Jupiter is afflicted you may be too reclusive.

Notes

1. Lois M. Rodden, *The American Book of Charts,* (San Diego, CA: Astro Computing Services, 1980).

16

The Eleventh House

Traditionally, the eleventh house rules friends, group activities, and social contacts. Because the eleventh is a succedent house—related to resources and self-worth—and above the horizon—involving outward expression—the core meaning of this house could be described as *self-expression socialized*. The eleventh house also shows a person's ability to function in social or group situations, where it is necessary to relate to several people at once and curb natural inclinations so as to "fit in." The eleventh house, along with the planets in and/or ruling it, illustrates an individual's basic need and desire to reach out and establish relationships with others. It also suggests inclinations toward involvement with clubs and organizations. A person whose eleventh house is emphasized often identifies his or her sense of self-worth with the group and its activities.

People with eleventh house emphasis in their birth charts spend a sizeable portion of their lives interacting with friends and/or societies. If the Sun, Moon, or Ascendant ruler is involved, these individuals experience their friends and social contacts as a part of their very being and may feel lost without them. These people become integral and important parts of any association they are involved with, and they give the group their complete support. In turn, the group will support them as well.

If you refer back to the chart of Doreen in chapter 3, you will note that both the Sun and Moon are in her eleventh house. Doreen was always at her best when surrounded by a group of friends who loved and depended upon her. Her childhood involvement with the Girl Scouts, later with the Army, then est, then with company softball and billiards teams gave her a sense of importance, of being needed, and of having some purpose in life. When she became involved with our group of metaphysical researchers, she seemed to have found her niche. However, whenever she was between associations, Doreen felt lost, as if she had no reason to live, and feared (erroneously) that people were no longer interested in her.

The chart of Ann on page 261 shows a heavy eleventh house concentration, which includes the Sun and the Ascendant ruler, Mercury. All her life, Ann has been a socially adept person. She thrives in large groups and enthusiastically joins any club or organization whose activities interest her. As a child, she was a Campfire Girl. In college, she was an avid joiner, becoming involved with creative organizations as well as a sorority. Her marriage to a military officer provided her with a rich source of social activities and many contacts with other officers and their wives. Ann became an active member of the Officers' Wives Club, and started bridge clubs and a dance group. Later in life, Ann joined the Daughters of the American Revolution and was president of her local chapter.

Her children also brought her outside contact. She took an active part in any activity that interested her children. When one of her daughters showed promise of becoming a champion swimmer, Ann began timing and judging swimming meets. Needless to say, Ann never lacked for companions. The friends she made enjoyed her enthusiasm, and looked to her not only for help or leadership, but for emotional support as well. (Notice the strong Cancer concentration in the eleventh house). But Ann attracted few close personal relationships—by choice.

The eleventh house rules group activities and casual friends to whom you relate on a "one-to-many" basis. Relationships that provide more personal, one-to-one encounters, your "face-to-face" friendships, are another matter. The "friends of your heart," your close personal friends for whom you have developed a deep and abiding love, are ruled by the fifth house. When a friendship progresses from one of occasional social contact to one of shared, mutual goals the relationship ceases to be an eleventh house one and falls under the rulership of the seventh house. Therefore, when judging an individual's capacity and need for friendship, we must look to all three relationship houses. My own chart, for example, contains a stellium in Libra in the seventh house. My closest and most abiding friendships have been more like partnerships.

When judging a person's innate drives toward forming friendships, determine which of the three relationship houses is the strongest. The strongest of the three houses tells which type of relationship the individual feels most comfortable in, and which one he or she will seek out unconsciously.

If a person has an eleventh house concentration, like Ann, he or she prefers many casual contacts and few close, one-to-one relationships. Only those with whom this individual has a strong synastric connection

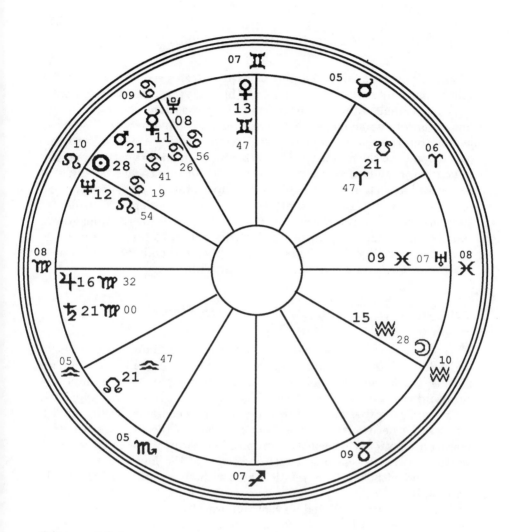

Figure 16.1
Ann
July 21,1921 9:35 am
Weatherford, Texas
Placidus house cusps

will become intimates. If the fifth house is dominant, the person is less inclined to develop low-key, superficial contacts, and has a very strong need for the intimacy and close love-bonds characteristic of the fifth house. If the seventh house is the strongest, the individual is more partnership-oriented and will gravitate toward friendships with people who have similar goals toward which they can work together.

The Sun In or Ruling the Eleventh House

This placement endows the person with a deep need and respect for others, particularly those with whom he or she is involved in a social way. Such individuals intuitively understand their associates and have innate knowledge of human nature. Their readiness to help others enables these people to make many contacts that reinforce their sense of self-worth.

If you have the Sun in the eleventh house, friends are very important to you and they give you a sense of purpose and meaning in life. If the Sun is well-aspected, your friends and group contacts are a source of great happiness to you. If the Sun is afflicted, you may experience frustrations, and perhaps believe you can never do enough to fulfill the obligations which you feel toward your friends. Particularly if Neptune is involved, inadequacy exists only in your own mind; your friends probably don't share your viewpoint and are quite happy with you.

The Moon In or Ruling the Eleventh House

This placement signifies a deep emotional need for many social contacts and a desire to make friends. This individual has a tendency to "mother" friends. He or she also possesses an understanding and sympathetic nature, and is always willing to help friends. If the Moon is well-aspected, the person will experience fruitful and nurturing contacts throughout life (though not necessarily with the same people). If the Moon is afflicted, however, emotional insecurity can interfere with the person's sense of worthiness. He or she might feel unworthy of the love and respect of friends and withdraw from relationships without a word, leaving friends upset and confused.

If you have an afflicted eleventh-house Moon, you need to develop your verbal skills so that you can communicate your insecurities to your friends and give them a chance to reassure you. If you have a friend with an afflicted eleventh-house Moon, you need to be aware of your friend's insecurities and try to reinforce that person's belief in his or her value. All people with eleventh-house Moons need to feel needed.

Mercury In or Ruling the Eleventh House

This placement indicates a tendency to flit from one friendship to another, enjoying intellectual input from as many people as possible. This person enjoys verbal communication with friends and is most attracted to those who can engage him or her in lively conversation. A progressive thinker, he or she probably has a strong interest in new and liberal ideas, as well as in modern technology and political reform. This individual is a gifted organizer and is often most comfortable serving in that capacity. He or she also may have a penchant for forming friendships with younger people. If Mercury is well-aspected, there will be many stimulating friendships throughout life. If Mercury is afflicted, however, the person might scatter energies among too many people. He or she also tends to lack understanding of others and is too critical. If Mars is involved, the individual can be argumentative.

If you have such a configuration in your chart, you need to try to curb your antagonistic tendencies. If you have a friend with such a placement, take care to keep your debates with your friend objective and intellectual, and do not take the acerbic comments associated with this position personally. Your friend simply seeks to gain from your intellect and may channel too much intense energy in this direction.

Venus In or Ruling the Eleventh House

This person has the ability to infuse all his or her friendships with love. Attractive and charming, this individual possesses considerable social skill which can be of benefit in group situations. Associations through friendship are of vital importance and he or she is capable of projecting love to everyone—even to all members of a large club or association. If Venus is well-aspected, the person has a positive outlook on life and this optimism insures many beneficial friendships throughout life. If Venus is afflicted, however, the person may experience disappointments through friendship and an overabundance of sentimentality (particularly if the afflicting planet is Jupiter). If Neptune is involved, there is a danger of unrealistic expectations, both of friends and self. If Venus is afflicted by Uranus, the individual might experience constant and sudden separations from friends, often without knowing why.

If you have this planetary placement in your chart, you might channel your energies into unusual or unconventional friendships, and perhaps groups that are associated with new and progressive ideas. If you have a friend with this placement of Venus, try not to be too possessive, for Venus/Uranus types need a lot of freedom in all relationships, including friendship.

Mars In or Ruling the Eleventh House

This placement signifies a large amount of energy channeled into friendships and group activities. This person has a powerful urge to bring about social or political reforms, and possesses talent for teamwork and organization. If Mars is well-aspected, the person's enthusiasm and energy appear limitless; this is the person you can always go to for favors. If Mars is afflicted, however, there is a danger of inconstancy and undependability. This individual can be argumentative and seem to have a "chip on the shoulder." If the afflicting planet is Jupiter or Neptune, he or she may promise everything but produce nothing.

If you have Mars in this position, it might be best to channel your energy into hard work toward your group's goals. If you have a friend with this placement, you may have to learn not to respond to his or her jibes, and accept your friend unconditionally. Unless other factors in the chart offset the tendency towards undependability, depend more on your other friends than you do on this person and you'll avoid problems with broken promises.

Jupiter In or Ruling the Eleventh House

This planet endows the individual with seemingly boundless gifts for sociability, camaraderie, and good fellowship. The person is generally surrounded by many friends who enjoy his or her good nature and joviality. A humanitarian, this individual manages to inculcate a sense of hope and optimism into all activities.

If you have Jupiter in this position, especially if he is well-aspected, you will always have a great deal to offer your friends, intellectually, emotionally, and otherwise. If Jupiter is afflicted, however, there is a danger of obstinacy, willfulness, and indecisiveness. You also have a tendency to scatter your energies and attention among too many different people or groups.

Saturn In or Ruling the Eleventh House

This placement can have any one of many possible effects—or all of them. The first, obvious possibility is that the individual is a loner, reluctant to seek out friends and social activities. Possibly this person believes that friends or associations of any sort might inhibit self-expression and involve too many binding responsibilities. Usually people with Saturn in the eleventh house form bonds only with those groups or individuals who do not limit them in any way. When these people do form friendships, the friends are usually older and often of a conservative, traditional frame of mind. In their youth these individuals can be so concerned with building careers that they have little time for social activities until later in life. When they do establish friendships, however, their relationships usually last a long time.

If Saturn is well-aspected, the person's friends find him or her capable of blending high social aspirations with practical creativity. If Saturn is afflicted, the person's hopes may lack a firm foundation and therefore lead to disappointments. If you have Saturn in this position, you need to use your natural gifts for practicality. If you have a friend with this planetary placement, be prepared to point out shortcomings in your friend's ideas (in a tactful and unthreatening manner) and work with him or her to make such dreams a reality.

Uranus In or Ruling the Eleventh House

This placement often renders the individual too independent to settle down and follow the collective aspirations of any one group, and he or she may have difficulty forming friendships and contacts. Generally, when this individual does establish bonds with individuals or associations, they are modern, progressive, and somewhat radical in nature. These people have an almost desperate need for freedom within their relationships and see the responsibilities of friendship as too binding.

If you have a friend with Uranus in the eleventh house, don't necessarily depend on him or her to give aid when it is needed. If other factors in the chart indicate generosity, however, such people can be very supportive and helpful—except when they feel it is expected of them. Then they rebel. If Uranus is well-aspected, the individual may have keen knowledge of human nature, and a talent for organizing others that can contribute greatly to any group. If Uranus is afflicted, however, particularly if Mars is involved, the person can be a troublemaker, likely to indulge in unpredictable or rebellious behavior—and he or she is not someone upon whom a friend can rely. If you know someone like this, it is best to simply enjoy his or her knowledge and unusual ideas, and look to others for help and support.

Neptune In or Ruling the Eleventh House

This person projects an almost hypnotic power of attraction. He or she has romantic and idealistic views of friendship and a tendency to search for soul-union through friendship. There may also be an unrealistic attitude towards friendship and an inclination to expect too much sacrifice from friends. Such individuals often are attracted to spiritual, psychic, or metaphysically-inclined groups and individuals.

If Neptune is well-aspected, the person's romantic attitudes towards relationships may be realized to some degree. If Neptune is afflicted, however, friendships may be fraught with insincerity and lies. This individual tends to be easily influenced by other people and has only a minimal ability to resist temptation. This becomes more dangerous when the person attracts friends who are addicted to alcohol or drugs.

If you have Neptune in this placement, you need to try to curb your impressionability. If you have a friend with this position of Neptune, you should try to influence your friend positively so as to offset any harmful influence others may have.

Pluto In or Ruling the Eleventh House

This placement indicates a powerful drive toward self-transformation through friendships. This person needs plenty of freedom in relationships; he or she will sever all attachments that restrict personal growth and seek out those which provide opportunities for growth. The person might distrust potential friends and group associations, possibly from fear that they will demand too much of him or her and thereby restrict the drive for self-expression.

If Pluto is well-aspected, a strong communal sense of purpose may accompany this individual's friendships and associations. This person may find that popularity and advancement in life come through friends and contacts. If Pluto is afflicted, however, there can be power struggles in friendships and groups which might result in disruption of the individual's self-expression. In the worst cases, power struggles, fear, and distrust can cause the person to wind up alone, a hermit, with no friends or associates at all.

If you have Pluto in this position, you should try to overcome your fear and distrust, and realize that your doubts may not come from the actual shortcomings of your friends. You should also try to avoid instigating any power struggles. If you have a friend with Pluto in this placement, you may need to go out of your way to convince him or her that you are worthy of trust and that there is no reason to fear you. Also, since this person needs to exercise power in order to reinforce self-worth, it is best to let your friend feel as if he or she is the power behind the relationship.

Notes

1. Samuel I and II, *The Living Bible,* (London, 1971).
2. Lillian Hellman, *Pentimento,* (NY: Simon and Schuster, 1975), p. 107.
3. Ibid., p. 127.

17
Case Studies

Henry II and Becket: Where Did They Go Wrong?

King Henry II of England (1132-1189) was a popular king. A capable administrator and warrior, Henry restored England to its former prosperity from the ruins left by his predecessor, Stephen. He also took time to become acquainted with the English people by traveling throughout the realm, speaking with mayors, feudal lords, and even the peasants themselves. Henry, who had grown up in northern France, wanted to learn all about the land he had inherited through his mother, but he also was interested in finding out what the people needed and what reforms were necessary to make England a safe and prosperous land.

Although he was only eighteen when he came to the throne, Henry was wise enough to know that he had an arduous task ahead of him. The damage done by the robber barons during the ineffectual rule of Stephen had been extensive. The process of restoration would take years, and, in order to perform the job properly, Henry needed competent advisors who were familiar with the ways and customs of the English people. One of the positions he needed to fill was that of chancellor.

For this important position, Henry chose Thomas à Becket, a Londoner in his middle thirties who had been a member of the household of the Archbishop of Canterbury for many years, and who had many times proven himself to be a man of understanding, purpose, diplomacy, and integrity. Becket certainly met Henry's requirements for the position. He had grown up in London, the son of a prosperous merchant, and had been educated in both rural schools in England and in the universities of Paris. He had also studied law in the famed colleges of Bologna and Auxerre.

Before the reign of Henry, the position of chancellor had simply been that of advisor to the king and keeper of the Great Seal. As soon as Becket assumed the post, however, the position took on new meaning. Becket was aware that Henry was anxious to keep in close contact with the needs of the people, and he soon assumed the position of King's lieutenant in charge of keeping this contact. The chancellor's staff rapidly grew to the then-incredible number of fifty-two clerks, all of whom were kept constantly busy—and the chancellor himself was busiest of all. He wrote dozens of letters every day, and consulted with many visitors and petitioners from all parts of the kingdom. Yet he still found time to hold long private consultations with the king. In this way, Henry managed to keep abreast of the activities of every earl and sheriff in the land—and to supervise and correct them whenever such action was necessary.

One of Henry's main concerns was justice; in fact, it was Henry who laid the groundwork for the English common law. He worked hard to establish trial by jury, and he wanted to place certain restrictions on the old law of church sanctuary—which, in short, stated that a felon was safe from secular law so long as he was inside a church and under its protection. Henry saw this custom as outdated, and sought to limit its practice. Becket stood beside him on this issue, as he did on many others.

Becket possessed many mental qualities that Henry lacked. Though Henry was well-educated for his time, he was mainly a soldier, and he admired Becket for his skills of debate and diplomacy. Henry respected the chancellor's talents so much that he began monopolizing Becket's time. Many were the occasions when Henry would dine with the chancellor. He was known to ride his horse into the dining hall, jump off, and bound across the table to the chair beside Becket (which was always reserved for him). These dinners often lasted late into the night and were animated with lively conversation and argument, questions and answers, and laughter.

In addition to being an excellent chancellor, Becket proved to be a fine military leader as well. When Henry took troops into France to assert his position as Count of Toulouse, Becket brought his own troops and fought beside him. Their bond was strengthened by their experiences as comrades in arms. They returned to England firmer friends than ever and they began spending much of their time together, hunting, playing chess, drinking, womanizing. In short, they were not only a fine team for leading a kingdom, they were inseparable companions as well.

As is usual when a king has a favorite, the English people began hearing of special favors being granted to Becket. The chancellor's household was nearly as sumptuous as the king's. Becket's clothes, though of simple design, were made of the finest fabrics and richest colors, and he enjoyed wearing gold chains at his neck and waist and jeweled rings on his fingers. His table was laid with the most expensive vessels and cutlery, and the food he and his staff enjoyed was plentiful and delicious. When Becket travelled to France in 1158 to negotiate the marriage of Henry's eldest son and the daughter of the French king, his entourage bespoke such wealth and luxury that the people of France gaped in awe. "If this is only the king's chancellor," it was whispered, "what then must be the wealth of the king?"[1]

However, it was difficult for the English people, even the nobles, to resent the favors granted Becket. Becket was a devoted, dedicated worker, and spent few hours on his own. There was no denying that Henry and Becket were improving conditions in the formerly war-torn kingdom. And no one was more aware of their effectiveness as a team than Henry. He knew that in Becket he had found a rare treasure—as a colleague and as a friend.

Then in 1162 an event occurred which changed everything. The old Archbishop of Canterbury died without an obvious successor. The Archbishop had trained no one, had groomed no protégé, had no close colleagues to whom he had entrusted the secrets of his position.

Henry had definite ideas of his own. In his efforts to establish the common law in England, the one obstacle he had confronted was the Church. The issue of sanctuary, the problem of lay courts versus church courts, and the debate over trying clerks and priests for crimes against the crown had been areas of dispute between the king and the bishops. Henry saw the Church's position as a powerful hindrance to an equitable system of justice for everyone. And so, while the old Archbishop lay dying, Henry spoke to Becket of his plan: Henry would unite the offices of chancellor and Archbishop by naming his friend Archbishop of Canterbury.

Of course, most of the English prelates opposed the plan. Becket was not even a priest, much less a bishop, and therefore they hardly considered him suitable for the job. Becket had been a member of the old Archbishop's household for about a dozen years, however, and this was the reasoning Henry used to justify his choice. Becket himself vehemently protested the idea, telling Henry, "If you do this, you will soon hate me as much as you love me now,"[2] but it is difficult to believe that Becket's objections ran too deeply. He was known to be an ambitious man, and enjoyed the power he had exercised as Henry's right-hand man. The formidable power in the position of Archbishop of Canterbury would probably have appealed to him immensely.

In the end, Henry got his way. Before the old Archbishop was even dead, Becket was consecrated a priest. Soon afterwards, the chancellor was made a bishop, and when the old prelate finally died, the miter was solemnly passed to Thomas à Becket. Then, Becket proved himself a prophet.

Historians have had a difficult time explaining exactly what happened to Becket after he became archbishop. He seemed to change totally.

He metamorphosed from a man who thrived on luxury to a grim ascetic. Gone were the expensive clothes. Becket assumed the traditional hair shirt, topped by the poorest of priestly garments. Gone was the sumptuous food; the new Archbishop was known to fast interminably, taking only enough nourishment to keep himself alive. He tore down the luxurious apartments inhabited by his predecessor and installed instead a bare, stark cell, furnished only with a meager pallet.

And he resigned as chancellor! Henry was aghast. The whole point of installing Becket as Archbishop of Canterbury had been to unite the offices of chancellor and archbishop, and to create a productive unit of church and lay powers. But Becket was adamant; he could not, he said, in all good conscience continue as chancellor. His new duties, he maintained, were to uphold the interests of the Church, and he could not do that and still be dedicated to the interests of the king.

Thus began a twelve-year battle between King and Archbishop. Becket seemed to have abandoned his role as the king's supporter; rather, he appeared to oppose him at every opportunity. In a complete about-face from his former viewpoint, he upheld the doctrine of church sanctuary. He opposed Henry on the issue of the trying of clerks and priests by secular courts; such people, Becket claimed, were under the protection of the Church and, therefore, should be tried by church courts. But, Henry protested, such a practice went against the very ideas of justice. The church courts, when trying a priest for high crimes, often gave him no more severe a punishment than a public flogging!

The quarrel became intensified when Becket himself physically rescued a murderer on his way to execution, whisking him to church sanctuary and granting him asylum. Henry was greatly affronted—and rightly so. The man had been convicted of murder and sentenced by the king's court. How dare the Archbishop interfere so blatantly!

Needless to say, all traces of friendship between Henry and Becket seemed to have disappeared. They were constantly quarreling, and, unlike before, they could not seem to agree on anything. To many people who were close to Henry, it appeared that Becket had engaged his former employer in a contest of wills, an intense power struggle, for Becket absolutely refused to compromise on any issue where he and Henry disagreed—particularly the reforms regarding the common law. Why? Had Becket, all the years he was serving Henry, actually resented the power of the young king? Had he seized upon the office of Archbishop of Canterbury solely as a means of putting his power on a par with Henry's?

Historians disagree. Some maintain that Becket was a consummate actor, throwing himself wholeheartedly into any role he assumed. Others state that his ascetic tendencies had shown themselves years before; he was known to prefer sleeping on the floor to resting in the comfortable goose-down beds used by the wealthy in that era. Still other historians speculate that Becket was sympathetic with the Church all along, because of his involvement with the prior Archbishop, and that his work for Henry as chancellor was simply "doing his job." But the actual answer remains an enigma. There is no denying that after his appointment as Archbishop, some of Becket's viewpoints grossly contradicted those he had espoused as chancellor—and some seem quite pointless *except* that by embracing these opinions, he was opposing Henry. Was this the case?

The rest of the story is history. Henry exiled Becket for several years, recalling him finally after receiving pressure from the Pope. For awhile Henry and Becket seemed to have re-established their old comradeship. But it was not to last. Once more they got into a bitter disagreement over the question of king's courts versus church courts, and Henry was almost at the end of his rope. In the presence of many others, he uttered the famous plea, "Will no one rid me of this meddlesome priest?"[3]

As is well-known, four knights who were present at that moment took Henry at his word. They travelled to Canterbury and found Becket in the cathedral, where they murdered him in cold blood. For his part—however unwitting—in Becket's murder, Henry allowed himself to be publicly flogged. Becket was later consecrated a saint.

Why would two staunch friends reach such an impasse that the relationship ended in murder?

The chart for Henry II reveals that he genuinely was interested in the welfare of his people. The presence of the Moon, Venus, and Mercury in Aquarius implies a strong humanitarian instinct, as well as a need for constant communication with those who shared his liberal, populist viewpoints. The presence of these planets in the seventh house indicates a pronounced preference for partnership-type relationships, such as that he thought he had with Becket. Saturn in Sagittarius reveals a staunch interest in justice and law, and Mars in Aries conjunct the MC denotes the energy to make his ideals a reality.

The Sun-Jupiter conjunction in Pisces indicates sensitivity to the needs and feelings of others. Hence we can see Henry's concern for his people, especially on the question of justice—and we can see as well that it was important to him for his friends and associates to share his views. Even though Henry was a trained and skilled soldier, (Mars in Aries conjunct the MC) his Sun was in Pisces, and therefore conflict, especially with those he loved, probably made him extremely uncomfortable. That he had high ideals regarding justice and his own friendships is shown by the trine between the Aquarian Venus and the Libran Neptune, blending an idealistic regard for the law with a love of his people—and a strong need to share that with those around him. (Aquarius rules friendships, Libra rules partnerships and relationships in general.)

Now let us consider the natal chart of Becket. Here we see an entirely different type of person. We know from his personality that Becket was

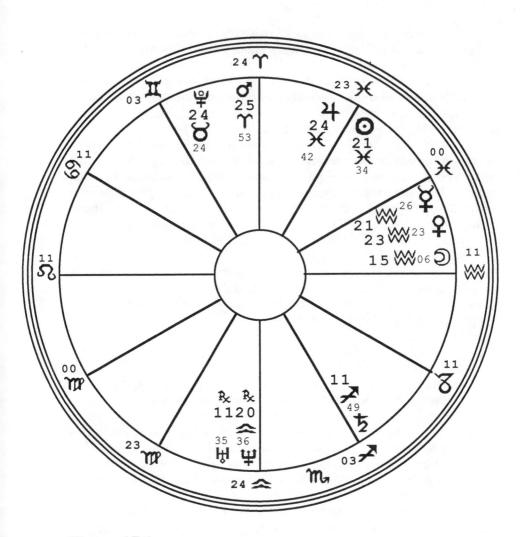

Figure 17.1
Henry II
March 5, 1133 2:00 pm (?)
Le Mans, France
Placidus house cusps

ambitious and power-oriented; we can deduce from his chart that those
drives ran very deep. He had the Sun, Mercury, and Jupiter in Capricorn,
as well as Pluto in Taurus in the eighth house, trining all his Capricorn
planets.

It is difficult to find any of Henry's humanitarianism in the chart of Becket. The Moon in Aries reveals a strong ego-drive, and the square between the Moon and the Capricorn planets suggests an almost obsessive concern with his own needs and desires. The Arien Moon also underscores the drive for power—and the Libran Ascendant indicates the ability to take either side of an issue for the sake of argument.

Becket's swing from luxurious living to severe asceticism is shown by the position of Mars and Venus in Scorpio in the second house. There are no halfway measures with Scorpio. Planets placed in Scorpio—especially Venus, and particularly in the second house of money and possessions—can represent either a love of wealth so pronounced it borders on decadence, or the most rigorous attachment to poverty. Or, this can imply alternating between the two extremes.

It appears from Becket's chart that he probably shared very few of Henry's actual concerns for the people. He was capable of seeing Henry's point of view, and of working toward any goal—so long as it aided him in his ambitions. The placement of Venus in Scorpio endowed Becket with a strong sense of loyalty and devotion, but the opposition between Venus and Pluto hints that this very loyalty could be sacrificed to his drive for power. This combination also suggests a penchant for vengeance against anyone who betrayed him.

Did Becket see Henry's decision to make him Archbishop as a betrayal, a rejection of his effectiveness as chancellor? Or did some other event, lost in the obscurities of history, occur to cause Becket to believe that Henry had betrayed him? Was the issue a woman, as was suggested in the famous Jean Anouilh play *Becket*?[4]

Scorpio, Capricorn, and Aries are not sociable signs; people who have these signs prominently figuring in their charts can be sociable, but the tendency needs support from other signs. From the heavy concentration of planets in these signs, it would appear that Becket was basically a loner. He may have cultivated his friendship with Henry (at least in the beginning) primarily to advance his own ambitions. And the fact that he supported Henry completely and worked hard toward the king's goals in the years as chancellor may have simply been a means to an end. He had the king's ear; other than the king himself, he was the highest secular power in the land.

But when he became Archbishop, another avenue of advancement was suddenly opened to him. Remember that the position of Archbishop of Canterbury, while the most powerful church position in England, was by no means the top rung of the ladder in the twelfth-century Church. There was the position of cardinal, and after that, the papal entourage at the Vatican, and then, the papacy itself. Some historians maintain that Becket aspired towards a cardinalship and perhaps even to be Pope—and, from the study of Becket's chart, it looks as if this might have been the

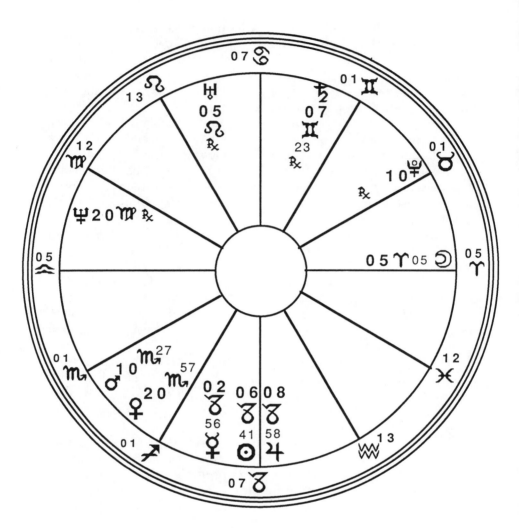

Figure 17.2
Thomas á Becket
December 21, 1118 12:30 am
London, England
Placidus house cusps

case. Was the fact that Becket turned on Henry in the issue of the common law, rigorously upholding the supremacy of the Church over the lay courts, not an expression of genuine commitment, but rather a way of impressing the higher church officials that Becket was dedicated to the interests of the Vatican—even if such dedication meant opposing the king and hurting a former friend?

From these two charts, then, we can deduce the basic character differences and relationship needs that caused these two friends to be torn apart. In terms of synastry, we actually find very little to signify a strong, lasting bond. The trines between Henry's Piscean planets and Becket's Scorpion ones indicate a bond of affection and good feelings; the trine between Henry's Saturn and Becket's Moon shows a karmic bond not easily severed. But other than these aspects, there appears to be little which would produce a lasting friendship. Henry's Aquarian Moon opposes Becket's Uranus in Leo. Becket's Virgoan Neptune opposes Henry's Piscean planets, suggesting deception throughout the relationship. There are wide trines between Becket's Geminian Saturn and Henry's air planets, however, this only emphasizes the karmic nature of the relationship.

We have here, then, what appears to be a relationship between two people with entirely different aims in life. Henry—most likely erroneously—believed that Becket shared his concern for the people. Becket's concern, however, was mainly for his own ambitions. Their Mercurys are not in aspect to each other, so there probably was little intimate communication between them. And people who have Mercury in Capricorn, like Becket, only communicate their feelings to others if they wish. Mercury in Capricorn hints at manipulativeness, and so once more we have indications that Becket, although he probably nourished some affection for Henry, may have used him. In true Libran fashion, he responded to Henry's humanitarian viewpoints, even if his adherence to them did not run very deep.

We can see that the friendship basically fell apart because of different goals in life. In spite of all that had happened between them, however, Henry mourned for his friend long after the murder in the cathedral. We cannot help wondering: If the situation had been reversed, would Becket have done the same?

Friendship and Politics:
Anne of Austria
and Marie de Rohan

Anne of Austria (1601-1666) had a special friend named Marie de Rohan who was her only support in her early years as Queen of France. Marie covered for Anne during her love affairs and sought to protect Anne's political position as much as was within her power. Anne and Marie were friends throughout life, and the friendship survived the efforts of nearly everyone at Court to break them up. The two women stubbornly kept in touch through secret correspondence and clandestine meetings, and there were times when Marie actually resorted to disguise in order to meet her friend undetected.

Anne of Austria (who, strangely enough, was a princess of Spain) married Louis XIII of France in 1615, when they were both fourteen years old. After one disastrous attempt to consummate the marriage, Louis either abandoned his wife's bed completely or slept with her only when pressure for an heir became strong. (Historians disagree on this point.) At any rate, there seems to be no doubt that Louis' main sexual inclinations were toward his own sex, and that he held his bride in little regard. To complicate matters further, Louis had a formidable and domineering mother, Marie de Medici, who was jealous of her son's young bride and did everything in her power to keep the two estranged.

In 1617, Anne was assigned two new ladies-in-waiting. One of them was the bright and charming Marie de Rohan. Marie immediately sensed the hurt and loneliness of the neglected young queen and set about to make life more bearable for Anne. She showered Anne with little gifts and attentions, and planned various amusements that were plainly designed to make the queen more happy with her lot. Marie was a lovely young woman, with bright golden hair and deep blue eyes. She was clearly aware of her beauty and intended to put it to work for her. She also put her attractiveness to work for Anne. Marie was known to engage Anne in hours of games, coupled with outrageous conversation which centered upon the handsome young men at Court and their possibilities. Marie, with her charms, would often draw the unsuspecting young men into their circle, and she and Anne would flirt openly with them. Marie also gave Anne a supply of rather earthy reading material.

Needless to say, Anne, who had been oppressed by her loneliness, was grateful for Marie's friendship and appreciated the amusement provided by her new friend. The two young women became inseparable.

When word of their activities reached the ear of Marie de Medici, the queen mother was greatly disturbed. It seems reasonable to assume that she did not wish for her hated daughter-in-law to enjoy life at all. She badgered her son with dire pronouncements of how Marie with her flirtatious nature and penchant for questionable books would corrupt the queen's morals. Louis paid a visit to his wife's household in order to investigate—and he, too, was swept away by Marie's charisma. He decided that Marie was no threat to his wife, and eventually began inviting both young women to his hunting parties—from which Anne had been excluded previously. This strengthened the bond between Anne and Marie—and thoroughly angered the queen mother.

The dowager queen began working behind Louis' back to separate the two friends. She went to the young king's regent, the notorious Cardinal Richelieu, and expressed to him her fears for the young queen's morals. Marie de Rohan, she declared, was a wanton who had cuckolded her husband, the Comte de Luynes, and could well influence Anne to do the same to Louis.

Cardinal Richelieu (whom some historians believe to have lusted after the young queen) immediately took steps and exiled Marie from Court. But he had underestimated her. She was determined that no one would keep her away from Court or from her friend. By this time, Marie's husband, the elderly Comte de Luynes, was dead and Marie wrote to her long-time lover, the Duc de Chevreuse, and asked him to marry her. He accepted.

Marie's new marriage changed her position with Court quite a bit. The Duc de Chevreuse was a wealthy, powerful, and influential French nobleman; he was also a prince of Lorraine, which in those days boasted of a strong army and fertile lands. It would be extremely poor politics to banish the wife of such a man from the French Court, and so when the Duc requested leave from Louis for Marie to return to Court, permission was granted. Marie was allowed to return to Versailles as an honored guest. The two friends had a joyous reunion.

The queen mother's condemnation of Marie as a wanton was not far from the truth. Indeed, during her first marriage Marie had had an affair with the Duc de Chevreuse, and now that they were married she and the Duc had an unspoken agreement: He had his lovers and she had hers. Therefore, while Marie was visiting at Court, she fell in love with Lord Holland, a handsome young envoy from King James I of England. Like Marie, Lord Holland sympathized with the plight of Anne of Austria, and decided that Anne would make a perfect lover for his friend, George Villiers, Duke of Buckingham, who would soon be arriving in Paris. When the Duke arrived, Marie and Lord Holland did everything they could to throw the two together, and the inevitable happened: Anne and young Villiers fell in love.

Historians disagree as to whether or not the love affair between Anne and the Duke was actually consummated, and about exactly how deep Anne's feelings ran. Nevertheless, Anne seems to have occasionally snuck out of the palace at night while Marie took her place in her bed. One cannot blame Anne for responding to the Duke's attentions, nor take issue with Marie for wanting her friend to steal a few moments of happiness even though the inevitable result was that Richelieu suspected what was going on and banished Buckingham from the French Court forever.

Perhaps the ultimate test of Marie's friendship with Anne came in 1626, when Louis' younger brother, Gaston, announced his intention to marry Mlle. de Montpensier. Since the marriage of Anne and Louis had (for obvious reasons) been childless, Gaston was presently heir to the throne of France and seemed likely to remain the heir. If Gaston married and had children, and Louis died, then what would become of Anne? She would undoubtedly be shut away in some distant household with a meager income for life. If Louis died while Gaston was unmarried, however, Gaston could conceivably marry Anne, and restore her to her position as Queen of France.

The problem intensified when Louis became gravely ill, and for a time everyone expected him to die. While the dowager queen and Anne cared for the dying king, Marie was not idle. Along with her husband, the Duc de Chevreuse, she paid Gaston a visit—and they convinced him that it would be far more politically expedient not to marry. If Louis did die, they maintained, Gaston would strengthen his support from other European nations, such as Anne's native Spain and her mother's native Austria, if he married Anne.

When Richelieu heard of the visit to Gaston by the Chevreuses, he grew quite concerned. By this time, he and Anne had an unquestioned enmity going, and he opposed any idea whatsoever of keeping Anne in power. Further, relations between France and Spain were becoming increasingly strained, and, unlike Marie and the Duc, Richelieu saw no advantage in cementing relations with that nation. Perhaps it would be best, he thought, to sever all ties with Spain and declare war on them. He began exerting pressure on Gaston to go ahead with the proposed marriage to Mlle. de Montpensier. Gaston was a weak-willed fellow with little mind of his own, and therefore, he was having a difficult time deciding which course of action was correct. He went for several weeks without making up his mind.

That Louis recovered from his illness did not alleviate the tension at all. Marie and Anne both knew now who their enemy was—not Louis, not Gaston, but Cardinal Richelieu. Therefore, a plot was hatched. Marie began using her vast network of friends in high places to promote an alliance between England, Lorraine, and the French Huguenot nobles—aided, perhaps, by Anne's relatives in Spain and Austria—to take the palace at Versailles by storm and force Louis to dismiss Richelieu. Richelieu would then be banished to his family's estates at Fleury, where he would subsequently be assassinated. Two innocent young noblemen, taken in totally by the combined charms of Anne and Marie, were induced to carry messages between the plotters. Richelieu was too experienced for the two women, however, and their messengers were taken prisoner and the plot uncovered. However, before they were executed, the two besotted messengers refused to implicate either Anne or Marie, and none of the letters which Richelieu had managed to intercept actually stated that Anne and Marie had plotted to overthrow and then assassinate Richelieu. Therefore, the cardinal could do nothing without risking the outrage of the French people, though his network of spies kept an eye on Anne.

In spite of her husband's influence, however, Marie was banished from Court and forbidden to see the queen. The two women kept their friendship going, however, with a series of clandestine meetings set up by secret correspondence. This went on for years, until the death (of natural causes!) of Cardinal Richelieu.

It was probably Marie who introduced Anne to Jean-Paul Claunet, the French nobleman who may have been the true father of Louis XIV. It was certainly Marie who promoted Anne's secret trysts with Jean-Paul, in secluded glades and deserted nunneries. And it was undoubtedly Marie's encouragement and enthusiasm which caused Anne to some degree to overcome her Virgoan self-effacement and glean what little happiness she could from her rather tedious and somewhat dangerous life.

After the death of Louis, when the young Dauphin became King Louis XIV, Anne was named Regent, along with Cardinal Mazarin, Richelieu's successor, who eventually became Anne's devoted lover for the rest of her life. During this period, the friendship between Anne and Marie underwent its first real strain. In previous years, Anne, in true Virgoan style, had assumed the more passive role in the relationship, allowing Marie to take the lead. After the deaths of Louis and Richelieu and her assumption of the Regency, Anne felt that she had finally come into her own, and she began to think for herself and make her own decisions, and to defer less and less to Marie's already-established cleverness and political skills.

Doubtlessly Marie was affronted by this abrupt change in her friend, and Anne began to view her companion's take-charge manner as arrogance rather than helpfulness. For several years there was a marked coldness between them. However, their friendship was strong enough to survive even this; Marie eventually became used to Anne's new assertiveness and Anne ultimately found her friend's ego amusing. When Marie died in 1679, she still remembered Anne as the only real friend she had ever had.

Let us now consider the natal charts of these two friends. The heavy

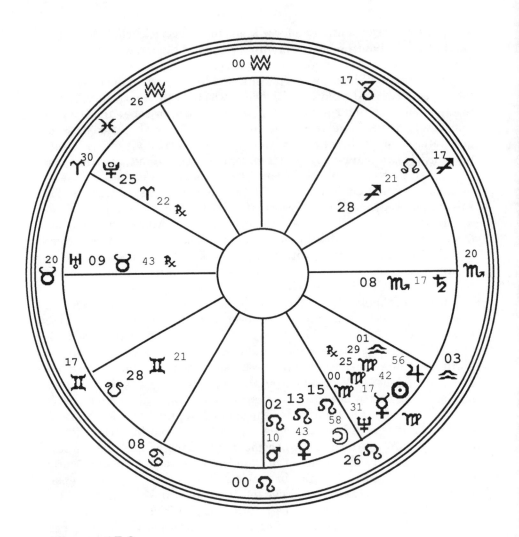

Figure 17.3
Anne of Austria
September 22, 1601
Valladolid, Spain
8:08 pm
Placidus house cusps

Virgoan concentration in Anne's chart shows her lack of assertiveness, and the Taurean Ascendant shows her inclination to accept a situation and "get caught in a rut." However, the Mars-Venus-Moon concentration in Leo shows that Anne was a very sensual person who needed to be liked and admired, and therefore we can see why she was so unhappy in the early years of her marriage. The conjunction of Mercury and the Sun to Jupiter shows that she was loving and good-natured, but the Virgoan reticence probably kept her from expressing those feelings until she met Marie. We can see, then, from studying Anne's chart, why she was so vulnerable and susceptible to the charms and affections of Marie.

Anne's Taurean Ascendant demonstrates her loyalty, and Mercury in Virgo denotes her skills at communication and her enjoyment of detailed work; hence we can see why, in the difficult years, Anne was capable of keeping her friendship with Marie alive through correspondence. The presence of Aquarius on the eleventh house cusp shows the unusual nature of Anne's friendships, and the placement of that house's ruler, Uranus, near the Ascendant indicates how important Anne's friendships were to her. However, this configuration also implies that she may have felt that becoming part of a group would limit her self-expression (she was, after all, a queen, with the Leo influence to support her regal nature). Her fifth house concentration suggests that she preferred the intimate, one-to-one type of relationship such as that she had with Marie.

The chart for Marie de Rohan is based on an approximate birth date and a rectified birth time. Historians are unsure of the exact date of her birth, knowing only that she was born in December of 1600. Several possible birth dates have been given for her, and this chart is based on the date where the planetary positions appear to have paralleled Marie's personality best. The time is rectified for that date. Even allowing for possible inaccuracies, we can tell what Marie needed from a relationship and what she had to offer in one.

It is fairly safe to assume that Marie was born in the first part of December, when the Sun was in Sagittarius, for in spite of the fact that she was ambitious and politically-oriented (which could be accounted for by the Mercury-Mars-Venus conjunction in Capricorn) she was the especially playful and fun-loving type which we associate with Sagittarius. She also loved to travel and journeyed extensively through Europe in the course of her life. If she had Leo rising, it is easy to see how she and Anne suited each other so well; they both would have had strong fifth-house planetary concentrations, indicating a need for deep love in a friendship and a desire to be admired and loved. As we have seen, each woman clearly fulfilled that need in the other.

Venus in Capricorn shows that Marie wanted friends in high places and that she was not above using her friends to advance herself. In the beginning, before she and Anne became close, is it possible that Marie saw in the lonely and vulnerable queen a chance to ingratiate herself with royalty? There is no doubt that their relationship was marked by pronounced deep affection—and if, in fact, Marie did have the Moon in Pisces and Leo rising, she was certainly capable of providing that affection.

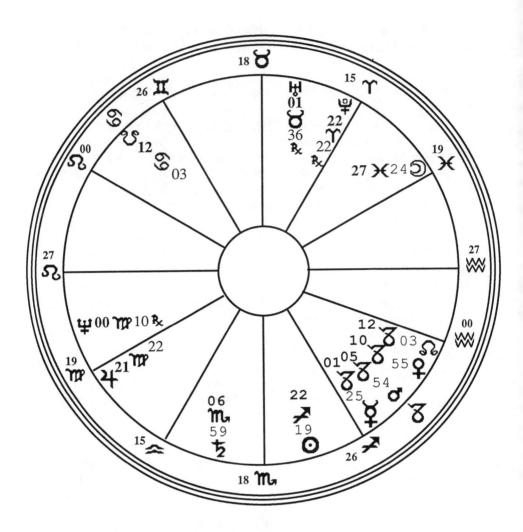

Figure 17.4
Marie de Rohan
December 13, 1600 (?)
Paris, France
Placidus house cusps

Still, it is quite possible that before Marie knew Anne well, she saw the lonely queen as a chance to advance herself. The trine between Jupiter and Venus adds to Marie's capacity for love—and Marie's loyalty is shown by Venus in Capricorn and (possibly) Leo rising. The cunning and sharp ears associated with Mercury in Capricorn show how Marie was able to keep abreast of the ominous undercurrents at court, thereby giving her an advantage and enabling her to do whatever she could to help her friend. The Piscean Moon demonstrates Marie's need to be of service to others—and Anne, in eagerly accepting all that Marie had to offer, certainly fulfilled that need for her.

The two charts present an interesting synastry comparison. The presence of Marie's Jupiter on Anne's Sun and Mercury denotes Marie's ability to bring Anne out of her shell and help her communicate her innermost feelings. The trine between Anne's Neptune and Marie's Mercury indicates the romantic nature of many of their shared communications; hence the notorious conversations regarding attractive young men and their complicity in romantic intrigue, as well as their idealistic attitude toward their own relationship. The trine between Anne's Moon and Marie's Pluto implies the tendency which the two of them shared for clandestine, underhanded activity. And above all, the lasting nature of their friendship is shown by the easy sextiles between Anne's Saturn and Marie's Capricorn planets, especially Venus, supported by the square between Marie's Saturn and Anne's Leo planets. As we know, Saturn ties are the hardest to break, because of their karmic nature.

Each of these women, therefore, served the needs and desires of the other with regard to friendship. Even their conflict after the death of Louis XIII (possibly due to the square between Anne's Sun-Jupiter conjunction and Marie's Capricorn planets) probably served only to strengthen the bond. The two women remained fast friends, and their story can be inspiring to the rest of us. When compared to the problems faced by Anne and Marie, the petty quarrels we may have with others seem minor.

A Tale of Two Musicians

John and Paul met when both of them were in their late teens. Fresh out of high school and full of ideals and ambitions, the two good-looking rock musicians believed that they could conquer the world. John was an excellent guitarist, Paul specialized in keyboards, and both were fine singers and songwriters. When they discovered their mutual interest, a bond was forged between them and they immediately made plans to become the next rock phenomenon, surpassing even the Beatles. They engaged other young musicians to join them and a band was formed. The leaders of the band were John and Paul, and the band bore their names.

They started playing in small clubs at night and writing and producing their own material during the day. The songs they wrote were exceptional and most were quite commercial in nature. The combination of their good looks, their professional voices, and their technical skills convinced many that the two had a brilliant future in the field of rock music.

Meanwhile, the two young men found that they had other things in common. Both were interested in metaphysics and meditation, and both were members of Self-Realization Fellowship. John was a black belt in karate, and Paul became interested as well. They soon became inseparable.

As the years went by, they saw each other through repeated crises. John married three times before he was thirty, and Paul was there to give help and support through each divorce. Paul suffered deaths in his family, and once was involved in a painful accident which threatened his musical career. The two apparently had formed an invaluable mutual support system as well as a promising musical partnership.

A career as a musician is a difficult path to follow. John and Paul continued playing in clubs throughout the Los Angeles area, but they were becoming worried. Some of their fellow band members were men in their late thirties and early forties. Would John and Paul eventually find themselves in the same position? Playing in clubs was not enough for John and Paul; they felt they deserved a better lifestyle. Their frustration grew daily.

Meanwhile, their personal relationship deteriorated. John seemed to run hot and cold in his relationship with Paul. When John was between marriages, he was devoted to their friendship, but when he was married, he seemed to have little interest in the relationship, except for professional contact. Paul was confused, especially since John, in true Capricorn fashion, was not a person to talk readily about himself and his feelings.

And Paul was harboring resentments as well. Although both young men were handsome and magnetic, John (a Leo) was most comfortable in the spotlight—and so when managers and investors came to hear the band, the one they noticed was John. Paul was reserved; John seemed to thrive in social situations, so people came to the conclusion that John was the "star." Paul, who believed in himself as well as his partner, could not understand this, and, unfairly, began focusing his bitterness on John.

Paul, a double Virgo, paid much attention to his own flaws, and he set about to eradicate as many of them as possible. He worked on his appearance, changed his diet, exercised regularly in health spas, and bought himself more becoming clothes. He began reading self-help books and started ridding himself of old hangups and phobias which had been holding him back. Slowly, but surely, his self-confidence and assurance grew. Suddenly people were interested in *him*.

At first, when Paul developed opportunities on his own, his inclination was to include John. But John, in true Leo-Capricorn fashion, was a bit affronted. He loved his friend, but he was used to calling the shots in their relationship, both professionally and personally. Paul's new assertiveness was a shock.

Where were they to go? Paul wanted desperately to stop playing in clubs and push their own original material, even if it meant losing the income. John wanted to continue. Paul believed that John was passing up opportunities; John felt Paul wanted to take undue risks. They talked, tried to compromise, and did everything they could to keep the partnership together. But nothing positive was accomplished. Finally Paul joined another band and the long-standing partnership ended. John and Paul saw little of each other for months afterwards, and it seemed as if the friendship was over. Paul often felt lonely, as though he had no friends at all.

Can their friendship survive a breach between them professionally? To consider this question, we must look to their natal charts.

It is easy to see why John was perceived as the more flamboyant of the two. The charisma inherent in Leo and the power conferred by the Sun-Pluto conjunction caused him to outshine others (such as Paul, whose Moon and Ascendant are in shy Virgo and whose Sun is in reclusive Scorpio). John's Capricorn Moon and Ascendant indicate an individual who is both magnetic and hardworking. John's elevated Venus in Libra conferred charm and sense of ease in social situations which obviously served him well in his career pursuit.

Paul's chart suggests that once the intrinsic reserve of Virgo and Scorpio is penetrated, he can be as open and charming as his friend, for he has Venus conjoining Jupiter in the first house.

A synastry comparison shows that the two men are a good match in many ways, especially the trine between Paul's Virgo concentration and John's Capricorn planets. Although the conjunction between their two Venuses is out of sign, the orb is so close it emphasizes the affection between them; the presence of Paul's Jupiter only adds to the relationship's strength. Paul's Uranus on John's Mercury suggests stimulating communication between them, and Paul's Mercury on John's Neptune indicates their mutual interest in metaphysical and spiritual studies. The placement of John's Saturn on Paul's Sun denotes the karmic nature of their friendship, and hints that the end of the business partnership might not necessarily mean the end of the relationship, for Saturn ties are notoriously difficult to break.

However, it is easy to see from John's chart that he functions best in a partnership-type of relationship. His eleventh house is empty, and its ruler, Jupiter, is posited in the seventh, along with four other planets, including the Sun. It was probably for this reason that John's personal friendship with Paul was shelved when John was married—and the impermanence of John's marriages is implied by the placement of the Jupiter-Uranus conjunction in the seventh house. The heavily-weighted sev-

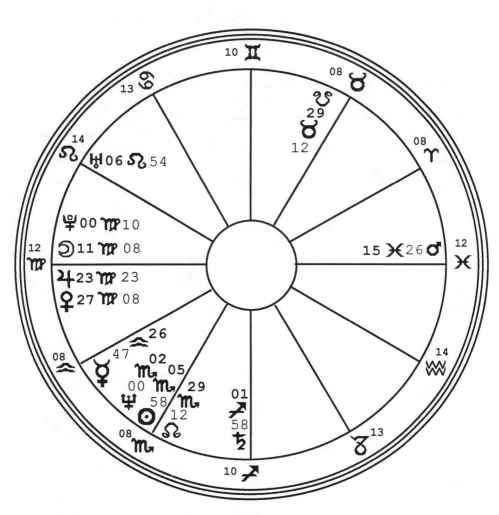

Figure 17.5
Paul
October 29, 1956 2:00 am
Santa Monica, California
Placidus house cusps

enth house denotes a self-image that functioned best when pursuing mutual goals and interests with another human being.

Though Paul is also drawn to partnerships (Mars in the seventh house), he apparently felt that they inhibited his self-image in some way.

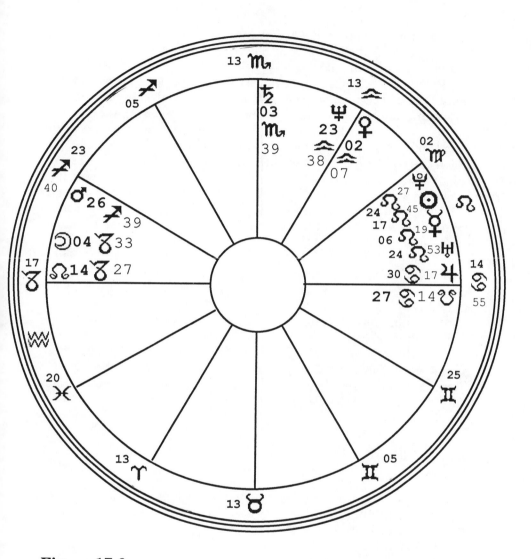

Figure 17.6
John
August 19, 1954 6:00 pm
Detroit, Michigan
Placidus house cusps

(The seventh house Mars, posited in Pisces, opposes Paul's Virgoan planets.) The presence of Uranus in the eleventh indicates that while Paul
is drawn to friendships in general, he often feels a need to break away
from them, and fears they may limit his self-expression. The happy-go-

lucky attitude conferred by Paul's Venus-Jupiter conjunction in the first house and the fact that the most highly elevated planet in his chart is Uranus reinforce his willingness to take risks.

Both men, however, are obviously quite capable of powerful affections. Both are capable of loyalty, John because of the strong Capricorn influence, and Paul because of his Scorpio Sun. It would appear then that the main problem with this relationship lies in different values regarding friendships in general and partnerships in particular.

If it were not for John's obvious need to make all his close relationships partnerships in some way, I would say that it might be best if they were not partners. However, if the two are to continue as friends, it seems that Paul would have to use his Virgoan adaptability and learn to accept John's need to be the central force in the relationship. If John could put his Leonine ego aside and let Paul lead from time to time (which Paul, reverberating to his Moon-Pluto conjunction, would need to do), and if Paul could realize that friends do not necessarily have to limit his self-expression, perhaps they could again function well, on both a personal and professional level.

This story has a happy ending. Another singing group is recording a song John and Paul wrote together. So, while John and Paul have not resumed their former intense alliance, they have lapsed into a modified partnership. They both take time to promote the results of their mutual efforts. Hopefully these two gifted young men will not drop their relationship; both they and the world can clearly benefit from their association.

Notes

1. Thomas B. Costain, *The Conquering Family,* (Garden City, NJ: Doubleday, 1962), p. 73. Also, Amy Kelly, *Eleanor of Aquitaine and the Four Kings,* (Cambridge, MA: Harvard, 1950), p. 107.

2. Costain, p. 74.

3. Costain, p. 107.

4. This story appears to be fictional, although the lives and characters of Henry and Becket indicate that it was possible.

Conclusion:

Astrology and Love

When I set out to write this book, my overall purpose was to learn about relationships myself. I had been a student of astrology for sixteen years and a certified professional astrologer for ten, and I had counseled many clients about their relationships. I still wondered, though, why human beings, who desperately needed others for their physical survival and emotional well-being, could never seem to make any kind of relationship really work. I had observed couples who had been married for forty years or more, who still spent most of their time fighting because they had not mastered the art (and it is an art) of living with other people in general and one other individual in particular. I had observed younger people, forever looking for the ideal, jumping from one relationship to another, going from the heights of ecstasy to the depths of despair.

I had watched as a couple whom I considered my friends split up, and I must admit it was a total surprise to me. I had grown to know them fairly well and had imagined them to be not only very much in love, but friends as well. I myself had recently gone through a traumatic relationship with a man who was clearly very attached to me and claimed to love me, but who was unwilling to commit to the partnership or even to acknowledge the contribution I had made to his life.

I once heard a popular radio psychologist, Dr. Toni Grant, speak of the "ghostly lover" for which everyone searches.[1] According to Dr. Grant, too many people, from the days of their early childhood, create within their imaginations a ghostly lover—an ideal to which they give absolute reality in their minds—and fall in love with that ghostly lover. They search constantly for this shadowy being, trying to find reflections of him or her in real people whom they meet, and as a result they never actually fall in love with anyone. They are too much in love with the figure they have created in their imaginations. When a genuine person—whom they may love more than they are aware of—doesn't measure up to the ghostly lover, they end the relationship and move on. My experience is that there can be another possible manifestation of this type of infatuation with the ghostly lover, too. Such people stay in relationships that are destroying them, trying desperately to change their partners Pygmalion-style into a facsimile of the partners of their dreams. Needless to say, neither approach makes for happiness in any kind of relationship.

In the meantime, while we constantly search for the perfect personification of our ghostly lovers, we meet many people with whom we have karma. Past-life experiences with these people have forged bonds that can be unbelievably strong. Even upon first meeting with these people, we are powerfully drawn to them; we feel as if we have known them all our lives. We find that we have incredible things in common with them; eventually, we may even find that we know what they are thinking before they say it aloud. We are comfortable with them; they make us feel good, as if we will never be alone again. No matter what happens, we feel a friend will be there. And then it happens: We begin to compete with the ghostly lover. How can any human being compete with someone that a lover's imagination has blown up into the ideal, perfect partner? We can't.

In the section on *Romance and Marriage* I proposed the idea that each ghostly lover is a composite of the individual's own view of the parent of the opposite sex, the animus or anima, and whatever romantic archetypes are popular at the moment—whether the archetype is Sir Galahad, Iseult the Fair, Lord Byron, Lily Langtry, Rudolph Valentino, Marilyn Monroe, or Charlie Sheen. We might add that complicating the issue are the archetypes which prevailed in past incarnations, all of which must have left a powerful impression on each psyche. It is easy to see why the specter of the ghostly lover can sabotage anyone's real-life relationship. Though it is difficult to exorcise the ghostly lover, it is possible to create a condition whereby the imaginary figure and a real-life partner can coexist.

Another problem is lack of self-esteem. Too many people are not conditioned to have high self-esteem. We are trained as children to be humble and self-effacing, and told continuously that it is "bad and wrong" to think highly of oneself. Parents, siblings, and peers reinforce this lack of confidence. Many of us end up thinking so little of ourselves that we believe, either consciously or unconsciously, that if someone actually gives us the unconditional love we need and want so desperately, there must be something wrong with that person—and therefore, we tend to fasten our affections on those who treat us more like the inferior creatures we believe ourselves to be than as divine beings created in the image of God. Too often, it becomes a challenge to the abused ones to *make* their partners love them—and thus, an involvement based not on love, but on addiction, is created.

Before I make situations sound utterly hopeless, let me say here that on the highest level, all relationships are perfect. Even the most traumatic and destructive involvements offer an opportunity for growth. If we are to become complete in ourselves, we need to accept and make use of what traits each person brings out in us—even though we might not like accepting some of them.

For example, psychologists and metaphysicians generally believe that when people allow themselves to take abuse from a romantic or marital partner, they are failing themselves, their partners, and the relationship. But try to convince anyone who is involved in an addictive relationship of that!

The key to understanding any situation is taking responsibility. Whatever your relationship, you have created it for the purpose of learning something from that relationship, whether the relationship is a loving and nurturing involvement or a destructive one. However, once the lesson is learned—meaning once you no longer feel the need for the relationship, or when it is becoming so negative a force in your life that you lose sight of all but the bad effects of it—it is best to accept that the lesson has been learned. The resultant growth, if not achieved, has at least begun.

If the relationship is not really destructive, but only seems inadequate because your partner is not living up to the standard set by your ghostly lover, (or if you are responding to your partner's love from a standpoint of low self-esteem) perhaps it is better to examine why the involvement seems inadequate. Is it impeding your growth or development—or your ability to serve others—in any way? Or is it contributing in all ways except the romantic ideals imbedded into your psyche by ancient romantic traditions, popular film or TV images, etc.?

There are all kinds of paths to understanding yourself and your relationships. One of the most valuable is astrology. Astrology can help you understand whether a person has a self-esteem problem. It also can reveal an individual's capacity to give and receive unconditional love.

The best advice I can offer for creating a relationship worth dying for (and don't we all wish for one?) is:

1. *Accept your own magnificence.* You have something to give another that no one else on this planet can offer. You are a unique individual, the only one of your kind—and for this reason alone you are worthy of the love of a devoted partner, whomever he or she may be.

2. *Communicate with your partner.* This doesn't mean speaking the unvarnished truth about everything that bothers you. You must commu-

nicate your dissatisfaction, but remember to reaffirm love at the same time. Communication involves expressing your expectations and even dislikes about your partner's behavior (notice I say about your partner's behavior—not about your partner) with good old-fashioned tact.

3. *Come to terms with your fantasies and those of your partner.* We all have our fantasies of Prince Charming and Sleeping Beauty—and there is nothing wrong with them. Fantasy lovers play roles in everyone's life; the problem is coming to terms with the fact that in the real world, such perfect lovers do not exist. Do not blame or penalize your partner for not living up to your ghostly ideal. At the same time, give your partner space to have his or her fantasies as well.

4. *Commit to the idea that you are worthy of a good relationship and take responsibility for creating one.* This may prove to be a painful process, and it may involve ending a relationship to which you have become quite attached. Sometimes severing your present bond is the only way to create a good relationship, for too many involvements have been entered into for the wrong reasons and simply should not be continued. If you are involved in a relationship that is far from ideal, but which for various reasons you are unwilling to leave, you must still commit to the idea that you are worthy of a good relationship and then create it from the one you have.

4. *Accept that the only ideal and perfect love is that which comes from God.* Though many are unaware of the fact, we as human beings do seek to recreate the continuous unconditional and eternal nature of the love we once experienced in the previous Night of Brahm, when all of us were one with God. Some human beings, such as Rama, Krishna, and Jesus, have found that perfect unity and ideal love while still in physical form—but they have not found it with another human being. They found it through enlightenment, and they lived their lives in continuous awareness and experience of the endless, unconditional love of God. Once we accept that the only truly unconditional love comes from God, it becomes easier to adjust to the conditional love of a human partner.

I wish all of you the exalted experience of being the recipient of the truest of love—both from your partners and from God. Peace, love, freedom.

Note

1. Dr. Toni Grant, *KABC Talkradio,* April, 1986.

Bibliography

Astrology

Arroyo, Stephen. *Relationships and Life Cycles.* Vancouver, WA: CRCS Publications, 1979.

George, Demetra with Robert Bloch. *Asteroid Goddesses.* San Diego, CA: ACS Publications, 1986.

Greene, Liz. *Relating: An Astrological Guide to Living with Others on a Small Planet.* York Beach, ME: Samuel Weiser, 1978.

Lantero, Erminie. *The Continuing Discovery of Chiron.* York Beach, ME: Samuel Weiser, 1983.

Lunstead, Betty. *Astrological Insights into Personality.* San Diego, CA: ACS Publications, 1980.

Rudhyar, Dane. *The Astrological Houses.* Reno, NV: CRCS Publications, 1972.

Sakoian, Frances and Acker, Louis. *The Astrology of Human Relationships.* New York: Harper & Row, 1975.

Tyl, Noel Jan. *Holistic Astrology: The Analysis of Inner and Outer Environments.* McLean, VA: TAI, 1980.

Psychology

Bell, Donald. *Being a Man: The Paradox of Masculinity.* Brattleboro, VT: Greene, 1982.

Benda, Clemens E., M.D. *The Image of Love.* New York: Glencoe, 1961.

Block, Joel D. and Greenberg, Diane. *Women and Friendship.* New York: Watts, 1985.

Branden, Nathaniel. *The Psychology of Romantic Love.* New York: Tarcher, 1980.

Cowan, Connell and Kinder, Melvyn. *Smart Women, Foolish Choices: Finding the Right Men and Avoiding the Wrong Ones.* New York: Crown, 1985.

Dass, Ram. *Grist for the Mill.* New York: Viking, 1976.

DeAngelis, Barbara. *How to Make Love All the Time.* New York: Rawson Associates, 1987.

Dowling, Colette. *The Cinderella Complex: Women's Hidden Fear of Independence.* New York: Summit, 1981.

Fields, Suzanne. *Like Father, Like Daughter.* Boston: Little, Brown, 1983.

Forward, Susan and Torres, Joan. *Men Who Hate Women and the Women Who Love Them.* New York: Bantam, 1986.

Ginott, Haim. *Between Parent and Child.* New York: MacMillan, 1965.

Johnson, Robert A. *He.* San Francisco: Harper & Row, 1983.

_____. *She.* San Francisco: Harper & Row, 1983.

_____. *We: The Psychology of Romantic Love.* San Francisco: Harper & Row, 1983.

Jung, Carl. *The Portable Jung.* Joseph Campbell, ed. New York: Viking, 1971.

Kiley, Dan. *The Peter Pan Syndrom: Men Who Have Never Grown Up.* New York: Dodd, Mead, 1983.

May, Rollo. *Love and Will.* New York: Dell, 1984.

_____. *Loving Each Other.* New York: Dell, 1984.

Peele, Stanton, with Archie Brodsky. *Love and Addiction.* New York: Signet, 1981.

Sager, C. J. and B. Hunt. *Intimate Partners: Hidden Patterns in Love Relationships.* New York: McGraw-Hill, 1978.

Mythology

Akananda, R. *Vedic Goddesses.* New Delhi: London Press, 1913.

Downing, Christine. *The Goddesses: Mythical Images of the Feminine.* New York: Crossroads, 1981.

Graves, Robert. *The Greek Myths.* New York: George Brazeller, 1957.

_____. *The White Goddess.* New York: Farrar, Strauss & Giroux, 1966.

Harrison, Jane Ellen. *Themis: A Study of the Social Origins of Greek Religion.* New York: Meridian Books, 1962.

_____. *Mythology.* New York: Harcourt-Brace, 1963.

MacCullough, J. A. *Religion of the Ancient Celts.* Edinburgh: Clark, 1911.

O'Flaherty, Wendy Doniger, ed. *The Rig-Veda.* Bungay, Suffolk, England: Penguin, 1981.

Rajagopalachari, C., ed. *The Ramayana.* Bombay: Bharatiya, 1979.

Sjoo, Monica, and Mor, Barbara. *The Great Cosmic Mother.* San Francisco: Harper & Row, 1985.

Woodroffe, Sir John. *Shakti and Shakta.* Madras, India: Ganesh and Company, 1918.

_____. *History of the Hindu Gods and Goddesses.* Madras, India: Ganesh and Company, 1920.

Biographical Information

Chapman, Hester W. *The Challenge of Anne Boleyn.* New York: Coward, McCann, 1974.

Costain, Thomas B. *The Conquering Family.* Garden City, NJ: Doubleday, 1962.

Erickson, Carolly. *Great Harry.* New York: Summit Books, 1980.

Flexner, James Thomas. *Washington: The Indispensible Man.* New York: Little, Brown, 1971.

Hallam, Elizabeth, ed. *The Plantagenet Chronicles.* New York: Weiderfeld & Nicolson, 1986.

Hellman, Lillian. *Pentimento.* New York: Simon & Schuster, 1975.

Huneker, James. *Chopin: The Man and His Music.* New York: Dover, 1960.

Kelly, Amy. *Eleanor of Aquitaine and the Four Kings.* Cambridge, MA: Harvard, 1950.

Niles, Blair. *Martha's Husband: An Informal Portrait of George Washington.* New York: McGraw-Hill, 1951.

Pollard, A. F. *Henry VIII.* New York: Harper & Row, 1966.

Prawdin, Michael. *Marie de Rohan, Duchess de Chevreuse.* London: George Allen, 1971.

Samuel I and II. *The Living Bible.* London: 1971.